SRA Reading Mastery Plus

Series Guide

Levels K–6

A Division of The McGraw·Hill Companies

Columbus, Ohio

Acknowledgments
SRA/McGraw-Hill gratefully acknowledges the
authors of the *Reading Mastery Plus* series:

Siegfried Engelmann

Elaine C. Bruner

Susan Hanner

Jean Osborn

Steve Osborn

Leslie Zoref

Owen Engelmann

Ann Arbogast

Karen Lou Seitz Davis

Tina Wells (K–2 Editor)

www.sra4kids.com

SRA/McGraw-Hill

A Division of The **McGraw·Hill** *Companies*

Send all inquiries to:
SRA/McGraw-Hill
4400 Easton Commons
Columbus, OH 43219

Printed in the United States of America.

ISBN 0-07-569187-6

7 8 9 10 11 DBH 09 08 07

Table of Contents

Introduction to *Reading Mastery Plus*

Reading Mastery Plus teaches the strategies that students in Kindergarten through Grade 6 need to achieve success in reading. Students learn new concepts at every level, in every book, and in every lesson. As strategies are taught, they are reviewed and applied in a variety of contexts. Through careful scaffolding and continuous performance assessment, all students can achieve reading success with *Reading Mastery Plus*.

Reading Mastery Plus is based on a few simple principles that have spelled reading success for students since the 1960s.

- The program provides for teaching all the skills students need to become proficient readers.
- All instruction is direct and unambiguous; exercises and activities are specified in detail.
- Every reading skill and strategy that students need is specifically taught, applied, and reviewed.
- Students receive consistent daily practice in reading, writing, listening, and speaking.
- Assessment is continuous; errors are corrected the instant they occur.

List of Materials

The table shows the program components for each level, K through 6.

	K	1	2	3	4	5	6
Teacher Materials							
Reading Presentation Book(s)	◆	◆	◆	◆	◆	◆	◆
Language Presentation Book(s)	◆	◆	◆				
Teacher's Guide	◆	◆	◆	◆	◆	◆	◆
Answer Key	◆	◆	◆	◆	◆	◆	◆
Audiocassette	◆	◆					
Spelling Book		◆	◆				
Writing and Spelling Guide				◆			
Language Arts Guide		◆	◆	◆	◆	◆	◆
Activities across the Curriculum				◆	◆	◆	◆
Seatwork		◆	◆				
Independent Readers Guide		◆	◆				
Literature Guide	◆	◆	◆	◆	◆	◆	◆
Literature Collection	◆	◆	◆				
Skills Profile Chart	◆	◆	◆	◆	◆	◆	◆
Behavioral Objectives	◆	◆	◆	◆	◆	◆	◆
Testing and Management Handbook						◆	◆
Student Materials							
Story-Picture Book	◆						
Storybook		◆	◆				
Textbook(s)		◆	◆	◆	◆	◆	◆
Workbook(s)	◆	◆	◆	◆	◆	◆	◆
Independent Readers		◆	◆				
Literature Collection			◆				
Literature Anthology				◆	◆	◆	◆

The Components

Teacher Materials

Reading Presentation Books (all levels)

Presentation books contain scripts for all lessons. The scripts tell you what to say and do. The scripts also specify the students' answers. Many scripts provide specific procedures for correcting the students' mistakes. Reduced student pages or portions of reduced student pages give you an easy reference to what the students see in their materials. Planning pages at every fifth lesson give you an overview of skills, concepts, and vocabulary being taught and reviewed.

Language Presentation Books (Levels K, 1, and 2)

These books specify activities that teach oral language skills.

Teacher's Guides (all levels)

These guides explain each level of the program in detail and indicate specific teaching techniques for many activities. The guides also contain correction procedures, suggestions for classroom management, placement information, and other information that will produce better student performance.

Behavioral Objectives (all levels)

For Levels K, 1, and 2, a complete listing of the behavioral objectives is in the *Behavioral Objectives* book. Behavioral objectives for Levels 3, 4, 5, and 6 are found in the *Teacher's Guides*.

Skills Profiles (all levels)

These charts for keeping track of an individual student's skill mastery are available as separate folders in Levels K, 1, and 2. In Levels 3, 4, 5, and 6, blackline masters of the charts are found in the *Teacher's Guides*.

Spelling Books (Levels 1 and 2)

These books contain spelling lessons that are scheduled to accompany the reading lessons.

Writing and Spelling Guide (Level 3)

This book contains spelling and writing lessons that are scheduled to accompany the reading lessons.

Language Arts Guides (Levels 1–6)

These books contain lessons and blackline masters for presenting additional language-arts lessons. The vocabulary and skill development of the language arts lessons are correlated with those of the reading lessons.

Independent Reader Lessons (Levels 1–2)

These lessons are to be presented after children have completed specific lesson ranges in the reading program. Materials consist of the Independent Readers Collection and blackline masters from the *Independent Readers Guide*. Students independently read a book from the collection and complete the accompanying worksheet. The text of each story consists of words that children have learned by the lesson the book is introduced.

Mastery Tests (all levels)

The mastery tests are designed to assess the performance of the students on the most important skills that were taught in the preceding lessons. In Levels K–4, mastery tests are incorporated in the reading lessons. In Levels 5 and 6, mastery tests are contained in the *Testing and Management Handbook*. The specifications for each test provide instructions for administration, student testing material, record-keeping charts, and remedial exercises.

Answer Keys (all levels)

These books contain the answers to the reading workbook and textbook activities.

Literature Collections (K–2) and Literature Guides (all levels)

These guides contain activities for presenting the literature selections. For Levels K, 1, and 2, you read the stories in the literature collection to the students. For Levels 3–6, students read selections from their *Literature Anthology*.

Activities across the Curriculum (Levels 3–6)

These activities are extensions of what students have been taught. They require students to integrate their writing, reading, and research skills.

Student Materials

Story-Picture Book (Level K)

This softbound, full-color pre-reading book contains illustrations for stories and activities that you present.

Storybooks and Textbooks (Levels 1–6)

These hardbound, full-color books contain the illustrated stories, novels, poems, information passages, and vocabulary words that the students read.

Workbooks (all levels)

These consumable books contain questions and exercises that the students complete during each reading lesson (Levels K–6) and language lesson (Levels K–2).

Literature Anthologies (Levels 3–6)

These anthologies, which are accompanied by a separate Literature Guide, contain classic and contemporary stories by well-known children's authors.

Independent Student Activities

Seatwork (Levels 1 and 2)

These blackline master books contain written activities that are coordinated with the reading. They present the same orthography, vocabulary, and skill requirements. Students are to complete all seatwork activities independently.

Skill Items (all levels)

The students complete exercises that teach specific decoding, comprehension, literary, and study skills.

Story Items (Levels 1–6)

The students answer questions about the stories.

Vocabulary Items (Levels 1–6)

The students use new vocabulary words to complete words and sentences, and to work crossword puzzles.

Review Items (all levels)

The students review previously taught stories, skills, and vocabulary.

Fact Games (Levels 3–5)

The students play games that involve facts they have learned.

Special Projects (Levels 3–6)

The students complete special projects that relate to their reading selections.

Writing Assignments (Levels 1–6)

The students write on assigned topics.

Independent Readers (Levels 1–2) and Supplementary Novels (Levels 4–6)

The students independently read independent readers or novels and complete comprehension activities for each selection.

Reading Component

Learning to Read—Levels K, 1, and 2

Reading Mastery Plus, Levels K, 1, and 2 focus on learning to read. This process involves decoding, but not only decoding. To read, students must be able to both decipher the symbols and understand what they mean. Initially, children learn to decode words through a special "orthography" that goes beyond phonics by showing letters that go together to make a unique sound. The orthography shows **th, sh, ch, wh,** and **er** as joined letters that make a single sound. The orthography also shows that letters with lines over them make a long-vowel sound. The orthography also provides for small letters that are silent. The net result is that all words in the program are spelled correctly but the long lines and joined combinations permit students to decode words (like **wer**e and **wher**e and **wāi**t) as perfectly regular words (and without ever having to learn verbal "phonics rules").

The special orthography is maintained through Levels K and 1. During this period, children learn to decode various words and engage in practice that builds greater fluency. After children have become fluent decoders, the prompted orthography is systematically replaced with details of standard orthography. This transition begins in Level 1 and is completed by lesson 20 of Level 2.

Throughout Levels K–2, decoding is taught explicitly and systematically. Students learn sounds, words presented in isolation, and stories. All words are composed entirely of letters and combinations that students have learned. All stories are composed entirely of words that students have learned as words presented in isolation. This sequence assures that students will be successful in reading stories and will be able to focus on the meanings. They will not tend to make word-reading mistakes because the words are familiar.

In *Reading Mastery Plus*, comprehension is specifically taught—not just tested— from the very first lesson. Students in *Reading Mastery Plus* learn how to answer questions and how to make stories come alive. *Reading Mastery Plus* places particular emphasis on the teaching of thinking skills and the acquisition of background knowledge. Specific step-by-step activities teach students not only how to infer, predict, and conclude, but also how to apply those skills to a variety of story contexts.

Reading to Learn—Levels 3 and 4

Reading Mastery Plus, Levels 3 and 4 focus on reading to learn. Levels 3 and 4 shift the emphasis from learning how to decode and understand what the text says and implies to using these skills as tools to learn new facts and relationships. Levels 3 and 4 have both information passages and related story sequences that teach students about different places in the world, different times—from the age of the dinosaurs to the present, different planets, different important events, and different activities. Students learn facts and rules that they apply to living near the North Pole, diving deep in the ocean, migrating with a flock of geese, traveling with a fly, and traveling through outer space and through the human body. The combination of information passages and engaging stories transforms science rules and historical facts into experiences that set the stage for content-area reading. It also provides a strong foundation of information and skill in different content areas.

Understanding Literature—Levels 5 and 6

In Levels 5 and 6, students extend what they have learned about reading stories and facts and begin to analyze and interpret literature. This transition involves learning to read new styles, new sentence forms, and new vocabulary. It also involves new comprehension skills for interpreting different types of literature. Students read classic and contemporary novels, short stories, poems, myths, folktales, biographies, and factual articles. Through daily writing activities, students compare different writers and analyze specific details of plots, characters, and themes. In addition to answering direct questions about the material they read, students complete a variety of comprehension activities that teach specific concepts and strategies. Students identify contradictions, interpret figurative language, draw inferences, and analyze the logic that characters use in making decisions. Students also interpret maps, graphs, and forms. Extended writing activities and explicit instruction in interpretation and analysis sharpen skills in understanding the perspective or viewpoint of a character, identifying motives, and identifying themes.

Language Component

Levels K through 2 have an oral-language component, which is the primary focus of the K program, and which becomes less central in Levels 1 and 2. The *Reading Mastery Plus* orientation is that reading-comprehension skills are not something that is completely unique to reading. They are simply a type of oral-language comprehension. The program establishes this comprehension and bridges the gap between speaking and listening and writing and reading.

Level K establishes the language of instruction—learning words and operations that the teacher uses to explain things. Children first learn the component skills that are required to understand what the teacher says when providing directions such as, "Touch the first sound of the next word." Students expand this learning in various ways to describe objects and actions. They learn important background knowledge and problem-solving strategies and applications. They learn how to draw conclusions from facts and observations.

In Levels 1 and 2, students continue to learn building-block language skills. In Level 1, students learn synonyms and opposites, larger and smaller classifications, part-whole relationships, absurdities, and contradictions. They also learn facts about the calendar, maps, types of material, and sentence skills.

At the same time, students learn about basic story grammars, how to predict what characters will do in new situations, storytelling, putting on plays, and collecting data to determine whether a character's opinion about something is correct.

In Level 2, the language skills support reading for meaning. The lessons focus on story grammars, drawing conclusions, making predictions based on evidence, and interpreting static diagrams and pictures as part of action sequences. Students also practice skills critical to learning to write. They report on main actions depicted in illustrations. They also identify parts of sentences that are unclear and change them so the sentences become clear.

Levels 3 through 6 build on the language foundations established in Levels K through 2 and extend what students have learned about speaking to writing. Students compare, report, and express their opinions on different matters. These activities are developed largely through the *Reading Mastery Plus* Language Arts Guides. In Level 4, for instance, students write passages based on a main idea, write narrative stories from pictures, and write on various topics such as "My Favorite Subject."

Literature

Students experience literature at all grade levels. The *Literature Guide* for each level details the literature activities and (in Levels 1–4) provides blackline masters for the literature lessons. In K–2, the teacher reads the literature selections and then presents activities that involve either groups or individual students. In Levels 3–6, each student has a *Literature Anthology*. New vocabulary, story background information, and comprehension-discussion items are presented on blackline masters (Levels 3–4) or in the anthology itself (Levels 5–6).

The literature that students study includes fiction, nonfiction, poetry, and drama—a mix of both modern and classic works.

Research

Research activities are presented in Levels K through 6. In Level K, students formulate specific questions and figure out reliable sources for providing information about teeth, books, what cows like to eat, and what paint is best on concrete. In Levels 1 and 2, students collect data to answer questions. For instance, they figure out the number of birds and other animals that are in a picture. They then complete a table that summarizes the types— red birds, blue birds, yellow birds, and other animals. In Level 2, students determine which of two conflicting reports is correct. Students gather evidence and summarize their findings.

In Levels 3 through 6, students engage in a variety of research activities. Some of these activities involve consulting reference books. Others require taking measurements. Still others require polling different people. Many of the special projects that follow story sequences in Levels 3 and 4 involve some form of research activity.

The research activities for Levels 3 through 6 give students practice in using and improving both content-area reading and study skills. Students develop research, writing, and presentation abilities.

Reading Mastery Plus, Level K

Reading Mastery Plus, Level K, contains 150 daily language lessons, over 50 pre-reading lessons, and 50 reading lessons that teach comprehension skills first, then basic decoding skills. Decoding is taught through an explicit phonics method that stresses letter sounds and blending. Students practice decoding by reading sounds, words, and one-sentence stories aloud. Comprehension activities include answering questions about pictures, following directions, and responding to a variety of questions based on the stories.

Materials

For the teacher:
- *Language Presentation Books* (3: Lessons 1–50, 51–100, 101–150)
- *Pre-Reading Presentation Book* (Lessons 51–100)
- *Reading Presentation Book* (Lessons 101–150)
- *Teacher's Guide*
- *Literature Guide*
- *Literature Collection* (Guide and seven Read-to Selections)
- *Answer Key*
- *Behavioral Objectives Book*
- *Skills Profile Folder*
- *A cassette* (Alphabet Song, sounds demonstration, and exercise demonstrations)
- *Letter Chart*

For the students:
- *Story-Picture Book*
- *Language/Reading Workbooks* (3)

Sample Activities

In *Reading Mastery Plus,* Level K, the students master decoding and comprehension readiness skills, learn 13 individual letter sounds, and learn how to read regularly-spelled words. The following exercises from lessons 130 and 139 are typical of those found in the reading portion of the program.

Sounds

Exercise 1 (shown below) prepares the students for decoding by teaching them how to pronounce specific sounds. First the teacher says a sound; then the students say the sound in unison. The teacher uses a simple signal to make sure the students respond together. After the group has mastered the sound, individual students say the sound.

Exercise 1 also prepares the students for comprehension by teaching them how to follow directions. Every exercise in the *Presentation Books* involves directions that the students must follow.

SAYING SOUNDS

EXERCISE 1

Children say the sounds

a. You're going to say some sounds. When I hold up my finger, say (pause) **c.** Get ready. (Hold up one finger.) *c.*
b. Next sound. Say (pause) ĭ̄ĭ. Get ready. (Hold up one finger.) *ĭ̄ĭ.*
c. Next sound. Say (pause) **nnn.** Get ready. (Hold up one finger.) *nnn.*
d. (Repeat *c* for sounds **c, ĭ̄ĭ,** and **nnn.**)
e. (Call on different children to do *a, b,* or *c.*)
f. Good saying the sounds.

Exercise 2 teaches the students how to read the letter **i**. The teacher holds the *Presentation Book* so that the students can see the large **i**. First the teacher touches under the **i** and says the letter's sound: **iii**. Then the students say the sound in unison as the teacher touches under the letter. The students practice saying the sound until every student has mastered it. Finally individual students say the sound.

LETTER SOUNDS

EXERCISE 2

Introducing the new sound i as in if

a. (Touch the first ball of the arrow for **i**.) Everybody what letter is this? (Signal.) *I*. My turn to say the sound for this letter. Get ready. (Move quickly to the second ball. Hold.) **iii**.

b. (Return to the first ball.) My turn again. Get ready. (Move quickly to the second ball. Hold.) **iii**.

c. (Repeat step *b*.)

d. (Return to the first ball.) Your turn. Get ready. (Move quickly to the second ball. Hold.) *iii*. Yes, **iii**.

e. (Return to the first ball.) Again. Get ready. (Move quickly to the second ball. Hold.) *iii*. Yes, **iii**.

f. (Repeat *e* until firm.)

g. (Call on different children to do *d*.)

h. Good saying **iii**.

A new letter sound is introduced every few lessons. The students learn 13 lower-case letters, as well as the sound combination **th**. Long and short vowels are treated as separate letters. For example, short **a** (as in *mat*) is taught in lesson 101, and it always looks like this: **a**. Long *e* (as in *me*) is taught in lesson 115, and it always has a macron over it: **ē**. In *Reading Mastery Plus*, Levels 1 and 2, students learn other ways of distinguishing between long and short vowels, and the macron is no longer used.

Reading Vocabulary

In exercise 13, the students learn how to read a regularly-spelled word. First the students identify the individual letter sounds in the word. Then they sound out the word. Finally they read the word by "saying it fast."

READING VOCABULARY

EXERCISE 13

Children say the sounds, then sound out the word

a. (Touch the first ball of the arrow for **am**.) You're going to sound it out. (Point to the ball for **a**.) What sound are you going to say first? (Touch the ball.) *aaa*. Yes, **aaa**. (Point to the ball for **m**.) What sound are you going to say next? (Touch the ball.) *mmm*. Yes, **mmm**.

b. (Return to the first ball.) Everybody, when I move my finger, say the sounds **aaammm**. Don't stop between the sounds. Get ready. (Move quickly under each sound. Hold.) *Aaammm*.

c. (Return to the first ball.) Again. Sound it out. Get ready. (Move quickly under each sound. Hold.) *Aaammm*.

d. (Repeat *c* until firm.)

e. (Return to the first ball.) Say it fast. (Slash.) *Am*.
Yes, **am**. You read the word **am**. Do you know who I (pause) **am**?

f. (Call on different children to do *c* and *e*.)

This simple and effective sound-out procedure allows the students to read hundreds of regularly-spelled words.

Story Reading and Worksheet Activities

The story-reading activities for lesson 139 are shown below.

The story word is **am** in exercise 13. The children sound out the story word and then say the word fast. Then individual children read the word. You model reading the word the fast way. In exercise 16, the children use the word as a basis for discussing what they will see in the story picture. The children look at the picture and answer some questions that relate to it.

After they finish the *Reading Presentation Book* activities, the students complete the reading exercises in their *Workbooks*.

The *Workbook* exercises develop and expand the skills taught in the *Language Presentation Book* (Side 1) and in the *Reading Presentation Book* (Side 2). First the teacher goes over the exercises with the students; then the students complete the exercises on their own.

On the reading worksheet for lesson 139 (side 2, below), the students copy the story word, match like sounds, cross out like sounds, circle like sounds, and write sounds.

STORY READING
EXERCISE 13

Children sound out the story word and say it fast

a. (Hold up worksheet. Point to **am**.) You're going to read this word. After you read this word, we'll talk about the picture.

b. Everybody, touch the first ball for the word. ✓
Look at the sounds in the word and figure out what you're going to say. (Pause three seconds.)

c. Sound it out. Get ready. (Tap for each sound, pausing about two seconds between taps. Children move their finger under each sound as they say *aaammm*.)

d. Again, finger on the first ball. ✓
Sound it out. Get ready. (Tap for each sound, pausing about two seconds between taps.) *Aaammm*.

e. (Repeat *d* until firm.)

f. Everybody, say it fast. (Signal.) *Am.*
What word? (Signal.) *Am.* Yes, **am.**

g. (Repeat *d* and *f* until firm.)

EXERCISE 14
Individual test

a. Everybody, follow along with your finger as I call on different children to read the word.

b. Everybody, touch the first ball for the word. ✓
(Call on a child.) Sound it out. Get ready. (Tap for each sound, pausing about two seconds between taps.) *Aaammm.*
Say it fast. (Signal.) *Am.* Yes, **am.**

c. (Call on different children to do *b*.)

EXERCISE 15
Teacher reads the fast way

a. (Hold up worksheet.)

b. (Touch the first ball of the arrow for **am**.) Everybody, I'm going to read this word the fast way. (Slash as you say:) **am.** I read it the fast way.

c. (Touch the first ball of the arrow for **am**.) I'll read it again. (Slash as you say:) **am.**

COMPREHENSION
EXERCISE 16

Picture comprehension

a. You've read the word (pause) **am.** The picture shows who I really . . . . (Signal.) *Am.* Yes, **am.**

b. Everybody, look at the picture. ✓

c. (Ask these questions:)
1. Is that who I really am? (Signal.) *No.* No, that's not who I am.
2. Who is that in the picture? (Call on a child.) *A tiger.* Yes, a big, mean tiger.
3. Am I really a big, mean tiger? (Signal.) *No.*
4. What would you do if you had that big, mean tiger? (Call on a child. Accept reasonable responses.)

Reading Mastery Plus, Level 1

Reading Mastery Plus, Level 1 contains 160 daily lessons that teach basic decoding and comprehension skills. Decoding is taught through an explicit phonics method that stresses letter sounds and blending. Students practice decoding by reading word lists and stories, both aloud and silently. Comprehension activities include answering questions about pictures, following directions, and responding to a variety of questions based on the stories.

Materials

For the teacher:
*   *Reading Presentation Books* (3)
*   *Language Presentation Book*
*   *Teacher's Guide*
*   *Spelling Book*
*   *Literature Guide*
*   *Literature Collection* (Guide and 15 Read-to Selections)
*   *Answer Key*
*   *Behavioral Objectives Book*
*   *Skills Profile Folder*
*   *Independent Readers Guide*
*   *Seatwork Blackline Masters*
*   *Language Arts Guide*
*   *Cassette Side B*
*   ★ Fast Start Kit *(Handbook, Presentation Book,* and *Cassette Side A)*

For the students:
*   *Storybook*
*   *Textbook*
*   *Reading Workbooks* (3)
*   *Language Workbook*
*   *Independent Reader Collection*

The *Workbooks, Storybook, Textbook,* and *Independent Readers* contain original stories written especially for the reading component of the program. There are both realistic and fantasy stories about animals and people.

> ★ **Fast Start**
> In *Reading Mastery Plus,* Level K, lessons 101–150, the students begin to master decoding and comprehension readiness skills, learn 13 individual letter sounds, and learn how to read a few regularly-spelled words. *Fast Start* covers this same material in 25 accelerated lessons designed to "catch up" children who did not complete *Reading Mastery Plus,* Level K. The *Fast Start Handbook* contains a Teacher's Guide, an Answer Key, and 25 reproducible blackline master worksheets.

Sounds in order of introduction

Review Sounds	New Sounds Book A
a as in am	ā as in ate
m as in man	h as in hat
s as in sat	u as in under
ē as in eat	g as in tag
r as in ran	l as in pal
d as in mad	w as in wow
f as in fan	sh as in wish
i as in if	I as in I'll
th as in this	k as in tack
t as in tap	ō as in over
n as in nap	v as in love
c as in cat	
o as in ox	

New Sounds Book B	
p as in sap	x as in ox
ch as in touch	oo as in moon
e as in end	j as in judge
b as in grab	ȳ as in my
ing as in sing	wh as in why
I as in ice	qu as in quick
y as in yard	z as in buzz
er as in brother	ū as in use

New Combinations Book C		
ar as in car	al as in ball	ou as in out

Sample Activities

In *Reading Mastery Plus*, Level 1, the students continue to master decoding and comprehension readiness skills, learn 27 more individual letter sounds, and learn how to read more regularly-spelled words.

Sounds

The following exercises from lessons 4 and 59 are typical of those found in the program.

Lesson 4, Exercise 2 teaches the students how to discriminate the new sound **ā** with the review sound **a**. The teacher holds the *Presentation Book* so that the students can see the large **a**'s. First the teacher touches under **ā** and says the letter's sound: **āāā**. Then the students say the sound in unison as the teacher touches under the letter. The students practice saying the sound until every student has mastered it. Finally the teacher alternates touching **ā** and **a** as students say the correct sound.

SOUNDS
EXERCISE 2
Teaching ā as in āte; children discriminate a—ā

a **ā**

ā

a

a. (Point to the first **ā**.) Everybody, this is **āāā**.
b. When I touch it, you say it. (Pause.) Get ready. (Touch **ā**.) *āāā*.
c. Again. (Touch **ā**.) *āāā*.
d. (Repeat c until firm.)
e. Get ready to do all these sounds. When I touch the sound, you say it. (Alternate touching the sounds. Before touching each **ā**, trace the line and say:) Remember—this is not **aaa**.
f. (Repeat e until all the sounds are firm.)

In the exercise shown below, from lesson 59, the teacher presents the sound combination **ch**. The two letters that make up this sound are connected by a heavy black line. This unique orthography is used for most sound combinations in *Reading Mastery Plus*, Level K and Level 1. In *Reading Mastery Plus*, Level 2, the students learn other means of recognizing sound combinations, and the letters are disjoined.

---

ch

SOUNDS
EXERCISE 1
Teaching ch as in chat

a. (Point to **ch**.) Here's a new sound. It's a quick sound.
b. My turn to say the sound. (Pause. Touch **ch** for an instant, saying:) **ch**. (Do not say **chuh**.)
c. Again. (Touch **ch** and say:) **ch**.
d. (Point to **ch**.) Your turn. When I touch it, you say the sound. (Pause.) Get ready. (Touch **ch**.) *ch*.
e. Again. (Touch **ch**.) *ch*.
f. (Repeat e until firm.)

A new letter sound is introduced every few lessons. The students learn every lowercase letter, as well as the joined sound combinations **th, sh, ch, iñg, er, oo, wh,** and **qu,** and the word **I**.

Long and short vowels are treated as separate letters. For example, short *a* (as in *mad*) is reviewed in lesson 1, and it always looks like this: **a**. Long *a* (as in *made*) is taught in lesson 4, and it has a macron over it: **ā,** until lesson 143, when students learn other ways of distinguishing between long and short vowels, and the macron is no longer used in *made* and other final *e* words.

The latter part of the program teaches three unjoined sound combinations: *ar* (as in *arm*), *al* (as in *ball*), and *ou* (as in *out*).

Reading Vocabulary

The following pages from lessons 4 and 61 are typical of those found in the program.

In lesson 4, exercises 5 through 9, the students practice reading regularly-spelled words. First the students sound out the word. Then they tell what word by "saying it fast." In exercise 8, the **k** is smaller than other letters; this means that it is silent.

This simple and effective sounding-out procedure allows the students to read hundreds of regularly-spelled words.

The students continue to learn new regularly-spelled words. They also learn how to read irregular words, how to read words "the fast way," and how to read words in lists.

A new irregular word is introduced every few lessons. The program teaches more than 50 irregular words.

In lesson 61, exercise 11, (shown on the next page), the students read an irregular word: **arm.** First the students sound out the word. Then the teacher tells the students how to say the word correctly. Finally the students practice reading the word.

In exercises 12 and 13, the students read a word that rhymes with *arm*: **farm.** Because this new word is so similar to the word presented before, the students are able to read the new word without first sounding it out.

In exercise 14, students sound out and read the word **tēₐch.** The *a* is smaller than the other letters in the word. The students have already

---

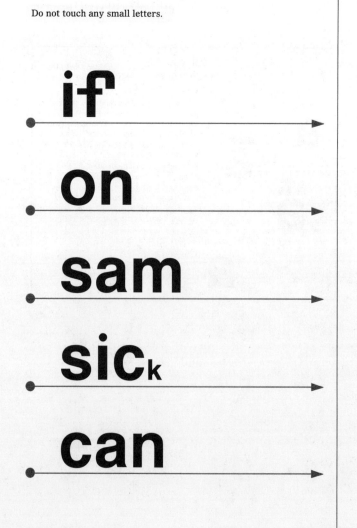

READING VOCABULARY

Get ready to read all the words on this page without making a mistake.

Do not touch any small letters.

EXERCISE 5

Children sound out the word and tell what word

a. (Touch the ball for **if.**) Sound it out.
b. Get ready. (Touch **i, f** as the children say *iiifff.*)
c. Again. (Repeat *b* until firm.)
d. Yes, what word? (Signal.) *If.*

EXERCISE 6

Children sound out the word and tell what word

a. (Touch the ball for **on.**) Sound it out.
b. Get ready. (Touch **o, n** as the children say *ooonnn.*)
c. Again. (Repeat *b* until firm.)
d. Yes, what word? (Signal.) *On.*

EXERCISE 7

Children sound out the word and tell what word

a. (Touch the ball for **sam.**) Sound it out.
b. Get ready. (Touch **s, a, m** as the children say *Sssaaammm.*)
c. Again. (Repeat *b* until firm.)
d. Yes, what word? (Signal.) *Sam.*

EXERCISE 8

Children sound out the word and tell what word

a. (Touch the ball for **sick.**) Sound it out.
b. Get ready. (Touch **s, i, c** as the children say *sssiiic.*)
c. Again. (Repeat *b* until firm.)
d. Yes, what word? (Signal.) *Sick.*

EXERCISE 9

Children sound out and tell what word

a. (Touch the ball for **can.**) Sound it out.
b. Get ready. (Touch **c, a, n** as the children say *caaannn.*)
c. Again. (Repeat *b* until firm.)
d. Yes, what word? (Signal.) *Can.*

Individual test

(Call on different children to sound out one word and tell what word.)

EXERCISE 11

Children sound out an irregular word (arm)

a. (Touch the ball for **arm.**) Sound it out.
b. Get ready. (Quickly touch each sound as the children say *aaarrrmmm.*)
c. Again. (Repeat *b* until firm.)
d. That's how we <u>sound out</u> the word. Here's how we <u>say</u> the word. **Arm.** How do we <u>say</u> the word? (Signal.) *Arm.*
e. Now you're going to <u>sound out</u> the word. Get ready. (Touch each sound as the children say *aaarrrmmm.*)
f. Now you're going to <u>say</u> the word. Get ready. (Signal.) *Arm.*
g. (Repeat *e* and *f* until firm.)

EXERCISE 12

Children rhyme with an irregular word (arm)

a. (Touch the ball for **arm.**) Everybody, you're going to read this word the fast way. Get ready. (Signal.) *Arm.*
b. (Touch the ball for **farm.**) This word rhymes with (pause) **arm.** Get ready. (Move to **f**, then quickly along the arrow.) *Farm.*
c. (Repeat *a* and *b* until firm.)

EXERCISE 13

Children sound out farm

(Have the children sound out **farm.**) *Fffaaarrrmmm.* How do we say the word? (Signal.) *Farm.* Yes, **farm.** Do you live on a **farm?**

EXERCISE 14

Children sound out the word and tell what word

a. (Touch the ball for **tēach.**) Sound it out.
b. Get ready. (Touch **t, ē, ch** as the children say *tēēēch.*)
• (If sounding out is not firm, repeat *b.*)
c. What word? (Signal.) *Teach.* Yes, **teach.**

EXERCISE 15

Children read the words the fast way

a. Now you get to read the words on this page the fast way.
b. (Touch the ball for **arm.** Pause three seconds.) Get ready. (Move your finger quickly along the arrow.) *Arm.*
c. (Repeat *b* for each word on the page.)

Do not touch any small letters.

EXERCISE 16

Individual test

(Call on different children to read one word the fast way.)

---

learned that "When a word has a little sound, you don't say the sound." This rule allows the students to sound out words with silent letters. From lesson 143, the students learn other means of identifying silent letters, and some letters become the same size.

In exercise 15, the students read all the words on the page "the fast way." When they read words "the fast way," the students simply read the words without sounding them out. Finally, in exercise 16, individual students take turns reading the words.

Story Reading and Worksheet Activities

As the program progresses, the students read longer, complete stories; answer comprehension questions; and learn how to complete a number of worksheet activities.

The first 36 stories appear in *Reading Workbook A.*

WORKSHEET **36** SIDE 1

.a fish māde a wish.
."I wish I had fēēt. I wish
.I had a tāil. I wish I had
.a hat. I wish I had a dish."

Beginning in lesson 37, the students read entire stories in their *Storybook.* These stories are written with words that the students have already learned. Initially, the stories are only a few sentences long. By the end of the program, however, the students are reading longer stories in their *Textbook,* which are serialized over a span of lessons.

The story-reading activities for lesson 61 are shown below. In exercise 21, the teacher reads the title of the story. The students learn that the title tells what the story is going to be about. In exercise 22, the students read the entire story "the fast way," without sounding out any words. After they finish this first reading, the students review any words they had trouble with. Then, in exercise 24, they read the story again, as the teacher asks literal and interpretive comprehension questions.

Most of the teacher's questions can be answered by specific words in the story. The students answer these questions in unison, at the teacher's signal. Some questions, however, require the students to make personal judgments or predictions. These questions are answered by individual students.

After the students finish the story, they predict what a picture of the story would look like. Then they turn the page and look at a picture of the story. The teacher presents comprehension questions about the picture. Later, the students will draw their own picture of the story.

On Side 1 and 2 of worksheet 61 (shown on the next page), the students copy letters and sentences, match words, follow pictured cross-out directions, and associate words with pictures. They also draw a picture of the day's story in the blank space on Side 2. The teacher explains all of the exercises before the students complete them.

Lesson 61 also includes an individual reading checkout (shown on the next page). The checkout requires the students to read for rate

---

Storybook

STORY
EXERCISE 21

Teacher introduces the title

a. (Pass out Storybook.)
b. Open your book to page 56. ✓
c. (Hold up your reader. Point to the title.) These words are called the title of the story. These words tell what the story is about. I'll read the title the fast way.
d. (Point to the words as you read:) Lots of cars.
e. Everybody, what is this story about? (Signal.) *Lots of cars.* Yes, **lots of cars.** This story is going to tell something about **lots of cars.**

EXERCISE 22

First reading—children read the story the fast way

(Have the children reread any sentences containing words that give them trouble. Keep a list of these words.)

a. Everybody, touch the title of the story and get ready to read the words in the title the fast way.
b. First word. ✓
   (Pause three seconds.) Get ready. (Tap.) *Lots.*
c. Next word. ✓
   (Pause three seconds.) Get ready. (Tap.) *Of.*
d. (Repeat c for the word **cars.**)
e. (After the children have read the title, ask:) What's this story about? (Signal.) *Lots of cars.* Yes, **lots of cars.**
f. Everybody, touch the first word of the story. ✓
g. Get ready to read this story the fast way.
h. First word. (Pause three seconds.) Get ready. (Tap.) *A.*
i. Next word. ✓
   (Pause three seconds.) Get ready. (Tap.) *Man.*
j. (Repeat i for the remaining words in the first sentence. Pause at least three seconds between taps. The children are to identify each word without sounding it out.)
k. (Repeat h through j for the next two sentences. Have the children reread the first three sentences until firm.)
l. (The children are to read the remainder of the story the fast way, stopping at the end of each sentence.)
m. (After the first reading of the story, print on the board the words that the children missed more than one time. Have the children sound out each word one time and tell what word.)
n. (After the group's responses are firm, call on individual children to read the words.)

EXERCISE 23

Individual test

a. Look at page 56. ✓
   I'm going to call on different children to read a whole sentence the fast way.
b. (Call on different children to read a sentence. Do not tap for each word.)

EXERCISE 24

Second reading—children read the story the fast way and answer questions

a. You're going to read the story again the fast way and I'll ask questions.
b. Starting with the first word of the title. ✓
   Get ready. (Tap.) *Lots.*
c. (Tap for each remaining word. Pause at least three seconds between taps. Pause longer before words that gave the children trouble during the first reading.)
d. (Ask the comprehension questions below as the children read.)

After the children read:	You say:
Lots of cars.	What's this story about? (Signal.) *Lots of cars.*
A man on a farm has lots of cars.	What does he have? (Signal.) *Lots of cars.*
He has little cars.	What kind of cars does he have? (Signal.) *Old cars and little cars.*
Are his cars for goats?	Are they for goats? (Signal.) *No.*
He has lots of cop cars.	What kind of cars does he have? (Signal.) *Cop cars.*

EXERCISE 25

Picture comprehension

a. What do you think you'll see in the picture? (Call on a child. Ideas: *A man with lots of cars; lots of cop cars.*)
b. Look at the picture on the next page. ✓
c. (Ask these questions:)
   1. Do you see lots of cop cars? (Signal.) *Yes.*
   2. What would you do if you had all those cop cars? (Call on a child. Accept reasonable responses.)

Lesson 61   Presentation Book B

and accuracy. As the group is working independently, the teacher calls on individual students to read the day's story aloud. The students earn stars if they can read the entire story (49 words) in less than two minutes (25 words per minute) while making no more than three errors (94% accuracy).

Reading Checkout

EXERCISE 28

2-minute individual checkout: rate and accuracy

a. As you are doing your worksheet, I'll call on children one at a time to read the whole story. Remember, you get two stars if you read the story in less than two minutes and make no more than three errors.

b. (Call on a child. Tell the child:) Start with the title and read the story carefully the fast way. Go. (Time the child. Tell the child any words the child misses. Stop the child as soon as the child makes the fourth error or exceeds the time limit.)

c. (If the child meets the rate-accuracy criterion, record two stars on your chart for lesson 61. Congratulate the child. Give children who do not earn two stars a chance to read the story again before the next lesson is presented.)

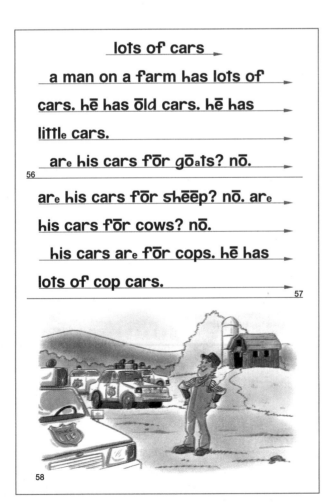

lots of cars

a man on a farm has lots of cars. hē has ōld cars. hē has littlₑ cars.

arₑ his cars fōr gōₐts? nō.

56

arₑ his cars fōr shēēp? nō. arₑ his cars fōr cows? nō.

his cars arₑ fōr cops. hē has lots of cop cars.

57

58

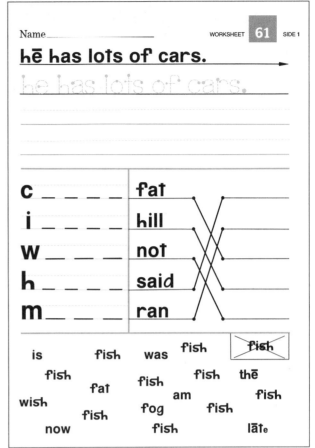

hē has lots of cars.

c _ _ _ _   fat
i _ _ _ _   hill
w _ _ _   not
h _ _ _ _   said
m _ _ _   ran

is   fish   was   fish   ~~fish~~
   fish   fat   fish   fish   thē
wish   am   fish
          fish   fog   fish
   now   fish   lātₑ

SIDE 2

man	rug
cat	rat
tāil	gātₑ
car	rākₑ

dog	log
rag	dish
rocₖ	shacₖ
cow	gōat

cōₐt	tāil
can	ātₑ
cōld	māil
car	shāvₑ

Reading Mastery Plus, Level 2

Reading Mastery Plus, Level 2 contains 160 daily reading lessons that expand basic reading skills. Students in the program learn strategies for decoding difficult words and for answering interpretive comprehension questions. They also learn basic reasoning skills, such as making inferences and drawing conclusions. The daily reading selections include realistic fiction, fantasy, and factual articles.

Materials

For the teacher:
- *Reading Presentation Books* (3)
- *Language Presentation Book*
- *Teacher's Guide*
- *Answer Key*
- *Spelling Book*
- *Literature Guide* (Blackline Masters)
- *Literature Collection* (Guide and 14 Read-to Selections)
- *Independent Readers Guide*
- *Behavioral Objectives Book*
- *Skills Profile Folder*
- *Seatwork Blackline Masters*
- *Language Arts Guide*

For the students:
- *Storybook*
- *Textbook*
- *Language/Reading Workbooks* (3)
- *Independent Reader Collection*

The *Storybook, Textbook,* and *Independent Readers* contain stories written especially for the program, as well as adaptations of famous children's stories. Many of the stories are serialized over a span of lessons.

Sample Activities—Lesson 32

Each lesson in *Reading Mastery Plus,* Level 2 begins with word practice exercises. The teacher presents lists of words that the students read aloud. In lessons 1–95, these word lists are in the *Reading Presentation Books.* In lessons 96–160, the lists are in the student *Textbook.* Often the teacher presents sound combinations and word parts in conjunction with the word lists.

In lessons 1–15, the unique *Reading Mastery* orthography is used for all words. In lessons 16–20, the *Reading Mastery* orthography is gradually phased out and replaced by standard orthography. During this transition period, the students practice the final-*e* rule and other guides for reading words in standard orthography. In lessons 21–160, standard orthography is used in all the student materials.

The following activities appear in lesson 32. The lesson begins with four separate word lists. The list in exercise 1 contains new words that are difficult to decode, as well as words that the students have already learned. The new words are printed in red. The teacher first reads the new words; then the students spell them. Finally the students read the new words. After the students have mastered the new words, they read the entire list.

The students read all of the words in unison. When the teacher points to a word, the students look over the word and get ready to read it. Then they read the word in unison as the teacher slashes under the word with a finger.

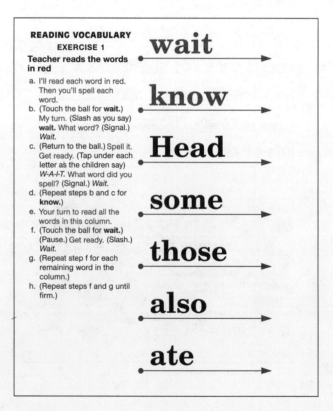

READING VOCABULARY
EXERCISE 1
Teacher reads the words in red

a. I'll read each word in red. Then you'll spell each word.
b. (Touch the ball for **wait**.) My turn. (Slash as you say) **wait**. What word? (Signal.) *Wait.*
c. (Return to the ball.) Spell it. Get ready. (Tap under each letter as the children say) *W-A-I-T.* What word did you spell? (Signal.) *Wait.*
d. (Repeat steps b and c for **know**.)
e. Your turn to read all the words in this column.
f. (Touch the ball for **wait**.) (Pause.) Get ready. (Slash.) *Wait.*
g. (Repeat step f for each remaining word in the column.)
h. (Repeat steps f and g until firm.)

wait
know
Head
some
those
also
ate

In exercise 2, the students read words that contain various sound combinations, word endings, or root words. Word elements are underlined in each word. The students first read the underlined part; then they read the entire word.

These underlined-part word lists teach students an important decoding strategy. The lists demonstrate that many unfamiliar words are made up of familiar parts. By identifying these familiar parts, the students are able to decode unfamiliar words.

In exercise 3, the students read new words that are easy to decode or words that they have already learned. The teacher points to each word; then the students read the word as the teacher slashes under it with a finger.

In exercise 4, the students spell each word before reading it. This procedure not only promotes accurate spelling, but also teaches the students to examine words carefully.

After the group finishes reading all the lists, individual students take turns reading one list each. In lessons 96–160, word lists appear in the student *Textbook*, not in the *Reading Presentation Book*.

EXERCISE 2
Words with underlined parts
a. First you're going to read the underlined part of each word in this column. Then you're going to read the whole word.
b. (Touch the ball for **string**.) Read the underlined part. Get ready. (Tap the ball.) *Ing.* Read the whole word. (Pause.) Get ready. (Slash.) *String.*
c. (Repeat step b until firm.)
d. (Repeat steps b and c for each remaining word in the column.)
e. (Repeat the column until children read all the words in order without making a mistake.)

To correct
word-identification errors (**note,** for example)
1. That word is **note.** What word? (Signal.) *Note.*
2. Spell **note.** Get ready. (Tap under each letter.) *N-O-T-E.*
3. What word did you spell? (Signal.) *Note.*
4. (Repeat 2 and 3 until firm.)
5. (Return to the first word in the column and present all words in order.) Starting over.

string

stand

stones

cash

pouch

smart

likes

EXERCISE 3
Read the fast way
a. You're going to read all the words in this column the fast way.
b. (Touch the ball for **Let's.**) (Pause.) Get ready. (Slash.) *Let's.*
c. (Repeat step b until firm.)
d. (Repeat steps b and c for each remaining word in the column.)
e. (Repeat the column until the children read all the words in order without making mistakes.)

Let's

who

ice cream

didn't

hopping

But

Liked

EXERCISE 4
Children spell, then read
a. First you're going to spell each word. Then you're going to read that word the fast way.
b. (Touch the ball for **hoping**.) Spell it. Get ready. (Tap under each letter as the children say) *H-O-P-I-N-G.* (Return to the ball.) Read it. Get ready. (Slash.) *Hoping.*
c. (Repeat step b for each remaining word in the column.)
d. (Repeat steps b and c until firm.)

hoping

tame

bite

then

cone

right

tiger

Individual test
a. (Call on different children to read one column of words from the lesson.)
b. (Praise children who read all words with no errors.)

After the word-practice exercises are completed, the teacher directs the students as they read aloud from their *Storybook* (lessons 1–95) or *Textbook* (lessons 96–160). During this group reading, the teacher monitors the students' decoding accuracy and also presents comprehension questions.

In exercise 5, the students begin the group reading by reading the first part of the *Storybook* story within a specified decoding error limit. The first part of the story extends from the title to the circled 5. The teacher calls on individual students to read two or three sentences in turn. The students must practice reading the story until they can read up to the circled 5 while making no more than five decoding errors.

In *Textbook* stories (lessons 96–160), the teacher writes the error limit on the board.

The *Reading Presentation Book* contains a reproduction of the *Storybook* page. Numbers are placed within these reproductions to indicate where the teacher is to present comprehension questions. The actual questions are printed near the reproduced pages.

After the group reads the first part of the story within the error limit, the teacher rereads the first part and presents the comprehension questions. Then the students take turns reading the rest of the story, as the teacher presents more comprehension questions.

The comprehension questions teach a variety of literal and interpretive comprehension skills. In this sample lesson, the students relate titles to story content, answer literal questions, identify the meanings of common words, and predict narrative outcomes.

Storybook

STORY 32

EXERCISE 5

Reading—decoding

a. (Pass out Storybook.)
b. Everybody, open your reader to story 32. ✓
c. Remember, if the group reads all the way to the red 5 without making more than five errors, we can go on.
d. Everybody, touch the title of the story. ✓
e. If you hear a mistake, raise your hand. Remember, children who do not have their place lose their turn. (Call on individual children to read two or three sentences. Do not ask comprehension questions. Tally all errors.)

To correct word-identification errors (**from**, for example)

1. That word is **from**. What word? *From.*
2. Go back to the beginning of the sentence and read the sentence again.

f. (If the children make more than five errors before they reach the red 5: when they reach the 5, return to the beginning of the story and have the children reread to the 5. Do not ask comprehension questions. Repeat step f until firm, and then go on to step g.)
g. (When the children read to the red 5 without making more than five errors: read the story to the children from the beginning to the 5. Ask the specified comprehension questions. When you reach the 5, call on individual children to continue reading the story. Have each child read two or three sentences. Ask the specified comprehension questions

The Tame Tiger Who Liked Ice Cream[1]

There once was a tame tiger. This tiger did not bite children.[2] He didn't eat goats or sheep.[3] He said, "I like ice cream.[4] So I will go to town and get some."

But the tiger didn't have any cash.[5] He said, "I will fill my pouch with round stones. I hope that the man at the ice cream store likes round stones."[6]

So the tiger filled his pouch with round stones. Then he walked to town. He went up to the man at the ice cream stand.

"I don't have any cash," the tiger said. "But I have a pouch filled with pretty round stones."[7]

"Let's see them," the man said.

So the tiger showed the man his stones. The man said, "I like those stones. They are pretty."[8]

The tiger gave the pouch to the man.⑤ Then the tiger said, "I want a big cone, and I want some string."[9]

The man said, "What will you do with a big cone and some string?"

"Wait and see," the tiger said.

What do you think the tiger did?[10] He ate the ice cream from the cone.[11] Then he put the big cone on his head with a string.[12]

The tiger said, "I love ice cream and I love hats. I ate the ice cream and now I have the best hat in town."[13]

The man at the ice cream stand said, "That tiger is very tame. He is also very smart."

The end

[1] What is this story going to be about? (Signal.) *The tame tiger who liked ice cream.* A tiger is an animal with stripes.
[2] Did this tiger bite children? (Signal.) *No.* Right. He was tame.
[3] I wonder what he did eat? Let's read some more.
[4] Now we know. What does he eat? (Signal.) *Ice cream.*
[5] What didn't he have? (Signal.) *Cash.* What's cash? *The children respond.* Right. He didn't have any money.
[6] What does the tiger want to do with the round stones? *The children respond.*
[7] Does he have cash? (Signal.) *No.* What does he have? (Signal.) *Pretty round stones.*
[8] Did the man like those stones? (Signal.) *Yes.*
[9] What did the tiger say? (Signal.) *I want a big cone, and I want some string.*
[10] What do you think? *The children respond.* Let's keep reading.
[11] What's the first thing the tiger did? (Signal.) *He ate the ice cream.*
[12] What's the next thing he did? (Signal.) *The children respond.*
[13] How did he get that hat? *The children respond.* Right. He made it from the cone and string.

After the students finish reading the story, they complete written exercises in their *Workbooks*. In lesson 32, the students answer questions about the story, follow written directions, and complete deductions. They also read a short passage and answer questions about the passage.

The teacher explains new exercises to the students. In this sample lesson, the teacher explains the deductions exercise. The students do the remaining exercises on their own.

Worksheet 32

DEDUCTIONS
EXERCISE 7
Picture deductions

a. (Hold up side 2 of your worksheet and touch the sentence in the box in the deductions exercise.)

b. Everybody, touch this sentence on your worksheet. ✓

c. (Call on a child.) Read the sentence in the box. *All the big horses are tired.*

d. Everybody, say that rule. (Signal.) *All the big horses are tired.* (Repeat until firm.)

e. You know that some of the horses in the picture are tired. What kind of horses are those? (Signal.) *All the big horses.* Everybody, touch a horse you know is tired. ✓

f. You don't know about the horses that are not big. Everybody, touch a horse you don't know about. ✓

g. (Call on a child.) Read the instructions below the box. *Circle every horse that is tired.*

h. Everybody, what are you going to do? (Signal.) *Circle every horse that is tired.* Yes, circle every horse that you know is tired.

i. Do it. (Observe children and give feedback.)

INDEPENDENT WORK
EXERCISE 8
Independent activity

Everybody, now you'll finish your worksheet. Remember to do all parts of the worksheet and to read all the parts carefully.

Worksheet **32**
Side 1

1. The tiger was _____.
       lame   old   tame   time

2. Did he bite children? _____

3. What did he like to eat? _____
       ice   ice bits   ice cream   ice skates

4. Did the tiger have any cash? _____

5. What were in his pouch? _____
       stops   cones   stones   rocks

6. Did the man like the stones? _____

7. Who said, "What will you do with a big cone and some string?" _____

8. Who said, "Wait and see"? _____

9. The tiger made the cone into a h_____.

The boy felt cold in the rain.

1. Make a box around the word that tells how the boy felt.
2. Make a box around the words that tell where the boy is.
3. Make a line over the words that tell who felt cold.

Worksheet **32**
Side 2

One day, the boss left a note for Sid. Here is what that note said: "Tape my cane with a bit of white tape. The white tape is in the tape can."
Do you think Sid did what the note said? Yes, he did. After he looked at the note, he got the white tape and taped the cane.

1. Who left the note for Sid? _____
2. The note told Sid to _____ a cane.
3. Where was the white tape? _____
       in the tap can   in the tape can
4. Sid got the tape and taped the _____.

All the big horses are tired.

Circle every horse that is tired.

Reading Mastery Plus, Level 3

Reading Mastery Plus, Level 3 contains 140 daily lessons that emphasize reasoning and reference skills. Students in the program learn how to apply rules in a wide variety of contexts and how to interpret maps, graphs, and time lines. The program also introduces a number of complex sentence forms and a range of vocabulary activities. The daily reading selections include realistic fiction, fantasy, and factual articles.

Materials

For the teacher:
* *Presentation Books* (3)
* *Teacher's Guide*
* *Answer Key*
* *Literature Guide*
* *Writing and Spelling Guide*
* *Language Arts Guide*
* *Activities Across the Curriculum*

For the students:
* *Textbooks* (3)
* *Workbooks* (3)
* *Literature Anthology*

The *Textbooks* contain stories and comprehension passages written especially for the program. Most of the stories are serialized over a span of lessons, and many of the stories incorporate science facts and rules. Here is a partial listing of the *Textbook* contents.

* **A Tricky Toad Named Goad**—A toad has amusing adventures in which she tricks people.
* **Nancy Learns About Being Small**—A girl becomes very small and learns important facts about common objects.
* **Herman Travels the World**—A fly goes around the world on a jet. The students use maps to follow the jet's progress.
* **Linda and Kathy Alone on an Island**—Two girls are shipwrecked and struggle to survive on an island.
* **Bertha and Her Nose**—A girl with a great sense of smell helps an investigator capture a group of polluters.

* **Andrew Dexter's Dreams**—A bank teller gets superhuman powers and is hired by a football team.
* **The Time Machine**—Two boys find a time machine and go back and forth in time.
* **Comprehension Passages**—Short passages that provide background information for the stories.

Sample Activities

The following vocabulary activities appear in lesson 52 of *Reading Mastery Plus,* Level 3.

The students begin lesson 52—and most other lessons—by working on model vocabulary sentences. These sentences contain selected vocabulary words. Students learn what each sentence means, practice saying the sentence, and respond to tasks about the meanings of specific words. In lesson 52, exercise 1, below, a new model sentence is introduced.

VOCABULARY SENTENCES

LESSONS 51–100

13. The smoke swirled in enormous billows.

EXERCISE 1

VOCABULARY

a. **Find page 397 in your textbook.** ✓
* Touch sentence 13. ✓
* This is a new vocabulary sentence. It says: The smoke swirled in enormous billows. Everybody, read that sentence. Get ready. (Signal.) *The smoke swirled in enormous billows.*
* Close your eyes and say the sentence. Get ready. (Signal.) *The smoke swirled in enormous billows.*
* Again. Say the sentence. Get ready. (Signal.) *The smoke swirled in enormous billows.*
* (Repeat until firm.)
b. When smoke **swirls,** it spins around as it drifts. If you mix chocolate syrup in milk, you'll see swirls of brown and white. What's a word that means **spun around?** (Signal.) *Swirled.*

---

c. Things that are **enormous** are very, very large. What's another way of saying **The building was very, very large?** (Signal.) *The building was enormous.*

d. **Billows** are large clouds or waves that are swelling up.

e. Listen to the sentence again: The smoke swirled in enormous billows.
- Everybody, say that sentence. Get ready. (Signal.) *The smoke swirled in enormous billows.*
- (Repeat until firm.)

f. What word means that the smoke spun around and around? (Signal.) *Swirled.*
- What word means **very, very large?** (Signal.) *Enormous.*
- What word tells you that the clouds were swelling up? (Signal.) *Billows.*
- (Repeat step f until firm.)

In the next exercise of lesson 52, students read word lists.

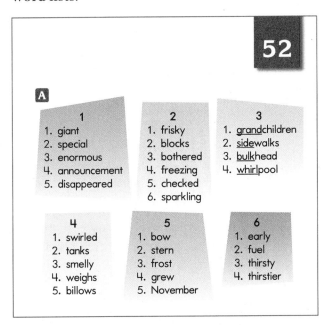

52

A

1	2	3
1. giant	1. frisky	1. grandchildren
2. special	2. blocks	2. sidewalks
3. enormous	3. bothered	3. bulkhead
4. announcement	4. freezing	4. whirlpool
5. disappeared	5. checked	
	6. sparkling	

4	5	6
1. swirled	1. bow	1. early
2. tanks	2. stern	2. fuel
3. smelly	3. frost	3. thirsty
4. weighs	4. grew	4. thirstier
5. billows	5. November	

There are three types of lists. The first type consists of words that are difficult to decode (such as **giant**). The teacher reads these words to the students. Then the students read the words and spell them.

READING WORDS

Column 1

a. Find lesson 52 in your textbook. ✓
- Touch column 1. ✓
- (Teacher reference:)

1. **giant**	4. **announcement**
2. **special**	5. **disappeared**
3. **enormous**	

b. Word 1 is **giant.** What word? (Signal.) *Giant.*
- Spell **giant.** Get ready. (Tap for each letter.) *G-I-A-N-T.*

c. Word 2 is **special.** What word? (Signal.) *Special.*
- Spell **special.** Get ready. (Tap for each letter.) *S-P-E-C-I-A-L.*

d. Word 3 is **enormous.** What word? (Signal.) *Enormous.*
- Spell **enormous.** Get ready. (Tap for each letter.) *E-N-O-R-M-O-U-S.*

e. Word 4 is **announcement.** What word? (Signal.) *Announcement.*

f. Word 5 is **disappeared.** What word? (Signal.) *Disappeared.*

g. Let's read those words again, the fast way.
- Word 1. What word? (Signal.) *Giant.*
- (Repeat for words 2–5.)

h. (Repeat step g until firm.)

The second type of list consists of words that have a common feature, such as a common sound or a common ending. The teacher explains the common feature; then the students read the words.

For each word in the lists with a meaning that may not be familiar to the students, (such as **frisky**), the teacher gives an explanation of the meaning.

Column 2

i. Find column 2. ✓
- (Teacher reference:)

1. frisky	4. freezing
2. blocks	5. checked
3. bothered	6. sparkling

- All these words have endings.
j. Word 1. What word? (Signal.) *Frisky.*
- **Frisky** means **playful** or **full of energy.** What's another way of saying **The cats were playful?** (Signal.) *The cats were frisky.*
k. Word 2. What word? (Signal.) *Blocks.*
- (Repeat for words 3–6.)
l. Let's read those words again.
- Word 1. What word? (Signal.) *Frisky.*
- (Repeat for words 2–6.)
m. (Repeat step l until firm.)

Column 3

n. Find column 3. ✓
- (Teacher reference:)

1. <u>grand</u>children	3. <u>bulk</u>head
2. <u>side</u>walks	4. <u>whirl</u>pool

- All these words are compound words. The first part of each word is underlined.
o. Word 1. What's the underlined part? (Signal.) *grand.*
- What's the whole word? (Signal.) *Grandchildren.*
p. Word 2. What's the underlined part? (Signal.) *side.*
- What's the whole word? (Signal.) *Sidewalks.*
q. Word 3. What's the underlined part? (Signal.) *bulk.*
- What's the whole word? (Signal.) *Bulkhead.*
r. Word 4. What's the underlined part? (Signal.) *whirl.*
- What's the whole word? (Signal.) *Whirlpool.*
s. Let's read those words again.
- Word 1. What word? (Signal.) *Grandchildren.*
- (Repeat for words 2–4.)
t. (Repeat step s until firm.)

Column 4

u. Find column 4. ✓
- (Teacher reference:)

1. swirled	4. weighs
2. tanks	5. billows
3. smelly	

- All these words have endings.
v. Word 1. What word? (Signal.) *Swirled.*
- (Repeat for words 2–5.)
w. Let's read those words again.
- Word 1. What word? (Signal.) *Swirled.*
- (Repeat for words 2–5.)
x. (Repeat step w until firm.)

Column 5

y. Find column 5. ✓
- (Teacher reference:)

1. bow	4. grew
2. stern	5. November
3. frost	

z. Word 1 rhymes with **how.** What word? (Signal.) *Bow.*
a. Word 2. What word? (Signal.) *Stern.*
- The bow is the front of a ship. The stern is the back of the ship. What do we call the front of a ship? (Signal.) *Bow.*
- What do we call the back of a ship? (Signal.) *Stern.*
b. Word 3. What word? (Signal.) *Frost.*
- Frost is frozen water that forms on grass during cold nights. When the temperature goes up in the morning, the frost disappears.
c. Word 4. What word? (Signal.) *Grew.*
- Word 5. What word? (Signal.) *November.*
d. Let's read those words again.
- Word 1. What word? (Signal.) *Bow.*
- (Repeat for words 2–5.)
e. (Repeat step d until firm.)

The third type of list consists of words that are easy to decode or words that the students have already learned. The teacher simply directs the students to read these lists.

Column 6

f. Find column 6. ✓
- (Teacher reference:)

1. **early**	3. **thirsty**
2. **fuel**	4. **thirstier**

g. Word 1. What word? (Signal.) *Early.*
- (Repeat for words 2–4.)

h. Let's read those words again.
- Word 1. What word? (Signal.) *Early.*
- (Repeat for words 2–4.)
i. (Repeat step h until firm.)

Individual Turns

(For columns 1–6: Call on individual students, each to read one to three words per turn.)

The next exercise in lesson 52, exercise 3, reviews the model sentence that was introduced in exercise 1. Students say the sentence and answer questions about word meanings.

EXERCISE 3
VOCABULARY REVIEW

a. Here's the new vocabulary sentence: The smoke swirled in enormous billows.
- Everybody, say that sentence. Get ready. (Signal.) *The smoke swirled in enormous billows.*
- (Repeat until firm.)
- What word means **very, very large?** (Signal.) *Enormous.*
b. What word tells you that the clouds were swelling up? (Signal.) *Billows.*
- What word means that the smoke spun around and around? (Signal.) *Swirled.*

The following group reading activities appear in lesson 16 of *Reading Mastery Plus,* Level 3. In lesson 16–and most other lessons–the students read their *Textbook* stories aloud. Many of these stories are preceded by comprehension passages. The comprehension passages present background information for the stories. The students will make use of this information as they read the stories.

The students read the comprehension passage aloud. Individual students take turns reading two or three sentences each. As the students read the passage, the teacher presents comprehension questions from the *Presentation Book.* These questions teach a variety of comprehension, reference, and study skills.

B **More Facts About** Toads and Frogs

Toads and frogs are members of the same family. But toads are different from frogs. Here are some facts about how toads and frogs are different:
- Toads have skin that is rough and covered with warts.
- No toads have teeth, but some frogs have teeth.
- The back legs of toads are not as big or strong as the back legs of frogs.

EXERCISE 3
COMPREHENSION PASSAGE

a. Find part B in your textbook. ✓
- The information passage gives some facts about toads and frogs.
b. Everybody, touch the title. ✓
- (Call on a student to read the title.) [More Facts About Toads and Frogs.]
- Everybody, what's the title? (Signal.) *More Facts About Toads and Frogs.*
c. (Call on individual students to read the passage, each student reading two or three sentences at a time.)

More Facts About Toads and Frogs

Toads and frogs are members of the same family. But toads are different from frogs. Here are some facts about how toads and frogs are different:
Toads have skin that is rough and covered with warts.

- Everybody, what is a toad's skin covered with? (Signal.) *Warts.*
- Warts are like rough bumps. Everybody, do **frogs** have skin that is rough and covered with warts? (Signal.) *No.*

No toads have teeth, but some frogs have teeth.

- Everybody, listen to that fact again: No toads have teeth, but some frogs have teeth.

- Say that fact. Get ready. (Signal.) *No toads have teeth, but some frogs have teeth.*
- (Repeat until firm.)
- Do any toads have teeth? (Signal.) *No.*
- Do any frogs have teeth? (Signal.) *Yes.*

The back legs of toads are not as big or strong as the back legs of frogs.

- Everybody, whose back legs are stronger, toads' or frogs'? (Signal.) *Frogs'.*
- So which animal could jump farther, a toad or a frog? (Signal.) *A frog.*

After they finish the comprehension passage, the students read the main story aloud within decoding error limits that are specified in the teacher's script.

As the students read the story, the teacher presents comprehension questions from the *Presentation Book.* The comprehension questions in *Reading Mastery Plus*, Level 3 emphasize interpretive comprehension skills, reasoning skills, and study skills. In the sample selections from lesson 16, the students interpret titles, infer story details, infer causes and effects, and predict outcomes.

C Goad Uses Her First Trick

Goad lived near Four Mile Lake. Down the road from the lake was a town. The name of that town was Toadsville. It was named Toadsville because so many people who visited the town had come to hunt for a big, smart, fast toad. And in the evening you could find hundreds of people sitting around Toadsville talking about Goad. First they would talk about some of the traps that had been made to catch Goad. Then they would tell how Goad escaped. One of their favorite stories is the one of the great big net.

Five hunters from Alaska had come to Four Mile Lake with a net that was nearly a mile wide. They waited until Goad was on a hill where there were no trees, just some white rocks. Then they flew over the hill in a plane and dropped the great big net over the hill. ★ Goad was under the net. The five hunters rushed to the place where Goad had last been seen. But there was no Goad. There was some grass and five large white rocks. The hunters removed the net and began to go over every centimeter of the ground.

Suddenly, one of the hunters noticed that the biggest rock was moving. The biggest rock wasn't a rock at all. It was Goad.

She had moved near the other rocks. Then she had turned over on her back so that her white belly was showing. That belly looked like a white rock. Suddenly, she turned over. "There she is," one of the hunters yelled, but before the others could turn around, Goad hopped down the side of the hill and was gone.

MORE NEXT TIME

EXERCISE 4

STORY READING

a. Find part C in your textbook. ✓
   - We're going to read this story two times. First you'll read it out loud and make no more than 6 errors. Then I'll read it and ask questions.
b. Everybody, touch the title. ✓
   - (Call on a student to read the title.) *[Goad Uses Her First Trick.]*
   - Everybody, what's Goad going to do in this story? (Signal.) *Her first trick.*

c. (Call on individual students to read the story, each student reading two or three sentences at a time.)

> • (Correct errors: Tell the word. Direct the student to reread the sentence.)
> • (If the group makes more than 6 errors, direct the students to reread the story.)

d. (After the group has read the selection making no more than 6 errors:)
Now I'll read the story and ask questions.

Goad Uses Her First Trick

Goad lived near Four Mile Lake. Down the road from the lake was a town. The name of that town was Toadsville. It was named Toadsville because so many people who visited the town had come to hunt for a big, smart, fast toad.

• Everybody, who is that big, smart, fast toad? (Signal.) *Goad.*

And in the evening you could find hundreds of people sitting around Toadsville talking about Goad. First they would talk about some of the traps that had been made to catch Goad. Then they would tell how Goad escaped. One of their favorite stories is the one of the great big net.

• How could you use a great big net to catch a toad? (Call on a student. Idea: *Drop it on top of the toad.*)

Five hunters from Alaska had come to Four Mile Lake with a net that was nearly a mile wide. They waited until Goad was on a hill where there were no trees, just some white rocks. Then they flew over the hill in a plane and dropped the great big net over the hill.

Goad was under the net. The five hunters rushed to the place where Goad had last been seen. But there was no Goad. There was some grass and five large white rocks. The hunters removed the net and began to go over every centimeter of the ground.

• The picture on the next page shows the hunters looking for Goad. You can see the trick that Goad is using. What is she doing? (Call on a student. Idea: *Pretending to be a rock.*)

Suddenly, one of the hunters noticed that the biggest rock was moving. The biggest rock wasn't a rock at all. It was Goad.

She had moved near the other rocks. Then she had turned over on her back so that her white belly was showing. That belly looked like a white rock. Suddenly she turned over. "There she is," one of the hunters yelled, but before the others could turn around, Goad hopped down the side of the hill and was gone.

MORE NEXT TIME

• Why didn't those hunters just grab her when she was hopping down the hill? (Call on a student. Idea: *Goad was too fast.*)

After the students finish the *Textbook* reading activities, they work independently in the *Workbook* and *Textbook*. The independent work includes items about the comprehension passage, story items, skill items, and review items.

The comprehension-passage items and story items are based on the comprehension questions presented during the group reading. In this sample lesson, the students recall narrative details, classify objects, explain causes and effects, and infer narrative events. Story items in other lessons involve skills such as sequencing narrative events, inferring details, and interpreting motives.

The skill items teach vocabulary and reasoning skills. In this sample lesson, the students make comparisons.

The review items review previously taught facts and skills. In this sample lesson, the students review map-reading skills, measurement information, and facts about fleas and apple trees.

A   16

1. At each dot, draw an arrow to show which way the string will move when the girl pulls it.

B

2. Which animal has smooth skin?   • toad   • frog
3. Which animal can jump farther?   • toad   • frog
4. Do any frogs have teeth? _____
5. **Make a box** around the toads in the picture.

A   B   C   D   E   F

C   Story Items

6. Goad was hard to catch because she was very ▆▆
   • old and slow   • fast and old   • smart and fast
7. What did the hunters from Alaska use when they tried to catch Goad?
   • a fish   • a box   • 12 dogs   • a big net
8. Goad fooled the hunters from Alaska by making herself look like a ▆▆
   • toad   • net   • rock
9. What part of Goad is white?   • nose   • belly   • back
10. **Underline** the picture of Goad using her first trick.

Review Items

11. Write **north, south, east,** and **west** in the right boxes.

12. An arrow goes from the **R.** Which direction is that arrow going?
    _____

13. An arrow goes from the **S.** Which direction is that arrow going?
    _____

14. An arrow goes from the **T.** Which direction is that arrow going?
    _____

▆▆▆▆▆ GO TO PART D IN YOUR TEXTBOOK. ▆▆▆▆▆

D Number your paper from 1 through 16.

Skill Items

Write the word from the box that means the same thing as the underlined part of each sentence.

weight	measure	leaves	paws
grove	family	hooves	evening

1. The deer ran into the <u>small group of trees</u> to hide.
2. The horse's <u>feet</u> were covered with mud.
3. She used a ruler to <u>see</u> how long the rope was.

4. Look at object A, object B, and object C. Write at least **2** ways all 3 objects are the same.

Object A   Object B   Object C

   • They are all big.   • They are striped.
   • They are pink.   • They are circles.
   • They are not round.

The workers propped up the cage with steel bars.
5. What 2 words refer to supporting something?
6. What word names a strong metal?
7. What objects were made of a strong metal?
8. What object was propped up?

Review Items
9. Which is longer, an inch or a centimeter?

10. Some of the lines in the box are one inch long. Some of the lines are one centimeter long. Write the letter of every line that is one centimeter long.
11. Write the letter of every line that is one inch long.

12. Where do the fleas in flea circuses usually come from?
13. What's the first thing that fleas must be taught?

14. What color are the flowers that apple trees make?
15. When do those flowers come out?
16. What grows in each place where there was a flower?

Reading Mastery Plus, Level 4

Reading Mastery Plus, Level 4 contains 140 daily lessons that emphasize problem-solving skills and reading in the content areas. Students in the program evaluate problems and solutions, learn facts about the world, and complete research projects. Many of the daily reading selections incorporate facts from science and social studies.

Materials

For the teacher:
- *Presentation Books* (2)
- *Teacher's Guide*
- *Answer Key*
- *Literature Guide*
- *Language Arts Guide*
- *Activities Across the Curriculum*

For the students:
- *Textbooks* (2)
- *Workbooks* (2)
- *Literature Anthology*

The *Textbooks* contain stories, factual articles, and comprehension passages written especially for the program. All of the stories are serialized over a span of lessons. Most of the stories incorporate science facts and rules. Here is a partial listing of the contents of the *Textbooks.*
- **Old Henry and Tim**–The story of two geese who each help the other in his own way.
- **Oomoo, Oolak, and a Polar Bear**–A realistic story about Alaskan Eskimos.
- **Leonard the Inventor**–A realistic story about a boy who invents things.
- **A Trip Through the Solar System**–A science-fiction story.
- **Waldo the Animal Trainer**–A realistic story about a boy who trains animals.
- **Go Anywhere—See Anything**–An imaginative story about two children who can go anywhere and see anything.
- **Comprehension Passages**–Short passages that provide background information for the stories.

- **Factual Articles**–Articles about people and the world.

Sample Activities—Lesson 43

The following activities appear in lesson 43 of *Reading Mastery Plus,* Level 4.

The students begin lesson 43—and most other lessons—by working on model vocabulary sentences. These sentences contain selected vocabulary words. Students learn what each sentence means, practice saying the sentence, and respond to exercises about the meanings of specific words. In lesson 43, exercise 1, below, a new model sentence is introduced:

> 10. The patent attorney wrote an agreement.

EXERCISE 1

VOCABULARY

a. **Find the vocabulary sentences on page 352 in your textbook.** ✓
- Touch sentence 10. ✓
- This is a new vocabulary sentence. It says: The patent attorney wrote an agreement. Everybody, say that sentence. Get ready. (Signal.) *The patent attorney wrote an agreement.*
- Close your eyes and say the sentence. Get ready. (Signal.) *The patent attorney wrote an agreement.*
- (Repeat until firm.)

b. A **patent** is a license that says that only one person can make a particular product. New inventions are patented so that not everybody can make the product.

c. A patent **attorney** is a lawyer whose special job is getting patents for new inventions.

d. The sentence says the patent attorney wrote an **agreement.** An agreement is a paper that tells what two people promise to do. If people make an agreement, they shouldn't break the agreement. They should keep their promises.

---

e. Listen to the sentence again: The patent attorney wrote an agreement. Everybody say that sentence. Get ready. (Signal.) *The patent attorney wrote an agreement.*

f. Everybody, what word means **lawyer?** (Signal.) *Attorney.*
 • What word names a license for somebody to be the only person who can make a product? (Signal.) *Patent.*
 • What do we call a lawyer whose special job is getting patents for new inventions? (Signal.) *Patent attorney.*
 • What word means **a promise made by people?** (Signal.) *Agreement.*
 • (Repeat step f until firm.)

In exercise 3 of lesson 43, students read word lists. There are three types: lists of words that are difficult to decode; lists of words with common features; and lists of words that are easy to decode.

The teacher directs the students as they read these lists in unison. For each word in the lists whose meaning may not be familiar to the students, the teacher gives an explanation of the meaning. Finally individual students take turns reading one to three words each.

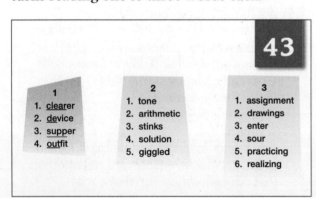

43

1	2	3
1. clearer	1. tone	1. assignment
2. device	2. arithmetic	2. drawings
3. supper	3. stinks	3. enter
4. outfit	4. solution	4. sour
	5. giggled	5. practicing
		6. realizing

EXERCISE 3

READING WORDS
Column 1
a. Find lesson 43 in your textbook. ✓
 • Touch column 1. ✓
 • (Teacher reference:)

1. clearer	3. supper
2. device	4. outfit

• All these words have more than one syllable. The first part of each word is underlined.
b. Word 1. What's the underlined part? (Signal.) *clear.*
 • What's the whole word? (Signal.) *Clearer.*
 • Spell **clearer.** Get ready. (Tap for each letter.) *C-L-E-A-R-E-R.*
c. Word 2. What's the underlined part? (Signal.) *de.*
 • What's the whole word? (Signal.) *Device.*
 • Spell **device.** Get ready. (Tap for each letter.) *D-E-V-I-C-E.*
d. Word 3. What's the underlined part? *Supp.*
 • What's the whole word? (Signal.) *Supper.*
 • Spell **supper.** Get ready. (Tap for each letter.) *S-U-P-P-E-R.*
e. Word 4. What's the underlined part? (Signal.) *out.*
 • What's the whole word? (Signal.) *Outfit.*
 • Spell **outfit.** Get ready. (Tap for each letter.) *O-U-T-F-I-T.*
f. Let's read those words again.
 • Word 1. What word? (Signal.) *Clearer.*
 • (Repeat for: **2. device, 3. supper, 4. outfit.**)
g. (Repeat step f until firm.)

Column 2
h. Find column 2. ✓
 • (Teacher reference:)

1. tone	4. solution
2. arithmetic	5. giggled
3. stinks	

i. Word 1. What word? (Signal.) *Tone.*
 • Your tone of voice tells what you are feeling. I can say "What are you doing?" so it sounds like a question or so it sounds like I'm scolding you. Which tone of voice do you want to hear? (Call on a student. Student preference.)
 • (Say "What are you doing?" using the selected tone of voice.)
j. Word 2. What word? (Signal.) *Arithmetic.*
 • (Repeat for words 3–5.)
k. Let's read those words again.
 • Word 1. What word? (Signal.) *Tone.*
 • (Repeat for words 2–5.)
l. (Repeat step k until firm.)

Column 3

m. Find column 3. ✓
   • (Teacher reference:)

1. assignment	4. sour
2. drawings	5. practicing
3. enter	6. realizing

n. Word 1. What word? (Signal.)
   Assignment.
   • (Repeat for words 2–6.)
o. Let's read those words again.
   • Word 1. What word? (Signal.)
   Assignment.
   • (Repeat for words 2–6.)
p. (Repeat step o until firm.)

Individual Turns

(For columns 1–3: Call on individual students, each to read one to three words per turn.)

Some of the lessons are preceded by comprehension passages. The students read the comprehension passage aloud. Individual students take turns reading two or three sentences each. As the students read the passage, the teacher presents comprehension passages that provide background information for the stories.

Next the students read their *Textbook* stories aloud.

ⓑ **A Good Idea**

The next evening, after supper, it happened. Leonard had no warning that it would happen. But it did. Everything in his mind suddenly came together and he had the idea for a great invention.

Here's how it happened: After supper, he went to his room to get a pencil. He was going to make some more drawings of ideas for inventions. When he started back to the kitchen, Grandmother Esther hollered at him, "Turn off the light in your room. Remember to save energy."

Leonard turned around, went back to his room, turned off the light, and stood there in the dark room. He felt the idea coming into his head. It got bigger and clearer and . . . "Hot dog!" he shouted. He shouted, "What an idea for an invention! Hot dog!"

He ran into the kitchen. "I've got it. What an idea! This is the best idea anybody ever had for an invention!"

His mother smiled. "I'll bet it's a machine that makes up a list of things you need at the store."

"Stop talking about that stupid machine," Grandmother Esther yelled from the other room. She ran into the kitchen. She was wearing her exercise outfit.

Grandmother Esther asked, "What's your idea, Leonard?"

Leonard said, "Let me explain how it's going to work. It's dark outside. And it's dark in the living room of your house. But when you walk through the door to the living room, the light goes on automatically. The light stays on as long as you're in the living room. But when you leave the living room, the light goes off."

Leonard's mother shook her head. "That sounds far too difficult."

Grandmother Esther said, "It sounds difficult to you because you don't know how the electric eye works."

"The electric eye?" Leonard's mother asked.

Leonard said, "Here's how it works, Mom. There's a little beam of light that goes across the doorway to the living room. When you enter the room, you break the beam. When you break that ✳ beam, the light turns on. Then when you leave the room, you break the beam and the light goes off."

"Oh, my," Leonard's mother said. He could tell from her tone of voice that she didn't understand what he said.

"Good thinking," Grandmother Esther said, and slapped Leonard on the back. "That's a fine idea for an invention, a fine idea."

"Thank you," Leonard said.

Grandmother Esther made a sour looking face. Slowly she said, "There's one big problem with being a good inventor. You have to think of all the things that could go wrong."

"What could go wrong?" Leonard asked.

Grandmother Esther explained. "When you break the beam one time, the light goes on. When you break the beam the next time, the light goes off. When you break the beam the next time, the light goes on."

"Right," Leonard said.

"That's the problem," Grandmother Esther said. "What if two people walk into a dark room? When the first one goes into the room, the light will go on. Now the second person goes into the room. What happens to the light?"

"It goes off," Leonard said very sadly. He shook his head. "Now both people are in the dark, and my invention stinks."

"Wrong!" Grandmother Esther shouted. "Both people are in the dark, but your invention does not stink. Every invention has problems. An inventor has to look at these problems and try to solve them. But you must remember that inventing something is more than just getting an idea. You must work on that idea until it is a good idea. Then you must take that good idea and make it into a good invention. Just because there's a problem doesn't mean that you give up. You've got a great idea."

Leonard's mother said, "I have a great idea for an invention. It's a machine that . . ."

"Not now," Grandmother Esther said. "We're close to a <u>real</u> invention."

Leonard said, "I'll just have to think about the problem and try to figure out how to solve it."

The students must read the first part of each story within a decoding error limit that is specified in the teacher's script. As the students read, the teacher presents comprehension questions from the *Presentation Book*. After the students complete their oral reading, they read the rest of the story silently. The teacher presents another group of comprehension questions at the end of the silent reading.

The comprehension questions in *Reading Mastery Plus*, Level 4 emphasize reasoning skills and character analysis. In this sample lesson, the students evaluate problems and solutions, use rules to predict outcomes, interpret a character's feelings and motives, and predict a character's actions.

EXERCISE 4

STORY READING

a. Find part B in your textbook. ✓
- The error limit for group reading is 11 errors. Read carefully.

b. Everybody, touch the title. ✓
- (Call on a student to read the title.) [A Good Idea.]
- Everybody, what's the title? (Signal.) *A Good Idea.*
- (Call on individual students to read the story, each student reading two or three sentences at a time. Ask the specified questions as the students read.)

- (Correct errors: Tell the word. Direct the student to reread the sentence.)
- (If the group makes more than 11 errors, direct the students to reread the story.)

A Good Idea
The next evening, after supper, it happened. Leonard had no warning that it would happen. But it did. Everything in his mind suddenly came together and he had the idea for a great invention.

- What happened that evening? (Call on a student. Idea: *Leonard got an idea for a great invention.*)
- Everybody, did Leonard know that this would happen? (Signal.) *No.*

Here's how it happened: After supper, he went to his room to get a pencil. He was going to make some more drawings of ideas for inventions. When he started back to the kitchen, Grandmother Esther hollered at him, "Turn off the light in your room. Remember to save energy."
Leonard turned around, went back to his room, turned off the light, and stood there in the dark room. He felt the idea coming into his head. It got bigger and clearer and . . . "Hot dog!" he shouted.

- Why did he shout? (Call on a student. Ideas: *He was excited; he had an idea.*)
- How did he feel? (Call on a student. Ideas: *Happy, excited.*)

He shouted, "What an idea for an invention! Hot dog!"
He ran into the kitchen. "I've got it. What an idea! This is the best idea anybody ever had for an invention!"
His mother smiled. "I'll bet it's a machine that makes up a list of things you need at the store."
"Stop talking about that stupid machine," Grandmother Esther yelled from the other room. She ran into the kitchen. She was wearing her exercise outfit.

- Look at the picture on the next page. ✓
- What is Grandmother Esther wearing? (Call on a student. Ideas: *Her exercise outfit; purple sweatsuit.*)

Grandmother Esther asked, "What's your idea, Leonard?"

Leonard said, "Let me explain how it's going to work. It's dark outside. And it's dark in the living room of your house. But when you walk through the door to the living room, the light goes on automatically. The light stays on as long as you're in the living room. But when you leave the living room, the light goes off."

- Leonard explained how the invention would work. Listen to that part again:

  Leonard said, "Let me explain how it's going to work. It's dark outside. And it's dark in the living room of your house. But when you walk through the door to the living room, the light goes on automatically. The light stays on as long as you're in the living room. But when you leave the living room, the light goes off."

- What happens when you walk **into** the room? (Call on a student. Idea: *The light goes on.*)
- What happens when you **leave** the room? (Call on a student. Idea: *The light goes off.*)
- What kind of thing could make the lights go on and off automatically? (Call on a student. Idea: *An electric eye.*)

Leonard's mother shook her head. "That sounds far too difficult."

Grandmother Esther said, "It sounds difficult to you because you don't know how the electric eye works."

- Everybody, did Grandmother Esther know how Leonard was thinking of making the lights go on and off? (Signal.) *Yes.*
- What was he going to use? (Signal.) *An electric eye.*

"The electric eye?" Leonard's mother asked.

Leonard said, "Here's how it works, Mom. There's a little beam of light that goes across the doorway to the living room. When you enter the room, you break the beam. When you break that ✳ beam, the light turns on. Then when you leave the room, you break the beam and the light goes off."

"Oh, my," Leonard's mother said. He could tell from her tone of voice that she didn't understand what he said.

"Good thinking," Grandmother Esther said, and slapped Leonard on the back. "That's a fine idea for an invention, a fine idea."

"Thank you," Leonard said.

- Everybody, do you think she feels that the electric eye invention is the right idea? (Signal.) *Yes.*

Grandmother Esther made a sour looking face. Slowly she said, "There's one big problem with being a good inventor. You have to think of all the things that could go wrong."

"What could go wrong?" Leonard asked.

Grandmother Esther explained. "When you break the beam one time, the light goes on. When you break the beam the next time, the light goes off. When you break the beam the next time, the light goes on."

"Right," Leonard said.

"That's the problem," Grandmother Esther said. "What if two people walk into a dark room? When the first one goes into the room, the light will go on. Now the second person goes into the room. What happens to the light?"

"It goes off," Leonard said very sadly. He shook his head. "Now both people are in the dark, and my invention stinks."

- What happens when the first person enters the room? (Call on a student. Idea: *The light goes on.*)
- What happens when the second person enters the room? (Call on a student. Idea: *The light goes off.*)
- Everybody, is that the way Leonard wants it to work? (Signal.) *No.*

- Read the rest of the story to yourself and be ready to answer some questions. Remember, Leonard has just said that he thinks his invention stinks. Raise your hand when you're finished.

> "Wrong!" Grandmother Esther shouted. "Both people are in the dark, but your invention does not stink. Every invention has problems. An inventor has to look at these problems and try to solve them. But you must remember that inventing something is more than just getting an idea. You must work on that idea until it is a good idea. Then you must take that good idea and make it into a good invention. Just because there's a problem doesn't mean that you give up. You've got a great idea."
>
> Leonard's mother said, "I have a great idea for an invention. It's a machine that . . ."
>
> "Not now," Grandmother Esther said. "We're close to a <u>real</u> invention."
>
> Leonard said, "I'll just have to think about the problem and try to figure out how to solve it."

- (After all students have raised their hand:) Why did Leonard think that his invention stinks? (Call on a student. Idea: *Because it has problems.*)
- Everybody, did Grandmother Esther think it stinks? (Signal.) *No.*
- She told him that every new invention has problems. So what does the inventor have to do? (Call on a student. Idea: *Solve the problems.*)
- Leonard's mother said she had a great idea for an invention. What do you think it was? (Call on a student. Idea: *The automatic grocery list-writer.*)
- Everybody, is Leonard going to give up? (Signal.) *No.*
- What is he going to do? (Call on a student. Idea: *Think about the problem and try to solve it.*)

- Everybody, look at the picture. The picture shows Leonard's invention. The lights in the box show what will happen each time the beam of light is broken. When we start out, the light is **not on**. What will happen when the beam is broken **one time?** (Signal.) *The light will go on.*
- What happens when the beam is broken two times? (Signal.) *The light will go off.*
- Look at the picture in the box and get ready to tell me what will happen when the beam is broken **five** times. (Pause.) Get ready. (Signal.) *The light will go on.*
- Everybody, get ready to tell me what will happen when the beam is broken **four** times. (Pause.) Get ready. (Signal.) *The light will go off.*
- Can you figure out what will happen when the beam is broken **six** times? (Call on a student. Idea: *The light will go off.*)

After the students finish the *Textbook* reading activities, they work independently in their *Workbooks* and *Textbooks*. The independent work includes comprehension-passage items, story items, skill items, vocabulary items, and review items.

In some lessons, additional activities include fact games and special projects.

In this sample lesson, the students complete story items and review items. The story items are based on the comprehension questions presented during the group reading. For the story items, the students recall narrative details, evaluate problems and solutions, and use rules to predict outcomes. The review items review previously taught facts. In this sample lesson, the students review facts they have learned about prehistoric eras, animal behavior, and geographic locations.

A Story Items

1. Leonard got his idea for a great invention when Grandmother Esther told him to do something. What did she tell him to do?

_____

Leonard's original invention had problems.

2. What does the light in a dark room do when you walk into the room?

_____

3. What does the light do when you leave the room?

_____

4. Let's say two people walk into a dark room. What happens to the light in the room when the first person enters?

_____

5. What happens to the light when the second person enters?

_____

6. What will Leonard use to make the lights work automatically?

_____

7. Did Leonard's mother understand how his invention would work?

_____

8. Grandmother Esther told Leonard that every invention has

_____

9. So what does the inventor have to do?
    • quit   • solve the problems   • hide the problems

Here's the rule about an electric eye: **Each time the beam of light is broken, the light changes.** Shade the bulbs that are off for each problem. The first problem is already done for you.

10. The light is off. The beam is broken 4 times.

Is the light **on** or **off** at the end? _____

11. Here's another problem. The light is off. The beam is broken 8 times.
    a. Shade the bulbs that are off.

    b. Is the light **on** or **off** at the end? _____

12. Here's another problem. The light is off. The beam is broken 3 times.
    a. Shade the bulbs that are off.

    b. Is the light on or off at the end? _____

GO TO PART C IN YOUR TEXTBOOK.

C   Number your paper from 1 through 24.

Skill Items

Use the words in the box to write complete sentences.

device	outfit	solution	entered
impressed	mentioned	responded	vocabulary

1. They were ▮▮▮ by her large ▮▮▮.
2. He ▮▮▮ to her clever ▮▮▮.

Review Items

Here's how an electric eye at a store works.
3. When somebody walks in the door, the body stops the beam of light from reaching the ▮▮▮.
4. When the body stops the beam, what does the device do next?
5. What does that tell the shopkeeper?

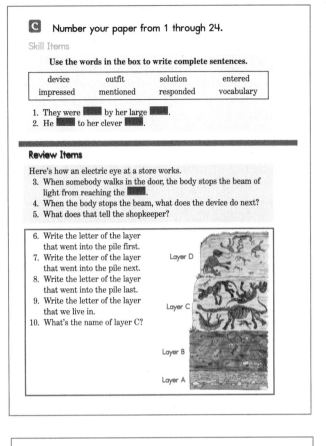

6. Write the letter of the layer that went into the pile first.
7. Write the letter of the layer that went into the pile next.
8. Write the letter of the layer that went into the pile last.
9. Write the letter of the layer that we live in.
10. What's the name of layer C?

11. Name the country that is just north of the United States.

12. Which letter shows where the United States is?
13. Which letter shows where Canada is?

14. The picture shows half a hailstone. How many times did the stone go through a cloud?

15. What's the name of geese that are all white?
16. What's the name of geese that are gray and white and black?
17. What color are all geese when they are born?
18. How old are geese when they mate for the first time?
19. After male and female geese mate, how long do they stay together?
20. Most geese live for about ▮▮▮ years.
21. When geese learn to fly, do they start in the water or on the land?
22. They run with their ▮▮▮ out to the side.
23. How many poles are there?
24. The farther you go from the equator, the ▮▮▮ it gets.
    • hotter   • colder   • fatter

Reading Mastery Plus, Level 5

Reading Mastery Plus, Level 5, contains 120 daily lessons that emphasize literary analysis and extended writing. Students in the program read a wide range of classic and modern fiction and prose, including two full-length novels, and they learn how to analyze characters, settings, plots, and themes. The daily writing assignments focus on the meaning of literature and encourage students to think critically. Other program activities include making outlines, inferring word meaning from context, and interpreting reference materials.

Materials

For the teacher:
- *Presentation Books* (2)
- *Teacher's Guide*
- *Answer Key*
- *Literature Guide*
- *Language Arts Guide*
- *Activities across the Curriculum*
- *Testing and Management Handbook*

For the students:
- *Textbooks* (2)
- *Workbook*
- *Literature Anthology*

The *Textbooks* and the *Literature Anthology* contain both classic and modern literature. Students read two full-length novels, as well as short stories, folktales, myths, factual articles, biographies, and poetry. Here is a partial listing:
- **Novels** by L. Frank Baum (*The Wonderful Wizard of Oz*) and Mark Twain (*The Prince and the Pauper*).
- **Short Stories** by well-known children's writers, including Toni Cade Bambara, Mavis Jukes, Jack London, Gary Soto, and Yoshiko Uchida.

- **Folktales and Myths** from around the world, including "Beauty and the Beast," "Hans in Luck," and "The Golden Touch."
- **Factual Articles** about endangered species, gold mining, Tudor England, animal migration, and other topics.
- **Biographies** of Jackie Robinson, Jane Addams, and Mark Twain.
- **Poetry** by Langston Hughes, Harry Behn, and Kathryn Jackson.

Sample Activities—Lesson 76

The following sample activities appear in the student *Textbook* and *Workbook* for lesson 76 of *Reading Mastery Plus,* Level 5. For an overview of student and teacher materials in lesson 76, turn to the sample lesson at the back of this guide, pages 170–180.

As with every other lesson in Level 5, students begin lesson 76 by reading in their *Textbooks.* Each *Textbook* lesson is divided into parts (part A, part B, part C, and so on). In part A of lesson 76, students read different types of word lists aloud and practice using the words in sentences.

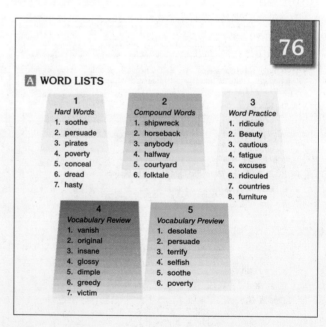

In part B, students read sentences that contain bold-faced vocabulary words. They then use context clues to determine the meanings of the vocabulary words.

B VOCABULARY FROM CONTEXT

1. There was nothing within a hundred miles of this lonely, **desolate** place.
2. She was good at talking people into doing things, but she could not **persuade** anybody to go to the beach with her.
3. The old house was frightening, and the sounds within it **terrified** me.
4. She seemed to be kind, but she was really very **selfish** and thought of nobody but herself.
5. He was so upset that nothing we could do would comfort or **soothe** him.
6. At first he was wealthy, but then he lost all his wealth and found himself in **poverty**.

In part C, students read a short "Story Background" passage that conveys important information about the story for lesson 76, "Beauty and the Beast." The passage explains that the story is a folktale and describes differences between folktales and myths. The teacher asks questions from the *Presentation Book* as individual students take turns reading the passage aloud.

In part D, students read the first chapter of "Beauty and the Beast." The first part of the chapter is done aloud, with individual students reading a few sentences each. During this oral reading, the teacher asks a range of interpretive and analytical comprehension questions. Afterwards, students read the rest of the chapter silently. The teacher asks more comprehension questions when everyone has finished reading.

C STORY BACKGROUND

Folktales

The next story you will read is a folktale called "Beauty and the Beast." Like myths, folktales are old stories that people told aloud before someone wrote them down. But folktales are usually much newer than myths. The myths you have just read, for example, take place about three thousand years ago. In comparison, "Beauty and the Beast" takes place just a few hundred years ago.

Another difference is that myths usually include gods and goddesses, but folktales do not. Instead, folktales often have witches, wizards, or other kinds of magic.

"Beauty and the Beast" is one of the most famous folktales of all time. Many movies have been made of the story, and many writers have retold it in their own words. The story comes from France, a large country in Europe.

D READING

Beauty and the Beast
Chapter 1

Once upon a time there lived a merchant who was enormously rich. The merchant had six sons and six daughters, and he would let them have anything they wanted.

But one day their house caught fire and burned to the ground, with all the splendid furniture, books, pictures, gold, silver, and precious goods it contained. Yet this was only the beginning of their misfortune. Shortly after the fire, the merchant lost every ship he had upon the sea, either because of pirates, shipwrecks, or fire. Then he heard that the people who worked for him in distant countries had stolen his money. At last, he fell into great poverty.

All the merchant had after those misfortunes was a little cottage in a desolate place a hundred miles from the town in which he used to live. He moved into the cottage with his children. They were in despair at the idea of leading such a different life. The cottage stood in the middle of a dark forest, and it seemed to be the most dismal place on earth.

The children had to cultivate the fields to earn their living. They were poorly clothed, and they missed the comforts and amusements of their earlier life. Only the youngest daughter tried to be brave and cheerful. She had also been sad at first, but she soon recovered her good nature. She set to work to make the best of things. But when she tried to persuade her sisters to join her in dancing and singing, they ridiculed her and said that this miserable life was all she was fit for. But she was far prettier and more clever than they were. She was so lovely that she was called Beauty.

After two years, their father received news that one of his ships, which he had believed to be lost, had come safely into port with a rich cargo. All the sons and daughters at once thought their poverty would be over, and they wanted to set out directly for the town. But their father was more cautious, so he decided to go by himself. Only Beauty had any doubt that they would soon be rich again. The other daughters gave their father requests for so many jewels and dresses that it would have taken a fortune to buy them. But Beauty did not ask for anything. Her father noticed her silence and said, "And what shall I bring for you, Beauty?"

"The only thing I wish for is to see you come home safely," she answered.

This reply angered her sisters, who thought she was accusing them of asking for costly things. But her father was pleased. Still, he told her to choose something.

"Well, dear Father," she said, "since you insist upon it, I want you to bring me a rose. I have not seen one since we came here, and I love them very much." ◆

So the merchant set out on horseback and reached the town as quickly as possible. But when he got there, he found out that his partners had taken the goods the ship had brought. So he found himself poorer than when he had left the cottage. He had only enough money to buy food on his journey home. To make matters worse, he left town during terrible weather. The storm was so bad that he was exhausted with cold and fatigue before he was halfway home. Night came on, and the deep snow and bitter frost made it impossible for the merchant's horse to carry him any further.

The merchant could see no houses or lights. The only shelter he could find was the hollow trunk of a great tree. He crouched there all night long. It was the longest night he had ever known. In spite of his weariness, the howling of the wolves kept him awake. And when the day broke, he was not much better off, for falling snow had covered up every path, and he did not know which way to turn.

At last, he made out some sort of path, and he started to follow it. It was rough and slippery, so he kept falling down. But the path soon became easier, and it led him to a row of trees that ended at a splendid castle. It seemed very strange to the merchant that no snow had fallen in the row of trees. Stranger still, the trees were fruit trees, and they were covered with apples and oranges. ★

The merchant walked down the row of trees and soon reached the castle. He called, but nobody answered. So he opened the door and called again. Then he climbed up a flight of steps and walked through several splendid rooms. The pleasant warmth of the air refreshed him, and he suddenly felt very hungry; but there seemed to be nobody in this huge palace who could give him anything to eat.

The merchant kept wandering through the deep silence of the splendid rooms. At last, he stopped in a room smaller than the rest, where a bright fire was burning next to a couch. The merchant thought this room must be prepared for someone, so he sat down to wait. But very soon he fell into a heavy sleep.

His extreme hunger wakened him after several hours. He was still alone, but a good dinner had been set on a little table. The merchant had eaten nothing for an entire day, so he lost no time in beginning his meal, which was delicious. He wondered who had brought the food, but no one appeared.

After dinner, the merchant went to sleep again. He woke completely refreshed the next morning. There was still no sign of anybody, although a fresh meal of cakes and fruit was sitting on the little table at his elbow. The silence began to terrify the merchant, and he decided to search once more through the rooms. But it was no use. There was no sign of life in the palace. Not even a mouse could be seen.

After students finish the reading activities, they work independently in their *Textbooks* and *Workbooks*. In the *Textbook* exercises for lesson 76, students write the main idea of a paragraph (part E), answer interpretive comprehension questions about the story (part F), and write a poem (part G).

E MAIN IDEA

For each paragraph, write a sentence that tells the complete main idea.

1. Saturday finally arrived. Janet took her camera out of her closet. Then she went outside to look for her friends. When she had found everybody, she told them to stand together on her porch. She looked through her camera and told everybody to stand closer together. Finally, she said, "Smile," and pressed the button on the camera. The camera went "click," and some of Janet's friends made faces.

2. William liked rowing boats. Last spring, William visited Swan Lake. He rented a rowboat for the whole day. He hopped into the boat and started to pull the oars. The boat started across the lake. William could see the boat rental place getting farther and farther away. William kept rowing. He looked at people fishing and at birds flying near the water. He had fun seeing how fast he could row. After a long time, he came to the opposite side of the lake.

F COMPREHENSION

Write the answers.
1. Why were most of the merchant's children greedy and spoiled?
2. Name at least three ways that Beauty was different from her sisters.
3. Why do you think Beauty asked her father for a rose?
4. Why did the merchant get lost on the way home?
5. Name at least three strange things about the palace.

G WRITING

What objects do you think are beautiful?
• Pick an object that you think is beautiful, such as a flower, a painting, or a river. Then write a poem about the object. Describe what the object looks like and tell why you think it's beautiful.

Students write the answers to *Workbook* exercises in the *Workbook* itself. In lesson 76, they answer literal comprehension questions about the story (part A), use vocabulary words in context (part B), sequence story events (part C), and review material from earlier lessons in the program (parts D and E).

76

Name_____

A STORY DETAILS

Write the answers.

1. At the beginning of the story, how rich was the merchant?

2. How many children did the merchant have?

3. What happened to his house?

4. What kind of house did the family move into?

5. Before her father left for town, what did Beauty ask him to bring back?

6. What kinds of things did the other children ask for?

7. Where did the merchant sleep during the storm?

8. What was strange about the row of trees the merchant found?

9. Why was the palace so silent?

B VOCABULARY

Write the correct words in the blanks.

shrewd	calculate
witty	century
appetite	secure
inhabitant	sympathy
discontented	defeat

1. Lillian was so _____ with her job that she quit.

2. The wise man made many _____ decisions.

3. A _____ is a long time.

4. The experts could not _____ the number of stars in the sky.

5. She was glad to see the food because she had an enormous _____.

6. The cat was _____ from dogs as long as it stayed inside the house.

7. After the child fell, her mother held her and showed great _____.

C SEQUENCING

Put the following events in the correct order by numbering them from **1** to **5**.

___ The merchant found a palace.
___ The merchant spent the night in a tree.
___ The merchant moved to a cottage.
___ The merchant's house burned down.
___ The merchant went back to the town.

D RELATED FACTS

Write which Greek god each statement describes. Choose **Hermes, Poseidon,** or **Zeus.**

1. The god of the sky
_____

2. The god of the ocean
_____

3. The god of travelers
_____

E STORY REVIEW

Write whether each statement describes **The Miraculous Pitcher** or **The Golden Touch.**

1. Zeus appeared in this story.
_____

2. The main character was a king.
_____

3. One of the characters had a magic staff.
_____

4. One of the characters was changed into a statue.
_____

5. The story showed how evil greed can be.
_____

6. The story showed why you should be kind to strangers.
_____

The *Textbook* and *Workbook* activities constitute the main part of lesson 76. Other activities can be found in the complete sample lesson at the back of this guide.

Reading Mastery Plus, Level 6

Reading Mastery Plus, Level 6, contains 120 daily lessons that focus on literary language, reasoning strategies, and extended writing. The reading selections include novels, short stories, poems, factual articles, biographies, and a play. Students in the program interpret complex sentence forms, figurative language, and literary irony; they also identify contradictions and faulty logic. In addition, students write a wide variety of essays, dialogues, short stories, and poems.

Materials

For the teacher:
- *Presentation Books* (2)
- *Teacher's Guide*
- *Answer Key*
- *Literature Guide*
- *Activities across the Curriculum*
- *Testing and Management Handbook*

For the students:
- *Textbooks* (2)
- *Workbook*
- *Literature Anthology*

The *Textbooks* and the *Literature Anthology* contain both classic and modern literature. Students read a full-length novel and three novellas, as well as short stories, folktales, myths, factual articles, poetry, biographies, and a play. Here is a partial listing:

- **Novels and Novellas** by Mark Twain (*Tom Sawyer*), Homer (*The Odyssey*), Frances Hodgson Burnett (*Sara Crewe*), and Jack London (*The Cruise of the Dazzler*).
- **Short Stories** by Mildred Taylor, Gary Soto, Isaac Bashevis Singer, Pam Conrad, Philippa Pearce, Robert McCloskey, and many other award-winning children's writers.
- **Folktales and Myths** from around the world, including "The Brave Little Tailor," "The Table, the Donkey, and the Stick," and "Persephone."
- **Factual Articles** about American history, the apprentice system, and San Francisco Bay.
- **Biographies** of Harriet Tubman and Jack London.
- **Poetry** by Walt Whitman, William Wordsworth, and Ernest Thayer.

Sample Activities—Lesson 57

The following sample activities appear in the student *Textbook* and *Workbook* for lesson 57 of *Reading Mastery Plus,* Level 6. For an overview of student and teacher materials in lesson 57, turn to the sample lesson at the back of this guide, pages 181–191.

As with every other lesson in Level 6, students begin lesson 57 by reading in their *Textbooks*. Each *Textbook* lesson is divided into parts (part A, part B, part C, and so on). In part A of lesson 57, students read different types of word lists aloud.

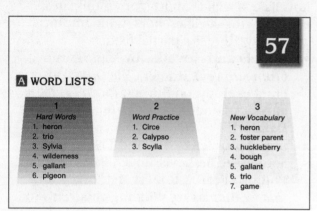

57

A WORD LISTS

1 Hard Words	2 Word Practice	3 New Vocabulary
1. heron	1. Circe	1. heron
2. trio	2. Calypso	2. foster parent
3. Sylvia	3. Scylla	3. huckleberry
4. wilderness		4. bough
5. gallant		5. gallant
6. pigeon		6. trio
		7. game

In part B, students read vocabulary definitions aloud and practice using the vocabulary words in context.

B VOCABULARY DEFINITIONS

1. **heron**—*Herons* are birds that wade through water and eat frogs and fish. Herons usually have tall, thin legs and a long, S-shaped neck. The picture shows a *white heron*.
   • Describe a heron.
2. **foster parent**—A *foster parent* is somebody who brings up a child but is not the child's real parent.
   • What do we call somebody who brings up a child but is not the child's real parent?
3. **huckleberry**—A *huckleberry* is a small purple or black berry that grows on bushes.
   • What is a huckleberry?
4. **bough**—A *bough* of a tree is a branch of the tree.
   • What is a branch of a tree?
5. **gallant**—Somebody who is *gallant* is brave and noble.
   • What's another way of saying *He was a noble warrior*?
6. **trio**—A *trio* is a group of three.
   • What's another way of saying *A group of three went to the river*?
7. **game**—Wild animals that are hunted are called *game*.
   • What do we call wild animals that are hunted?

In part C, students read the first part of "A White Heron," a classic short story by Sarah Orne Jewett. The story includes a focus question that draws attention to a central theme. Students have the option of reading the first part of the story aloud; the second part is always read silently. After the reading, the teacher asks comprehension questions.

C READING

A White Heron
*by Sarah Orne Jewett**
Part 1

Focus Question: How did Sylvia feel about living on her foster mother's farm?

The woods were filled with shadows one June evening, but a bright sunset still glimmered faintly among the trunks of the trees. A girl named Sylvia was driving a cow from the pasture to her home. Sylvia had spent more than an hour looking for the cow and had finally found her hiding behind a huckleberry bush.

Sylvia and the cow were going away from the sunset and into the dark woods. But they were familiar with the path, and the darkness did not bother them.

Sylvia wondered what her foster mother, Mrs. Tilley, would say because they were so late. But Mrs. Tilley knew how difficult it was to find the cow. She had chased the beast many times herself. As she waited, she was only thankful that Sylvia could help her. Sylvia seemed to love the out-of-doors, and Mrs. Tilley thought that being outdoors was a good change for an orphan girl who had grown up in a town.

The companions followed the shady road. The cow took slow steps, and the girl took very fast ones. The cow stopped at the brook to drink, and Sylvia stood still and waited. She let her bare feet cool themselves in the water while the great twilight moths struck softly against her. She waded on through the brook as the cow moved away, and she listened to the waterbirds with pleasure.

There was a stirring in the great boughs overhead. They were full of little birds that seemed to be wide awake and going about their business. Sylvia began to feel sleepy as she walked along. However, it was not much farther to the house, and the air was soft and sweet.

She was not often in the woods so late as this. The darkness made her feel as if she were a part of the gray shadows and the moving leaves. She was thinking how long it seemed since she had first come to her foster mother's farm a year ago. Sylvia wondered if everything was still going on in the noisy town just the same as when she had lived there. ♦

It seemed to Sylvia that she had never been alive at all before she came to live at her foster mother's farm. It was a beautiful place to live, and she never wished to go back to the town. The thought of the children who used to chase and frighten her made her hurry along the path to escape from the shadows of the trees.

_____
* *Adapted for young readers*

After students finish the reading activities, they work independently in their *Textbooks* and *Workbooks*. In the *Textbook* exercises for lesson 57, students make inferences (part D), complete deductions (part E), review vocabulary words (part F), answer interpretive comprehension questions about the story (part G), and write an essay (part H).

Suddenly, she was horror-struck to hear a clear whistle not very far away. It was not a bird's whistle. It sounded more like a boy's. Sylvia stepped aside into the bushes, but she was too late. The whistler had discovered her, and he called out in a cheerful voice, "Hello, little girl, how far is it to the road?"

Trembling, Sylvia answered quietly, "A long distance."

She did not dare to look at the tall young man, who carried a gun over his shoulder. But Sylvia came out of the bushes and again followed the cow, while the young man walked alongside her.

"I have been hunting for some birds," the stranger said kindly, "and I have lost my way. Don't be afraid," he added gallantly. "Speak up and tell me what your name is and whether you think I can spend the night at your house and go out hunting early in the morning." ★

Sylvia was more alarmed than before. Would her foster mother blame her for this? She hung her head, but she managed to answer "Sylvia" when her companion again asked her name.

Mrs. Tilley was standing in the doorway when the trio came into view. The cow gave a loud moo as if to explain the situation.

Mrs. Tilley said, "Yes, you'd better speak up for yourself, you naughty old cow! Where'd she hide herself this time, Sylvia?" But Sylvia kept silent.

The young man stood his gun beside the door and dropped a heavy gamebag next to it. Then he said good evening to Mrs. Tilley. He repeated his story and asked if he could have a night's lodging.

"Put me anywhere you like," he said. "I must be off early in the morning, before day, but I am very hungry indeed. Could you give me some milk?"

"Dear sakes, yes," said Mrs. Tilley. "You might do better if you went out to the main road, but you're welcome to what we've got. I'll milk the cow right now, and you make yourself at home. Now step round and set a plate for the gentleman, Sylvia!"

Sylvia promptly stepped. She was glad to have something to do, and she was hungry herself.

D INFERENCE

Write the answers for items 1–8.

You have to answer different types of questions about the passages you read. Some questions are answered by words in the passage. Other questions are *not* answered by words in the passage. You have to figure out the answer by making a deduction.

The following passage includes both types of questions.

More about Ecology

Two hundred years ago, many people were not concerned with ecology. They believed there was no end to the different types of wildlife, so they killed wild animals by the hundreds of thousands. When we look back on these killings, we may feel shocked. But for the people who lived two hundred years ago, wild animals seemed to be as plentiful as weeds.

Because of these killings, more than a hundred types of animals have become extinct since 1800. An animal is extinct when there are no more animals of that type.

One type of extinct animal is the passenger pigeon. At one time, these birds were so plentiful that flocks of them used to blacken the sky. Now the passenger pigeon is gone forever. Think of that. You will never get to see a living passenger pigeon or any of the other animals that have become extinct. The only place you can see those animals is in a museum, where they are stuffed and mounted.

1. Are house cats extinct?
2. Is that question answered by **words** or a **deduction**?
3. Name one type of extinct animal.
4. **Words** or **deduction**?
5. How many types of animals have become extinct since 1800?
6. **Words** or **deduction**?
7. The dodo bird is extinct. How many animals of that type are alive today?
8. **Words** or **deduction**?

E DEDUCTIONS

Write the answers about the deductions.

Oliver believed that if he studied, he would pass the test. Oliver studied for the test.

1. So, what did Oliver believe would happen?

Nadia believed that if you ate an apple a day you would stay healthy. Nadia ate an apple every day.

2. So, what did Nadia believe would happen?

F VOCABULARY REVIEW

unprecedented
maneuver
devoted
spurn
endured
regard

For each item, write the correct word.
1. When you move skillfully, you ▓▓▓.
2. When you consider something, you ▓▓▓ it.
3. Something that has never occurred before is ▓▓▓.

G COMPREHENSION

Write the answers.
1. How did Sylvia feel about living on her foster mother's farm?
2. Why didn't Sylvia like the town?
3. Why do you think Sylvia didn't dare to look at the young man?
4. How do you think Sylvia feels about hunting? Explain your answer.
5. What do you think will happen in the next part of the story?

H WRITING

Where would you rather live, on a farm or in a town?

Write an essay that explains your answer. Try to answer the following questions:
• What are the advantages of living on a farm?
• What are the disadvantages of living on a farm?
• What are the advantages of living in a town?
• What are the disadvantages of living in a town?
• Where would you rather live? Why?
Make your essay at least sixty words long.

Students write the answers to *Workbook* exercises in the *Workbook* itself. In lesson 57, they answer literal comprehension questions about the story (part A), use vocabulary words in context (part B), identify different types of figurative language (part C), complete deductions (part D), distinguish characters by trait (part E), and make comparisons (part F).

The *Textbook* and *Workbook* activities constitute the main part of lesson 57. Other activities can be found in the complete sample lesson at the back of this guide.

57

A STORY DETAILS

Write or circle the answers.

1. Sylvia was ___ who lived on a farm.
   • a vacationer • a farmhand • an orphan

2. Where had Sylvia lived before coming to the farm?
   _____

3. Sylvia thought she had never been ___ at all before coming to the farm.
   • scared • alive • punished

4. Which place did Sylvia enjoy more, the town or the farm?
   _____

5. How had the children in town treated Sylvia?
   _____

6. What was the young man doing in the woods?
   _____

7. Was Sylvia bold or shy?
   _____

8. What was the name of the person who owned the farm?
   _____

9. That person was Sylvia's ___.
   • employer • mother • foster parent

B VOCABULARY

Write the correct words in the blanks.

regarded	suitable
appealed	humiliating
unprecedented	maneuvered

1. The starving boy _____ to the sympathy of the crowd.

2. They _____ the criminal as a dangerous person.

3. He _____ the shopping cart past the fallen cans.

4. The pitcher made an _____ number of strikeouts.

C FIGURATIVE LANGUAGE

For each statement, write **simile, metaphor,** or **exaggeration.**

1. Her face was like a pale star.
   _____

2. The apartment was a prison.
   _____

3. The day was like a dream.
   _____

D DEDUCTIONS

Complete each deduction.
Every element has an atomic weight. Argon is an element.

1. What's the conclusion about argon?
   _____
   _____

Horses eat grass. A palomino is a horse.

2. What's the conclusion about a palomino?
   _____
   _____

E CHARACTER TRAITS

Write whether each phrase describes **Sylvia, Mrs. Tilley,** or **the stranger.**

1. Very shy
   _____

2. Whistled loudly
   _____

3. An orphan
   _____

4. Owned a farm
   _____

5. Felt like a part of the woods
   _____

6. Hunted for animals
   _____

F COMPARISONS

Write **Odyssey** if the event occurred in *The Odyssey.* Write **Yarn** if the event occurred in "Mystery Yarn."

1. Telemachus was one of the suitors.
   _____

2. Telemachus helped defeat the suitors.
   _____

3. The suitors took a test that involved unwinding string.
   _____

4. The suitors took a test that involved a bow and arrow.
   _____

Testing and Management

The seven *Reading Mastery Plus* placement tests determine the level in which students should be placed. The in-program mastery tests measure student progress within each level. The specifications for each test provide instructions for administration, student testing material, record-keeping charts, and remedial exercises.

Placement Tests

The students should generally be placed in the level of *Reading Mastery Plus* that corresponds with their grade level. To ensure accurate placement, each level of the series includes a placement test. These tests should be administered at the beginning of the school year.

The placement test results will provide you with

- information about the students' decoding and comprehension skills,
- a means of identifying which students should be placed in another level of the *Reading Mastery Plus* program,
- guidelines for grouping the students.

Copies of the placement tests and accompanying instructions appear on pages 70–87 of this guide as well as in the *Teacher's Guides.* These pages may be reproduced for classroom use.

In-Program Mastery Tests

The *Reading Mastery Plus* series is designed so that the students are constantly tested on their reading skills as they progress through each level of the series. Each student's decoding skills are periodically measured through rate-and-accuracy checkouts. For these checkouts, the student reads a passage aloud as you record the student's decoding errors. Comprehension, reference, and study skills are measured through the daily independent work. Because the independent work is directly related to other program material, it serves as a continuous test of each student's skill mastery. You check the independent work every day and use a chart to keep track of each student's performance.

You can use the rate-and-accuracy checkouts and the independent work to identify students who need remedial help. The *Teacher's Guides* contain specific remedial procedures for students who do not perform well on these exercises. These procedures include a review of program material and additional practice with specific skills. The procedures can be used with individual students or with an entire group.

In-program mastery tests are integrated into the main program components in Levels K–4 and appear in a separate *Testing and Management Handbook* in Levels 5 and 6. These criterion-referenced tests are scheduled intermittently in Levels K–2 and every tenth lesson in Levels 3–6. Each test item measures student mastery of a specific skill taught in the *Reading Mastery Plus* series.

Instructions for administering the mastery tests appear in the *Reading Presentation Books* in Levels K–4 and in the *Testing and Management Handbooks* for Levels 5 and 6. These instructions give you remedial exercises for students who do not perform well on the mastery tests. Each test has its own set of remedial exercises, and there is a specific remedial exercise for every tested skill.

Grouping the Students

Reading Mastery Plus can be presented either to small groups of students or to the entire class. In general, Levels K–4 should be presented to small groups of students, while Levels 5 and 6 should be presented to the entire class.

Small-group instruction offers several advantages. If you use small-group instruction, the students can be grouped according to their ability levels: above-average, average, below-average. This homogeneous grouping will allow you to spend more time with the below-average students, who will need the most help. You can use the placement test results as a guideline for grouping the students.

Small-group instruction also allows you to monitor individual performance more closely. In small groups, individual students will have more opportunities to read aloud and to answer your questions. The students will also get a better view of any material presented. This is particularly important in *Reading Mastery Plus,* Levels K–2, where you often point to pictures, words, and letters in the *Presentation Books.*

Small-group instruction is simple with *Reading Mastery Plus* because you can teach one group of students while the rest of the students are doing their independent work. Ideally, for *Reading Mastery Plus,* Levels K–2, the class should be divided into three groups: higher-performing, middle-performing, and lower-performing. The lower-performing group should be the smallest. For *Reading Mastery Plus,* Levels 3 and 4, the class can be divided into just two groups: one for the lower-performing students and another for the rest of the class. *Reading Mastery Plus,* Levels 5 and 6 are usually presented to the entire class, but they can also be presented to small groups.

Scheduling the Reading Period

Generally, one reading lesson of *Reading Mastery Plus* should be presented on each day of the school year. Every lesson is divided into three parts: group instruction, independent work, and workcheck. The group instruction usually requires thirty minutes; the independent work, between twenty and thirty minutes; the workcheck, ten minutes. The students should generally complete the independent work immediately after finishing the group instruction. However, they can also complete the independent work later in the day or even as homework.

The following chart shows one possible schedule for reading lessons in a class with two groups of students.

	Group A	Group B
8:45–9:15	group instruction	
9:15–9:45	independent work	group instruction
9:45–10:15	workcheck	independent work
10:15–10:25		workcheck

Note: Spelling lessons (Levels 1–3), Language lessons (Levels K–2), Language Arts lessons (Levels 1–6), and Literature lessons (Levels K–6) are not to be presented as part of the reading lessons. Present them at a different time.

Motivating the Students

Reading Mastery Plus is designed so that every student can succeed. Each lesson is a series of exercises. The students are able to succeed on each and every exercise, and their success is consistently rewarded. As soon as the students learn a new skill in one exercise, they apply that skill in another exercise and review it in still another. This constant application and review provides a consistent reward for learning. Students are motivated to learn each new skill because they know that they will soon be using that skill.

Teaching Techniques

Arranging the Classroom

The classroom should be arranged differently for different levels of the program.

In *Reading Mastery Plus,* Levels K–2, you will usually be presenting the program to small groups of students. The group that is being taught should be seated in a small semicircle in front of you. The students should sit on chairs, not at desks, and you should be within touching distance of every student. Every student in the group must be able to see the pictures or words that you present from the *Presentation Book.* The lowest performers in the group should be seated directly in front of you where you can monitor them closely.

Reading Mastery Plus, Levels 3 and 4 are usually presented to somewhat larger groups of students. The group that is being taught should face you. The students may sit at their desks, or simply on chairs. The group can be arranged in any form as long as all students are facing you. The lowest performers should be seated directly in front of you.

Reading Mastery Plus, Levels 5 and 6 are usually presented to the entire class. The class should be facing you and the students should be seated at their desks. The lowest performers should be seated directly in front of you.

Using the Presentation Books

The *Presentation Books* contain complete scripts for presenting every lesson in *Reading Mastery Plus.* The scripts are carefully written so that all instruction is clear and unambiguous. The program will be most effective if the scripts are followed closely.

Each lesson shows you what to say, what to do, and what the students' responses should be.

- What you say appears in blue type.
  You say this.
- What you do appears in parentheses.
  (You do this.)

- The responses of the students are in italics. *Students say this.*

Pacing the Lesson

Present the daily lessons at a lively pace. Fast pacing offers several advantages.

- Fast pacing generates student interest. Students are likely to pay attention if the lesson is presented at a lively pace.
- Fast pacing encourages student achievement. With fast pacing, you can cover more material and the students can receive more practice.
- Fast pacing keeps the students thinking. If a lesson is presented slowly, the students' minds may wander. With fast pacing, the students are constantly thinking, and they are unlikely to become distracted.
- Fast pacing reduces management problems. With fast pacing, the students are involved in their work and unlikely to misbehave.

To set a fast pace, you should move quickly, but you should not rush the students into making mistakes. Experience will show you the pace that is appropriate for each group. You should read over the material before presenting it. Fast pacing is easier if you do not have to refer to the *Presentation Book* for every word.

Using Signals

For many of the exercises in *Reading Mastery Plus,* the students must answer aloud and in unison. This group response is very important because

- every student must initiate a response,
- every student is able to practice the exercise,
- you can monitor every student,
- you can hear any incorrect answers and correct them immediately.

For the students to answer simultaneously, you must use a signal. The signal eliminates the problem of one student leading the rest of the group.

There are two basic types of signals: visual and auditory. The visual signals are used when the students are looking at you or at the *Presentation Book.* You signal the students by making some type of hand motion (quickly dropping your hand, touching a word or picture, slashing under a word). Auditory signals are used in all levels. The students answer on signal as they read word lists, stories, and skill exercises. Auditory signals are used for these exercises because the students are looking at what they are reading, not at you. You can use either a foot tap, a clap, a finger snap, or a tap on a desk as an auditory signal.

You should use the following procedure for both visual and auditory signals.

1. Ask the specified question.
2. Pause for about one second.
3. Give the auditory or visual signal.
4. Listen to the group response and correct any errors.
5. Move quickly to the next question.

The one-second pause is very important. It clearly separates the question from the signal and ensures that every student sees or hears the signal. The pause should always last for about one second. When the pause is of a consistent length, the group is able to answer more effectively.

Praising the Students

The students will work harder if they receive praise for their work. Each lesson provides many opportunities for praise. You can praise the students when they learn a new sound, when they read lists of words, or when they read a story without making any errors. You can also praise students when they behave well and when they work particularly hard.

Praise should be simple and positive. You can say things such as, Great. You read the entire list without making any mistakes. or Good talking. I could hear everybody. The students are especially reinforced when you repeat a correct answer; for example, Yes, that word is **am.**

Praise should be an integral part of your presentation, but don't overdo it. Every statement of praise should clearly result from a specific student action. If praise is indiscriminate and undeserved, it will lose all meaning for the students. Generally, students in the lower levels of the program will require more praise than students in the upper levels.

Correcting Mistakes

The *Reading Mastery Plus* program includes correction procedures for many of the mistakes that the students are likely to make. These mistakes fall into two categories: general and specific. The general mistakes include not paying attention and not answering on signal. The specific mistakes include misidentifying words and giving the wrong answers to questions.

General Mistakes

The general mistakes are most likely to occur when students are beginning the program. It is very important to correct these mistakes as soon as they occur so that students do not fall into bad habits.

In *Reading Mastery Plus,* Levels K–2, the students must always pay attention when you are pointing to letters or words in the *Presentation Book.* If a student is not paying attention, you should use the following procedure.

1. Look at the student.
2. Say, Watch my finger. Let's try it again.
3. Repeat the question as soon as the student is paying attention.
4. Return to the beginning of the exercise.

Variations of this procedure can be used whenever a student is not paying attention. You should always look at the student, tell the student to pay attention, repeat the question, and then return to the beginning of the exercise.

If a student is paying attention, but does not answer a question, you should use the following procedure.

1. Look at the student.
2. Say, I have to hear everybody.
3. Repeat the question.
4. Return to the beginning of the exercise.

Every student must answer exactly on signal. A student who does not answer on signal may begin to depend on the other students for the correct answers. The correction procedure shows the students that you expect everyone to answer on signal.

If a student answers early or late, you should use the following procedure.

1. Look at the student.
2. Say, You're early, or You're late.
3. Repeat the question until all the students answer on signal.
4. Return to the beginning of the exercise.

By requiring a simultaneous response, you eliminate the problem of one student leading and the others following. When the students answer simultaneously, they have to think for themselves, and they will pay closer attention to you.

In all of these procedures, you must first correct the mistake and then return to the beginning of the exercise. By repeating the exercise, you demonstrate to the students that mistakes will not be ignored. The students must work on an exercise from beginning to end until they get it right. If general mistakes are properly corrected in the early lessons of a level, the students will make far fewer mistakes in the later lessons.

Specific Mistakes

When students misidentify a word or give a wrong answer, they are making a specific mistake. Many of the exercises in the *Presentation Books* contain correction procedures for specific mistakes. There are two basic types of correction procedures for specific mistakes. The first type is the *model-lead-test-retest* procedure. The second type is the *process-test-retest* procedure.

Here is an example of the *model-lead-test-retest* procedure.

To correct
(If the children do not say *aaa:*)
1. **aaa.**
2. (Touch the first ball of the arrow.) Say it with me. Get ready. (Move quickly to the second ball of the arrow. Hold for two seconds. Say **aaa** with the children.) *aaa.*
3. (Touch the first ball of the arrow.) Your turn. Get ready. (Move quickly to the second ball of the arrow. Hold for two seconds.) *aaa.*

In step 1, you *model* the correct answer. In step 2, you *lead* the students by saying the correct answer with them. (Sometimes, the *lead* step is not used.) In step 3, you *test* the students by having them say the correct answer by themselves. At a later point in the lesson, you *retest* the students by presenting the exercise again.

Here is an example of the *process-test-retest* procedure.

> **To correct**
> 1. Everybody, sound out the word. (Touch each sound as the children sound out the word.)
> 2. What word? (Signal.) a m

In step 1, the students use a particular *process* to correct their mistakes. In this case, the process is to sound out the word. In step 2, you *test* the students by asking, What word? At a later point in the lesson, you *retest* the student by presenting the exercise again.

The specific correction procedures typically appear when a new skill is introduced because that is when the students are most likely to make mistakes. If the students are properly corrected at this time, they are unlikely to make mistakes when the skill appears in subsequent exercises. Nevertheless, you should memorize the correction procedure for a particular skill so that it can be administered at any time.

Teaching to Mastery

Every skill in *Reading Mastery Plus* should be taught to mastery. When a skill is taught to mastery, every student in the group is able to perform the skill independently, without making any mistakes.

Teaching to mastery is of critical importance because the students are constantly applying each new skill. When a skill is taught to mastery, the students are able to apply the skill and are prepared to learn related skills. By teaching every skill to mastery, you ensure that each student is able to succeed throughout the program.

Practice Scripts

This section contains representative teacher presentation scripts from each level of the *Reading Mastery Plus* series. If you will be teaching *Reading Mastery Plus,* you should practice the appropriate scripts before presenting the program to your students. You can practice these scripts on your own, with another teacher, or at a training session conducted by an experienced trainer.

Script 1 - Letter Sounds

Script 2 - Letter Sounds

Script 3 - Sounds Firm-up

Script 4 - Reading Vocabulary

Script 5 - Reading Vocabulary

Script 6 - Reading Words

Script 7 - Reading Words

Script 8 - Metaphors

Script 9 - Story Reading

Script 10 - Reading Aloud

Full lesson scripts appear in the sample lessons at the end of this guide. To practice a script or a lesson, first read each script carefully and become familiar with it. Then present the script aloud several times, with only brief glances at the actual text. During these presentations, you should execute the proper signals and develop a rapid pace. Finally present the script to another person, who will play the role of the student. This "student" can then answer on signal and can also make intentional errors that you have to correct.

You should practice the scripts that are relevant to the program level you will be teaching. The following chart shows the practice scripts that are relevant to each level.

If time permits, you should practice the remaining scripts. This additional practice will give you a valuable perspective on the entire program.

Practice Scripts	Level							Sounds	Words	Story
	K	1	2	3	4	5	6			
Script 1 - Letter Sounds	◆							✔		
Script 2 - Letter Sounds	◆							✔		
Script 3 - Sounds Firm-up	◆	◆						✔		
Script 4 - Reading Vocabulary	◆	◆							✔	
Script 5 - Reading Vocabulary		◆	◆						✔	
Script 6 - Reading Words			◆						✔	
Script 7 - Reading Words			◆	◆	◆	◆	◆		✔	
Script 8 - Metaphors							◆		✔	
Script 9 - Story Reading		◆	◆							✔
Script 10 - Reading Aloud			◆	◆	◆	◆	◆			✔

Practice Script 1

The following script appears in lesson 104 of *Reading Mastery Plus,* Level K. The script introduces the continuous sound **mmm.**

LETTER SOUNDS
EXERCISE 5

Introducing the new sound mmm as in mat

a. (Touch the first ball of the arrow.) You're going to learn a new sound. My turn to say it. When I move under the letter, I'll say the sound. I'll keep on saying it as long as I touch under it. Get ready. (Move quickly to the second ball of the arrow. Hold for two seconds.) **mmm.**

b. (Touch the first ball of the arrow.) My turn again. Get ready. (Move quickly to the second ball of the arrow. Hold for two seconds.) **mmm.**

c. (Touch the first ball of the arrow.) My turn again. Get ready. (Move quickly to the second ball of the arrow. Hold for two seconds.) **mmm.**

d. (Touch the first ball of the arrow.) Your turn. When I move under the letter, you say the sound. Keep on saying it as long as I touch under it. Get ready. (Move quickly to the second ball of the arrow. Hold for two seconds.) *mmm.* Yes, **mmm.**

To correct

(If the children do not say *mmm:*)

1. **mmm.**
2. (Touch the first ball of the arrow.) Say it with me. Get ready. (Move quickly to the second ball of the arrow. Hold for two seconds. Say **mmm** with the children.) *mmm.*
3. (Touch the first ball of the arrow.) Your turn. Get ready. (Move quickly to the second ball of the arrow. Hold for two seconds.) *mmm.*

e. (Touch the first ball of the arrow.) Again. Get ready. (Move quickly to the second ball of the arrow. Hold for two seconds.) *mmm.* Yes, **mmm.**

f. (Repeat *e* until firm.)
g. (Call on different children to do *d.*)
h. Good saying **mmm.**

Description

In steps a–c, you model the correct way to say the sound. In step d, you test the students by having them say the sound. Step d also includes a correction procedure. In steps e and f, you continue to test the group until all of the students have mastered the sound. Finally, in step g, individual students take turns saying the sound.

Teaching Techniques

You should hold the *Presentation Book* so that all the students can see the sound. Hold the book with one hand and point with the other hand. Use the following procedures to present the sound.

1. Touch the large ball of the arrow and say, Your turn. Get ready.
2. Pause for one second.
3. Quickly move your finger to the second ball of the arrow. This movement acts as a signal for the student to say the sound.
4. Touch the second ball for two seconds. Because **mmm** is a continuous sound, the group says the sound for as long as you touch the second ball.

When presenting this exercise, make sure that you do not block the students' view of the letter. Always touch the balls, not the letter. Also, make sure that your signal timing is consistent. Always pause for one second before moving to the second ball, and always point to the second ball for two seconds.

Step f requires you to repeat step e until all students are "firm." Students are "firm" when every one of them has mastered the sound. Every student must be able to say the sound for as long as you touch it.

In step g, you test individual students. You do not have to give an individual test to every student on every exercise. However, during the course of a lesson, every student should receive at least two or three individual tests. Try to give more individual tests to the lowest performers in the group, so that you can be sure that they have mastered each exercise.

Corrections

To correct mistakes, use the specified correction procedure.

1. *Model* the correct sound.
2. *Lead* the students by saying the sound with them.
3. *Test* by having the students say the sound by themselves.
4. *Retest* by presenting the sound again at a later point in the lesson.

Practice Script 2

The following script appears in lesson 123 of *Reading Mastery Plus,* Level K. The script introduces the stop sound **d.**

Description

This script is similar to Practice Script 1, except that the presentation has been streamlined and the correction procedure no longer appears. (Printed correction procedures are included only in the first few appearances of an exercise, but they can still be used to correct student errors on subsequent appearances of the exercise or on similar exercises.)

In step a, you model the correct way to say the sound. In step b, you test the students by having them say the sound. In step c, you continue to test the group until all of the students have mastered the sound. Finally, in step d, individual students take turns saying the sound.

LETTER SOUNDS
EXERCISE 2
Introducing the new sound d as in dad

a. (Touch the ball of the arrow for **d.**) Everybody, what letter is this? (Signal.) *D.* Listen: We always have to say the sound for this letter fast. The little arrow under the sound tells me that I can't stop under this sound. My turn to say it fast. (Slash to the end of the arrow as you say **d.** Return to the ball.) My turn to say it fast again. (Slash to the end of the arrow as you say **d.**)
b. (Touch the ball of the arrow.) Your turn. Say it fast. (Slash to the end of the arrow.) *d.* Yes, **d.**
c. (Repeat *b* until firm.)
d. (Call on different children to do *b.*)

Teaching Techniques

Because *d* is a stop sound, you signal differently than for **mmm.**

1. Touch the large ball and say, Your turn. Say it fast.
2. Pause for one second.
3. Slash your finger under the sound. This slash acts as a signal. When your finger passes under the sound, the students "say it fast."

Corrections

To correct mistakes, use the *model-lead-test-retest* procedure.

1. *Model* the correct sound.
2. *Lead* the students by saying the sound with the group.
3. *Test* by having the students say the sound by themselves.
4. *Retest* by presenting the sound again at a later point in the lesson.

Practice Script 3

The following script appears in lesson 4 of *Reading Mastery Plus,* Level 1. The script reviews sounds that the students have learned.

SOUNDS

EXERCISE 3

Sounds firm-up

a. (Point to **ā**.) When I touch the letter, you say the sound.
b. (Pause.) Get ready. (Touch **ā**.) *āāā*.
c. Again. (Repeat *b* until firm.)
d. Get ready to say all the sounds when I touch them.
e. (Alternate touching **o, ā, c,** and **n** three or four times. Point to the sound. Pause one second. Say:) Get ready. (Touch the sound.) *The children respond.*

EXERCISE 4

Individual test

(Call on different children to identify one or more sounds in exercise 3.)

Description

In step b, you test the students by having them say the first sound. In step c, you retest the group. In step e, you test the sounds three or four times. Finally, you administer individual tests.

Teaching Techniques

Your presentation is different from the preceding scripts because after Level K, lesson 146, there are no arrows under the sounds.

1. Point just below a sound, with your finger about an inch from the page.
2. Say, Get Ready.
3. Pause for one second.
4. Touch under the sound. Your touch acts as a signal. Always touch under the letter so that all the students can see the letter.

Corrections

To correct mistakes, use the specified correction procedure.

1. *Model* the correct sound.
2. *Lead* the students by saying the sound with the group. (You may need to repeat this step several times.)
3. *Test* by having the students say the sound by themselves.
4. *Retest* by proceeding with step e.

Practice Script 4

The following script appears in lesson 142 of *Reading Mastery Plus,* Level K. The script introduces the word **meat.**

READING VOCABULARY

EXERCISE 9

Children sound out the word and say it fast

a. (Touch the first ball of the arrow for **mēat.**) Sound it out. Get ready. (Move quickly under each sound.) *Mmmēēēt.*

b. (Return to the first ball.) Again, sound it out. Get ready. (Move quickly under each sound.) *Mmmēēēt.*

c. (Repeat *b* until firm.)

d. (Return to the first ball.) Say it fast. (Slash.) *Meat.* Yes, what word? (Signal.) *Meat.* A hamburger is made of (pause) **meat.**

Description

In steps a-c, the group sounds out the word by saying each sound in sequence. Then, in step d, the group reads the word normally by "saying it fast."

Teaching Techniques

To present the word, follow this procedure.

1. Touch the large ball and say, Sound it out. Get ready.
2. Pause for one second.
3. Quickly move your finger to the second ball of the arrow. Hold your finger on the second ball for about one second as the students say, **mmm.**
4. Move your finger to the third ball and hold it there for about one second as the students say, **ēēē.**
5. Move your finger to the fourth ball and hold it there for just an instant as the students say, **t.**

Note that the small **a** does not have a ball under it. The students do not say any small silent letters; you simply move your finger past them.

After the students are proficient at sounding out the word, they "say it fast." Use the following procedure.

1. Touch the large ball of the arrow and say, Say it fast.
2. Pause for one second.
3. Quickly slash under the word as the students "say it fast."

Corrections

Some students may have trouble "saying it fast." To correct mistakes, use a *model-test-retest* procedure.

1. *Model* the correct answer by sounding out the word and saying it fast.
2. *Test* by having the group sound out the word and say it fast.
3. *Retest* by presenting the task again at a later point in the lesson.

Practice Script 5

The following script appears in lesson 106 of *Reading Mastery Plus,* Level 1.

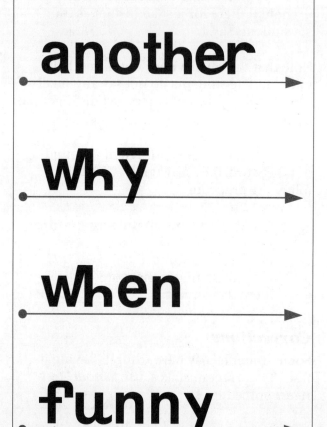

READING VOCABULARY

EXERCISE 10

Read the fast way

a. Read these words the fast way.
b. (Touch the ball for **another.** Pause two seconds.) Get ready. (Signal.) *Another.* Yes, **another.**
c. (Repeat *b* for **whȳ, when,** and **funny.**)

another

whȳ

when

funny

Description

This exercise reviews words that the group has already learned. The group reads all the words "the fast way," without first sounding them out.

Teaching Techniques

To present the words, follow this procedure.

1. Touch the ball of the arrow.
2. Pause for two seconds. This pause gives the students time to examine the word.
3. Say, Get ready.
4. Pause for one second.
5. Quickly slash under the word with your finger, as the students read the word.
6. Reinforce the students by repeating the word out loud.

Corrections

Correct mistakes by using a *process-test-retest* procedure.

1. Tell the students to use the sounding-out *process,* and direct them as they sound out the word.
2. *Test* the students by asking, What word?
3. *Retest* by returning to the top of the column and presenting all of the words in order.

Practice Script 6

Beginning in *Reading Mastery Plus,* Level 2, the word lists appear in the students' *Textbooks.* Students spell each word instead of sounding it out. The *Presentation Books* contain presentation scripts for the word lists, as well as reproductions of the student lists.

The following script appears in lesson 96 of *Reading Mastery Plus,* Level 2.

Description

In steps c–f, you direct the group to spell and read each word aloud. In step g, you direct the group to reread the words the fast way.

Teaching Techniques

To present the word lists, follow this procedure.

1. Direct the students to locate a list of words.
2. Check. Observe to confirm that students have found the list.
3. Say, Spell word 1. Get ready.
4. Give a series of auditory signals—one for each letter. You must give auditory signals, such as taps, claps, or finger snaps because the students are looking at their books and not at you.
5. Listen carefully as the students spell the word.
6. Say, What word?
7. Give an auditory signal. Students say the word "the fast way."

EXERCISE 2

READING WORDS

a. Find the fence. ✓
• (Teacher reference:)

> 1. noon
> 2. tubby
> 3. boat
> 4. contest

b. You'll spell each word and then tell me the word.
c. Spell word 1. Get ready. (Tap 4 times.) *N-O-O-N.*
• What word? (Signal.) *Noon.*
d. Spell word 2. Get ready. (Tap 5 times.) *T-U-B-B-Y.*
• What word? (Signal.) *Tubby.*
e. Spell word 3. Get ready. (Tap 4 times.) *B-O-A-T.*
• What word? (Signal.) *Boat.*
f. Spell word 4. Get ready. (Tap 7 times.) *C-O-N-T-E-S-T.*
• What word? (Signal.) *Contest.*
g. Let's read those words again the fast way.
• Word 1. What word? (Signal.) *Noon.*
• (Repeat for remaining words: **tubby, boat, contest.**)

Practice Script 7

In *Reading Mastery Plus,* Levels 2–6, you present vocabulary information about specific words that the students read.

The following vocabulary exercise appears in lesson 34 of *Reading Mastery Plus,* Level 3.

1
1. neither
2. remind
3. manage
4. prove

EXERCISE 2
READING WORDS
Column 1
a. **Find lesson 34 in your textbook.** ✓
 • Touch column 1. ✓
 • (Teacher reference:)

1. neither	3. manage
2. remind	4. prove

b. Word 1 is **neither.** What word? (Signal.) *Neither.*
 • Spell **neither.** Get ready. (Tap for each letter.) *N-E-I-T-H-E-R.*
c. Word 2 is **remind.** What word? (Signal.) *Remind.*
 • Spell **remind.** Get ready. (Tap for each letter.) *R-E-M-I-N-D.*
d. Word 3 is **manage.** What word? (Signal.) *Manage.*
 • Spell **manage.** Get ready. (Tap for each letter.) *M-A-N-A-G-E.*
 • When you work hard to do something, you manage to do it. Here's another way of saying **He worked hard to keep swimming: He managed to keep swimming.**

 • Your turn. What's another way of saying **He worked hard to keep swimming?** (Signal.) *He managed to keep swimming.*
 • What's another way of saying **The baby worked hard to walk?** (Signal.) *The baby managed to walk.*
e. Word 4 is **prove.** What word? (Signal.) *Prove.*
 • Spell **prove.** Get ready. (Tap for each letter.) *P-R-O-V-E.*
 • When you prove something, you show that it is true. When you prove that you can stand up, you show it's true that you can stand up.
 • What would you have to do to prove that they are serving spaghetti for lunch? (Call on a student. Idea: *Show it's true that they are serving spaghetti for lunch.*)
 • What would you have to do to prove that it is raining outside? (Call on a student. Idea: *Show it's true that it's raining outside.*)
f. Let's read those words again, the fast way.
 • Word 1. What word? (Signal.) *Neither.*
 • (Repeat for words 2–4.)
g. (Repeat step f until firm.)

Description

In steps a-e, you direct the students as they read and spell the four vocabulary words. In steps d and e, you also teach the meaning of two of these words. In step d, you *model* how to use the word in context and then *test* by asking the students to use it in a different context. In step e, you give the meaning of the word and then call on a student to paraphrase a sentence containing the new word.

Teaching Techniques

When presenting the word list, use the same audible signaling discussed in Practice Script 6. When presenting the word meanings, you will either call on the group or call on individual students. When the group is tested in step d, the students must answer in unison. When you call on individual students, answers may vary. Accept sentences that express the correct meaning. Rephrase by referring to the sentence in the script. "Yes, you show it's true that they are serving spaghetti for lunch."

Corrections

Some students may have trouble using the vocabulary words in context. For example, in step d they may say, *He worked hard to keep swimming,* instead of, *He managed to keep swimming.* Use a *model-test-retest* procedure to correct mistakes.

1. *Model* the correct answer.
2. *Test* the students by having the group repeat the correct answer.
3. *Test* the group again by repeating the question.
4. *Retest* the students by repeating the question at a later point in the lesson.

Practice Script 8

In certain lessons, you direct the students as they read skill exercises that appear in their *Textbooks* (Levels 3–6). The following script appears in lesson 49 of *Reading Mastery Plus*, Level 6.

Description

The students take turns reading parts of the exercise aloud. After they complete each section, you present the questions specified in the *Presentation Book*. These questions are always presented to individual students.

EXERCISE 3

METAPHORS

1. Everybody, turn to part D at the end of today's story. ✓
- (Call on individual students to read several sentences each.)
- (At the end of each section, present the questions for that section.)

Write the answers for items 1–6.
   A metaphor is like a simile except it doesn't use the word *like*.

- Name the kind of figurative language that is like a simile. (Response: *Metaphor.*)
- How is a metaphor different from a simile? (Idea: *It doesn't use the word* like.)

   Here's an accurate statement: *The woman was very smart.* Here's a metaphor: *The woman was a walking encyclopedia.*
   1. What two things are the same in that metaphor?

- What's the answer? (Response: *The woman, an encyclopedia.*)

2. How could they be the same?

- What's the answer? (Idea: *Both are full of information.*)

   Here's another metaphor: *The man was a rattlesnake.*
   3. What two things are the same in that metaphor?

- What's the answer? (Response: *The man, a rattlesnake.*)

4. How could they be the same?

- What's the answer? (Ideas: *Both are dangerous.*)
- You'll write the answers to the items later.

D METAPHORS

Write the answers for items 1–6.

A metaphor is like a simile except it doesn't use the word *like*.

Here's an accurate statement: *The woman was very smart*. Here's a metaphor: *The woman was a walking encyclopedia*.

1. What two things are the same in that metaphor?
2. How could they be the same?

Here's another metaphor: *The man was a rattlesnake.*

3. What two things are the same in that metaphor?
4. How could they be the same?

Here's another metaphor: *Miss Minchin was a jailer.*

5. What two things are the same in that metaphor?
6. How could they be the same?

Teaching Techniques

Because all of the questions are presented to individual students, no signals are used. Call on a different student to answer each question. Lower-performing students should be called on more frequently so you can be sure they have mastered the skill.

Corrections

Use a *model-test-retest* procedure to correct mistakes.

1. *Model* by calling on another student to give the correct answer.
2. *Test* the student who made a mistake by repeating the question.
3. *Retest* the student by repeating the question at a later time in the lesson.

Practice Script 9

There are two basic procedures for presenting the Group Reading. The first procedure is used in *Reading Mastery Plus*, Level 1, and lessons 1–15 of *Reading Mastery Plus*, Level 2. The following script shows the first procedure. It appears in lesson 109 of *Reading Mastery Plus*, Level 1.

Description

In exercise 12, the students read the title and the first part of the story aloud and in unison. In exercise 13, the students take turns reading the rest of the story aloud. You call on individual students to read one sentence each. Occasionally you direct the group to read a sentence in unison. In exercise 14, the students take turns reading the story again as you present comprehension questions.

STORY 109

EXERCISE 12

First reading—title and three sentences

a. Everybody, open your reader to page 6. ✓
b. Everybody, touch the title. ✓
c. I'll tap and you read each word in the title the fast way.
d. First word. ✓
   (Pause two seconds.)
   Get ready. (Tap.) *The.*
e. Next word. ✓
   (Pause two seconds.)
   Get ready. (Tap.) *Cow.*
f. (Repeat e for the remaining words in the title.)
g. Everybody, say the title. (Signal.) *The cow boy and the cow.* Yes, **the cow boy and the cow.**
h. Everybody, get ready to read this story the fast way.
i. First word. ✓
   (Pause two seconds.)
   Get ready. (Tap.) *A.*
j. Next word. ✓
   (Pause two seconds.)
   Get ready. (Tap.) *Cow boy.*
k. (Repeat j for the remaining words in the first three sentences. Have the children reread the first three sentences until firm.)

EXERCISE 13

Remaining sentences

a. I'm going to call on different children to read a sentence. Everybody, follow along and point to the words. If you hear a mistake, raise your hand.
b. (Call on a child.) Read the next sentence.
c. (Call on a different child.) Read the next sentence.

d. (Repeat c for most of the remaining sentences in the story.)
e. (Occasionally have the group read a sentence. When the group is to read, say:) Everybody, read the next sentence. (Pause two seconds. Tap for each word in the sentence. Pause at least two seconds between taps.)
f. (After underlined sentence ④ has been read, ask:) Do you think the cow will really jump better than the horse? (Call on a child. Accept reasonable responses.)
g. We'll see. (Repeat d and e for the remaining sentences.)

EXERCISE 14

Second reading—sentences and questions

a. You're going to read the story again. This time I'm going to ask questions.
b. Starting with the first word of the title. ✓ Get ready. (Tap as the children read the title.)
c. (Call on a child.) Read the first sentence.

> **To correct** word-identification errors (**from,** for example)
> 1. That word is **from.** What word? *From.*
> 2. Go back to the beginning of the sentence and read the sentence again.

d. (Call on a different child.) Read the next sentence.
e. (Repeat d for most of the remaining sentences in the story.)
f. (Occasionally have the group read a sentence.)

---

g. (After each underlined sentence has been read, present each comprehension question specified below to the entire group.)

[1] What's this story going to be about? (Signal.) *The cow boy and the cow.* What do cow boys usually ride on? (Signal.) *Horses.*

[2] Why was this cow boy sad? (Signal.) *He did not have a horse.*

[3] What did the cow say? (Signal.) *But I can run as fast as a horse.*

④ What did the cow say? (Signal.) *And I can jump better than a horse.*

[5] Is the cow boy going to give the cow a try? (Signal.) *Yes.*

[6] Why did the other cow boys make fun of him? (Call on a child. Accept reasonable responses.)

[7] Is this the end of the story? (Signal.) *No.* What do you think is going to happen? (Let the children comment for 10 seconds.) Next time we'll read more about the cow boy and the cow.

---

the cow boy and the cow[1]

a cow boy was sad. hē did not havₑ a hōrsₑ.[2] the other cow boys said, "hō, hō, that funny cow boy has nō hōrsₑ."

a cow cāmₑ up to the cow boy. the cow said, "if you arₑ a cow boy, you nēēd a cow. I am a cow."

the cow boy said, "do not bē funny. cow boys do not rIdₑ on cows."

the cow said, "but I can run as fast as a hōrsₑ.[3] and I can jump better than a hōrsₑ."④

the cow boy said, "I will givₑ you a trȳ. but I·will fēēl very funny rIdiñg on a cow." sō the cow boy got on the cow.[5]

then the other cow boys cāmₑ up the rōₐd. "hō, hō," they said. "look at that funny cow boy.[6] hē is trȳiñg to rIdₑ a cow."

stop[7]

Teaching Techniques

Use the following procedure to conduct the reading.

1. Direct the students to touch under each word by saying, First word or Next word.
2. Pause for two seconds as the students figure out the word.
3. Say, Get ready.
4. Pause for one second.
5. Tap or clap as the students read the word in unison.

The comprehension questions are cued by little numbers in your copy of the story. When the students read up to a number, you present the questions for that number. Sentences that contain numbers are always underlined. The student version of the text does not contain any numbers or underlines.

The students should be looking at you when you present the questions, but they should continue to touch the current word in the story. For questions that require precise answers, you will need to use a hand-drop signal.

1. Hold out one hand, as if you were stopping traffic.
2. Present the question.
3. Pause for one second.
4. Quickly drop your hand. Your hand-drop acts as a signal. If you want, you can also snap your fingers as you drop your hand.
5. Listen carefully to the students' answers and correct any mistakes.

Some comprehension questions do not require precise answers. You simply present these questions to the group and accept all reasonable answers.

Corrections

The students will make two basic types of mistakes during the Group Reading: word-identification errors and comprehension errors. To correct word-identification errors, follow the procedure specified in exercise 14.

1. *Model* the correct word.
2. *Test* the student by having the student say the word.
3. *Retest* the student by having the student reread the sentence.

Comprehension errors tend to fall into two groups. For some questions, the students will give the right answer, but they will say it incorrectly. For other questions, the students will simply give the wrong answer.

When the students do not word the answer correctly, use the following procedure.

1. *Model* the correct answer.
2. *Test* by having the students say the answer correctly.
3. *Retest* the students by repeating the question.

The corrections for wrong answers are a little more complicated. If the question is clearly answered by a sentence in the story, use the following procedure.

1. Demonstrate a *process* for answering the question by reading the appropriate sentence.
2. *Test* the students by repeating the question.
3. *Retest* the students by repeating the question again at a later time in the lesson.

If the question is not clearly answered by a sentence in the story, use the following procedure.

1. *Model* the correct answer.
2. *Test* by having the students say the correct answer.
3. *Test* the students again by repeating the question.
4. *Retest* the students by repeating the question at a later time in the lesson.

Practice Script 10

The following script for a story background comprehension passage is typical of the second type of Group Reading procedure. It appears in lesson 6 of *Reading Mastery Plus*, Level 5.

EXERCISE 9

READING ALOUD

1. The error limit for this chapter is six.
2. (Call on individual students to read two or three sentences each.)
3. (After students complete each section, ask the questions for that section.)

There was no attic at all and no cellar—except a small hole, dug in the ground, called a cyclone cellar. The family could go into the cellar in case one of those great whirlwinds arose, mighty enough to crush any building in its path. The cellar was reached by a trapdoor in the middle of the floor. A ladder inside led down into a small, dark hole.

When Dorothy stood in the doorway and looked outside, she could see nothing but the great, gray prairie on every side. No trees or houses could be seen on the flat country that reached the edge of the sky in all directions.

- What is the "great whirlwind"? (Idea: *A cyclone.*)
- What was the hole under the floor called? (Response: *A cyclone cellar.*)
- What did they use the cyclone cellar for? (Idea: *To hide from cyclones.*)
- How would you climb down into the cellar after you opened the trapdoor? (Idea: *On a ladder.*)
- Everybody, look at the picture. The picture shows what you have just been reading about. The horizon is the line where the land meets the sky. Run your finger along the horizon. ✓
- What is the funny cloud on the left side of the picture? (Response: *A cyclone.*)
- Who is standing in the doorway of the house? (Idea: *Dorothy.*)
- What people are standing in the field? (Idea: *Uncle Henry and Aunt Em.*)

The sun had baked the plowed land into a gray mass with little cracks running through it. Not even the grass was green, for the sun had burned the tops of the grass blades until they were the same gray color as the land. Once, the house had been painted white, but the sun blistered the paint and the rains washed it away, and now the house was as dull and gray as everything else.

When Aunt Em came here to live, she was young and pretty. The sun and wind had changed her, too. They had taken the sparkle from her eyes and left them a sober gray. They had taken the red from her cheeks and lips, and they were gray also. She was thin and she never smiled, now. ♦

- What color is the house now? (Response: *Gray.*)
- Had the house always been gray? (Response: *No.*)
- Name two things that made the house's color change. (Ideas: *The sun blistered the paint; the rain washed the paint away.*)
- What other things in the story are gray? (Ideas: *Prairie; grass; land; Aunt Em.*)
- Had Aunt Em's eyes, cheeks, and lips always been gray? (Response: *No.*)
- What made Aunt Em change? (Ideas: *The sun and wind; her hard life.*)

Description

Individual students take turns reading the passage aloud. After students complete each section, ask the questions for that section.

For questions that require precise answers, the answers are preceded by the word "Response." For questions that do not require precise answers, the answers are preceded by the word "Idea."

Teaching Techniques

In this practice script, all of the questions are presented to individual students, and no signal is required. However, in some Group Reading scripts, certain questions are presented to the entire group. Use a hand-drop signal for these questions. (The hand-drop signal is discussed in Practice Script 9.)

Corrections

The students will make two basic types of mistakes during the Group Reading: word-identification errors and comprehension errors. To correct word-identification errors, use the following procedure.

1. *Model* the correct word.
2. *Test* the student by having the student say the word.
3. *Retest* the student by having the student reread the sentence.

To correct comprehension errors, use the following procedure.

1. *Model* the correct answer by calling on another student to give the correct answer.
2. *Test* the student who gave an incorrect answer by repeating the question.
3. *Retest* the student by repeating the question at a later time in the lesson.

Scope and Sequence

The scope and sequence chart on the following pages provides an overview of the skills taught in the reading and language components of the *Reading Mastery Plus* series. The reading component is divided into four principal areas: decoding skills, comprehension skills, literary skills, and study skills.

Reading Component— Decoding Skills

Reading Mastery Plus uses a widely acclaimed phonics method that features step-by-step instruction for all decoding skills.

Decoding Readiness: Students learn blending, sequencing, and matching skills that prepare them for decoding.

Sounds and Letters: Students learn letter sounds in a carefully programmed sequence. New letters are introduced every few lessons, and then systematically reviewed.

Words: Students learn how to sound out and read regularly-spelled words and how to read irregularly-spelled words.

Sentences and Stories: Students learn how to read sentences and then entire stories. Individual checkouts monitor reading rate and accuracy.

Reading Component— Comprehension Skills

Reading Mastery Plus provides thorough instruction in reading comprehension. Oral questions, written questions, and skill exercises develop comprehension in five important areas.

Comprehension Readiness: Students learn how to follow directions and how to answer questions about pictures.

Vocabulary: Students learn how to identify word meanings and how to interpret definitions.

Literal Comprehension: Students learn how to understand the explicit meaning of a text.

Interpretive Comprehension: Students learn how to interpret the implicit meaning of a text.

Reasoning: Students learn how to analyze the underlying logic of a text.

Reading Component—Literary Skills

Reading Mastery Plus stresses literary appreciation and interpretation. Students read a wide range of literature and carefully analyze content and style.

Characters and Settings: Students learn how to interpret complex characters and settings.

Literary Devices: Students learn how to interpret figurative language and other elements of literary style.

Types of Literature: Students learn about various types of literature and read examples of each type.

Reading Component—Study Skills

Reading Mastery Plus teaches the writing and reference skills that are necessary for effective studying.

Writing: Students gradually develop writing skills, first by copying words and stories, then by writing answers to questions, and finally by writing whole paragraphs, stories, and poems.

Reference Materials: Students learn how to interpret a wide variety of reference materials, such as maps, diagrams, time lines, and graphs.

Language Components

The Language component comprises three *Language Presentation Books* in Level K, one *Language Presentation Book* in Level 1, one *Language Presentation Book* in Level 2, and one *Language Arts Guide* for each level, Levels 1 through 6.

Language Presentation Books—Skills

Reading Mastery Plus, Levels K, 1, and 2 teach language skills students need to succeed in the classroom.

Actions: Students learn concepts by performing and describing actions.

Patterns: Students learn to match patterns and to complete patterns.

Descriptions of Objects/Word Skills: Students learn language conventions for describing and defining objects.

Information and Background Knowledge: Students learn basic information to build their background knowledge for understanding of a wide variety of concepts such as the calendar, the relationship between objects and their parts, locations, colors, and shapes.

Spatial and Temporal Relations: Students learn conventions for describing sequences that occur over time, sequences that are shown in space, and actions that relate to points in time or space.

Instructional Words and Problem-Solving Concepts: Students learn the language of instruction and the concepts needed to follow instruction, solve logical problems, and draw conclusions from evidence.

Classification: Students learn common classification words, names of objects found in each class, statements for describing objects and the classes they are in, and rules for classifying objects.

Problem-Solving Strategies and Applications: Students apply previously learned concepts to problem-solving applications.

Story Grammar: Students first learn to analyze stories the teacher tells in terms of the major parts and themes, then they practice using story grammars to create new stories and new endings.

Questioning Skills: Students formulate specific questions.

Reasoning Skills: Students learn the full range of reasoning skills needed to present evidence, draw conclusions, and analyze arguments that others present.

Sentence Skills: Students learn to test sentences for whether they accurately report, whether they are unambiguous, and whether they are consistent in their use of tense.

Language Arts Guides—Skills

The *Language Arts Guides* for levels 1 through 6 provide additional instruction to help extend the students' language foundations from speaking to writing. The specific skill areas taught in each level are listed below.

Level 1: Main-Idea Sentence Writing; Editing and Rewriting; Writing Notes and Lists; Reporting and Writing Directions

Level 2: Writing Parallel Sentences; Reporting on an Illustrated Sequence; Writing Directions about Making Two Things the Same; Reference Skills; Table of Contents; Alphabetizing Skills; Writing about Personal Experiences; Reference Skills

Level 3: Reference Material; Grammar; Alphabetical Order; Study Skills; Fact and Opinion; Listening Skills; Writing Skills; Technology Skills; Vocabulary Skills

Level 4: Writing Skills; Vocabulary Skills; Listening Skills; Speaking Skills; Reference Material

Level 5: Developing and Writing Reports; Figurative Language; Grammar; Punctuation; Reading and Writing; Using Context to Gain Meaning; Using Reference Materials; Vocabulary Development; Word Parts; Writing

Level 6: Book Parts; Capitalization; Comprehension Skills; Grammar; Punctuation; Reference Sources; Vocabulary; Word Parts; Writing Skills

Reading Component — Decoding Skills

	K	1	2	3	4	5	6
Decoding Readiness							
pronouncing individual sounds	◆	◆	◆				
sequencing from left to right	◆	◆					
blending sounds orally	◆	◆	◆				
identifying rhyming sounds	◆	◆	◆				
Sounds and Letters							
reading short vowels	◆	◆	◆				
reading long vowels	◆	◆	◆				
reading voiced consonants	◆	◆	◆				
reading unvoiced consonants	◆	◆					
reading sound combinations	◆	◆	◆	◆			
identifying vowel names	◆		◆				
identifying consonant names	◆		◆				
identifying alphabetical order	◆		◆	◆			
Words							
reading regularly–spelled words	◆	◆	◆	◆	◆	◆	◆
reading irregularly–spelled words		◆	◆	◆	◆	◆	◆
recognizing rhyming words	◆	◆	◆	◆	◆	◆	◆
recognizing inflected endings		◆	◆	◆	◆		
recognizing compound words		◆	◆	◆	◆	◆	
reading word lists for accuracy		◆	◆	◆	◆	◆	
spelling difficult words			◆	◆	◆		
Sentences and Stories							
reading aloud	◆	◆	◆	◆	◆	◆	◆
reading silently		◆	◆	◆	◆	◆	◆
reading aloud for rate and accuracy		◆	◆	◆	◆	◆	
identifying punctuation marks		◆			◆	◆	

Reading Component — Comprehension Skills

	K	1	2	3	4	5	6
Comprehension Readiness							
following oral directions	◆	◆	◆	◆	◆	◆	◆
answering questions about pictures	◆	◆	◆	◆	◆	◆	◆
associating pictures with words	◆	◆	◆				
drawing pictures based on a story	◆	◆					
repeating sentences	◆	◆	◆	◆	◆		
Vocabulary							
identifying the meanings of common words		◆	◆	◆	◆	◆	◆
writing the names of pictured objects			◆				
comprehending vocabulary definitions				◆	◆	◆	◆
using vocabulary words in context			◆	◆	◆	◆	◆
identifying homonyms and homographs			◆	◆		◆	
comprehending contractions				◆			
using context to predict word meaning						◆	◆
Literal Comprehension							
answering literal questions about a text	◆	◆	◆	◆	◆	◆	◆
identifying literal cause and effect	◆	◆	◆	◆	◆	◆	◆
recalling details and events	◆	◆	◆	◆	◆	◆	◆
following written directions		◆	◆	◆	◆	◆	◆
memorizing facts and rules	◆		◆	◆	◆		
sequencing narrative events	◆			◆	◆	◆	◆
Interpretive Comprehension							
predicting narrative outcomes	◆	◆	◆	◆	◆	◆	◆
relating titles to story content		◆	◆	◆	◆	◆	
inferring causes and effects	◆		◆	◆	◆	◆	◆
inferring story details and events	◆		◆	◆	◆	◆	◆
making comparisons				◆	◆	◆	◆
inferring details relevant to a main idea			◆		◆	◆	◆
inferring the main idea				◆		◆	◆
outlining						◆	◆
inferring story morals					◆	◆	
Reasoning							
using rules to classify objects	◆		◆	◆	◆		
completing written deductions			◆	◆			◆
drawing conclusions				◆	◆	◆	◆
using rules to predict outcomes			◆	◆	◆		
evaluating problems and solutions					◆	◆	◆
identifying relevant evidence					◆		◆
identifying contradictions							◆
identifying inferential questions							◆
identifying logical fallacies							◆

Reading Component — Literary Skills

	K	1	2	3	4	5	6
Character and Settings							
interpreting a character's feelings	◆	◆	◆	◆	◆	◆	◆
pretending to be a character	◆	◆	◆	◆	◆	◆	◆
interpreting a character's motives	◆	◆	◆	◆	◆	◆	◆
inferring a character's point of view	◆	◆	◆	◆	◆	◆	◆
predicting a character's action				◆	◆	◆	◆
identifying features of a setting				◆	◆	◆	◆
identifying a character's traits				◆	◆	◆	◆
Literary Devices							
interpreting figurative language							◆
interpreting extended dialogues							◆
interpreting substitute words							◆
interpreting shortened sentences						◆	◆
interpreting combined sentences						◆	◆
interpreting literary irony							◆
Types of Literature							
reading realistic fiction		◆	◆	◆	◆	◆	◆
reading fantasy		◆	◆	◆	◆	◆	◆
reading factual articles			◆	◆	◆	◆	◆
distinguishing between realism and fantasy				◆		◆	
distinguishing between fact and fiction					◆		
reading biographies						◆	◆
reading poetry						◆	◆
reading drama						◆	◆

Reading Component — Study Skills

	K	1	2	3	4	5	6
Writing							
copying letters	♦	♦	♦				
copying words	♦	♦	♦				
copying sentences	♦	♦	♦				
writing answers to questions		♦	♦	♦	♦	♦	♦
organizing information					♦	♦	♦
completing writing assignments			♦			♦	♦
Reference Materials							
interpreting maps		♦		♦	♦	♦	♦
interpreting standard measurements				♦	♦		
interpreting diagrams		♦		♦	♦	♦	♦
interpreting time lines				♦	♦	♦	
filling out forms				♦			♦
using reference sources				♦	♦	♦	♦
interpreting glossaries				♦	♦	♦	
interpreting indexes				♦	♦	♦	
interpreting graphs			♦	♦	♦	♦	♦

Language Presentation Books—Skills

Actions	K	1	2
beginning actions/action games	◆	◆	
actions—pronouns	◆	◆	◆
Patterns			
matching	◆		
pattern completion (pair relations)	◆		
Descriptions of Objects/ Word Skills			
object identification/ definition	◆	◆	◆
identity statements/ common objects	◆		
missing objects	◆		◆
opposites	◆	◆	
synonyms	◆	◆	
plurals	◆		◆
comparatives	◆		
rhyming	◆		
Information and Background Knowledge			
days of the week	◆	◆	◆
months of the year	◆	◆	
seasons	◆	◆	
colors and shapes	◆		
names	◆		◆
parts of the body	◆	◆	
school information	◆		
part/whole	◆	◆	◆
materials	◆	◆	◆
common information	◆		◆
locations	◆		◆

Spatial and Temporal Relations	K	1	2
picture completion	◆		◆
top/bottom/middle/ front/back	◆		
prepositions (on/over/in, etc.)	◆		
sequence actions	◆	◆	◆
before/after	◆	◆	
first/next/last	◆	◆	◆
following spatial directions	◆	◆	◆
map skills		◆	◆
north/south/east/west		◆	◆
from/to		◆	
continuous movement		◆	◆
Instructional Words and Problem-Solving Concepts			
directions with and/or/maybe	◆		
same–different	◆	◆	
some, all, none	◆	◆	
if–then rules	◆	◆	◆
where, who, when, what, how, why	◆	◆	◆
Classification			
classification names	◆	◆	
classification rules	◆	◆	
classification and clues			◆
Solving Strategies and Applications			
applications involving: actions, color, opposites, parts, multiple-descriptive terms, tense, plurals, prepositions, classification, comparatives, or, all/some/none, *and* only	◆	◆	◆

Language Presentation Books—Skills

	K	1	2
Story Grammar			
story-related activities	◆	◆	◆
retelling	◆	◆	◆
prediction	◆	◆	◆
putting on a play		◆	◆
Questioning Skills			
inquiry—finding best source	◆		
inquiry—identifying objects		◆	
question formulation and research			◆
Reasoning Skills			
if–then rules	◆	◆	
true/false		◆	
analogies		◆	
deductions			◆
data collection		◆	
reporting and inference			◆
absurdities involving function/parts/location	◆		
absurdities and contradictions		◆	
can do/can not do		◆	
Skills			
tense (past, present, future tense words)	◆	◆	◆
identifying and correcting errors		◆	◆
constructing sentences for illustrations		◆	◆
main idea and clues			◆
clarity—pronoun ambiguity			◆

Language Arts Guides—Skills

1	2	3	4	5	6
◆	◆	◆	◆	◆	◆

Level 1: Main-Idea Sentence Writing; Editing and Rewriting; Writing Notes and Lists; Reporting and Writing Directions

Level 2: Writing Parallel Sentences; Reporting on an Illustrated Sequence; Writing Directions about Making Two Things the Same; Reference Skills; Table of Contents; Alphabetizing Skills; Writing about Personal Experiences; Reference Skills

Level 3: Reference Material; Grammar; Alphabetical Order; Study Skills; Fact and Opinion; Listening Skills; Writing Skills; Technology Skills; Vocabulary Skills

Level 4: Writing Skills; Vocabulary Skills; Listening Skills; Speaking Skills; Reference Material

Level 5: Developing and Writing Reports; Figurative Language; Grammar; Punctuation; Reading and Writing; Using Context to Gain Meaning; Using Reference Materials; Vocabulary Development; Word Parts; Writing

Level 6: Book Parts; Capitalization; Comprehension Skills; Grammar; Punctuation; Reference Sources; Vocabulary; Word Parts; Writing Skills

Placement Tests

The placement tests can be used to determine the level of *Reading Mastery Plus* in which your students should be placed. There is a separate test for each level.

Ideally, placement testing should be conducted at the beginning of the school year. Begin placement testing by giving your students the placement test that corresponds with their grade level. For example, students in third grade should be given the placement test for *Reading Mastery Plus*, Level 3.

The following sections give specific instructions for each placement test.

Reading Mastery Plus, Level K

The placement test for *Reading Mastery Plus*, Level K is administered individually to each child before instruction begins. All testing should be completed during the first week.

The test items use several typefaces.

- This blue type indicates what you say.
- (This type in parentheses indicates what you do.)
- *This italic type shows the student's answers.*

The score sheet appears in the next column. Make one copy of the score sheet for each child. You should administer the test in a place that is somewhat removed from the other children so that they will not overhear the testing.

Level K Placement Test Directions

Some test items require you to point to pictures in this book. For these items, hold the book so that the child can see the pictures.

Placement Guidelines

- Children who score six or more errors begin at lesson 1, Level K Language.
- Children who score four or five errors begin at lesson 11, Level K Language.
- Children who score less than four errors begin at lesson 21, Level K Language.

PLACEMENT SCORING SHEET

Student's Name _____ Date _____

Items	Correct Responses	Incorrect Responses
1	0	1
2	0	1
3	0	1
4	0	1
5	0	1
6	0	1
7	0	1
8	0	1
9	0	1 1 1 1
10	0	1
11	0	1 1 1 1
12	0	1
13	0	1 1 1 1
14	0	1
15	0	1

Total of All Incorrect Responses

Score

Student's Score	Starts at Lesson
6 or more	1
4 or 5	11
less than 4	21

(Circle the lesson)

PLACEMENT TEST

1. Show me your nose.
   (The child must point to his/her nose.)

2. Show me your head.
   (The child may point anywhere on his/her head.)

3. Show me your ear.
   (The child may point to one or both ears.)

4. Show me your hand.
   (The child may hold up one hand or both hands.)

5. Show me your chin.
   (The child must point to his/her chin.)

6. Show me your cheek.
   (The child may touch one cheek or both cheeks.)

7. Show me your shoulder.
   (The child may point to one shoulder or both shoulders.)

8. (Point to the man.)
   What is this man doing?
   (Accept *Sleeping, going to sleep,* or *lying down.* Don't accept *Sleep, eyes shut,* or *got to sleep.*)

9. My turn to say the whole thing.
   This man is sleeping. Say that.
   This (or *that*) *man is sleeping.*

10. (Point to the girl.)
    What is this girl doing?
    (Accept *Eating, eating a hamburger,* or an entire correct sentence. Don't accept *Eat* or *eat a hamburger.*)

11. My turn to say the whole thing.
    This girl is eating. Say that.
    This girl is eating or
    This girl is eating a hamburger.

12. (Point to the cat.)
    What is this cat doing?
    (Accept *Climbing the tree, going up the tree, climbing on a tree, climbing up there,* or *climbing.*)

13. My turn to say the whole thing.
    This cat is climbing the tree. Say that.
    This cat is climbing the tree.

14. What's your whole name?
    (The child must give first and last name; middle name is optional.)

15. What's your first name?
    (The child must give first name only.)

Reading Mastery Plus, Level 1

The placement test for *Reading Mastery Plus,* Level 1, is administered to individual students in turn. You present test items aloud and tally the student's correct answers on a score sheet. You should administer the test in a place that is somewhat removed from the other students so that they will not overhear the testing.

The test items use several typefaces.
- This blue type indicates what you say.
- (This type in parentheses indicates what you do.)
- *This italic type shows the student's answers.*

Some test items require you to point to the large letters that appear in this book. For these items, hold the book so that the student can see the letters.

The placement test appears on pages 74–75.

The score sheet appears on page 73. Make one copy of the score sheet for each student. To use the score sheet, simply circle 1 point if the student answers correctly.

Placement Guidelines

Part 1 of the Placement Test

Children who made 0–8 points begin with *Reading Mastery Plus,* Fast Start, lesson 1.

Children who made 9–13 points continue testing in Part 2.

Part 2 of the Placement Test

Children who made a combined score of 0–15 points begin with *Reading Mastery Plus,* Fast Start, lesson 1.

Children who made a combined score of 16–24 points begin with *Reading Mastery Plus,* Level 1, lesson 1.

Placement Test Scoring Sheet for *Reading Mastery Plus*, Level 1

Student's Name _____ Date _____

Circle 1 point if the student answers or responds (touches) correctly.

PART 1: SOUNDS				PART 2: SENTENCE			
th	item 1	0	1 point	(Touch.)	item 1	0	1 point
t	item 2	0	1 point		item 2	0	1 point
c	item 3	0	1 point	it	item 3	0	1 point
n	item 4	0	1 point		item 4	0	1 point
a	item 5	0	1 point		item 5	0	1 point
d	item 6	0	1 point	is	item 6	0	1 point
o	item 7	0	1 point		item 7	0	1 point
s	item 8	0	1 point		item 8	0	1 point
i	item 9	0	1 point	fat	item 9	0	1 point
r	item 10	0	1 point		item 10	0	1 point
ē	item 11	0	1 point		item 11	0	1 point
m	item 12	0	1 point		Total Points ☐		
f	item 13	0	1 point				
	Total Points ☐						

Number of Points

9–13   Continue testing in part 2. (Check box) ☐

0–8   Start at *Reading Mastery Plus,* Fast Start, lesson 1. (Check box) ☐

Combined Number of Points (Parts 1 & 2)

16–24   Start at *Reading Mastery Plus,* Level 1, lesson 1.

0–15   Start at *Reading Mastery Plus,* Fast Start, lesson 1.

Placement Test Directions

Note: If a child makes 5 or more errors, do not present part 2.

Part 1

You're going to tell me the sound of each letter, not the name but the sound that it makes.

(Touch under each letter. Child says sounds:)

a. (test item 1) (Touch under **th.**) What sound? (Signal.) *ththth.*
b. (test item 2) (Touch under **t.**) What sound? (Signal.) *t.*
c. (test item 3) (Touch under **c.**) What sound? (Signal.) *k.*
d. (test item 4) (Touch under **n.**) What sound? (Signal.) *nnn.*
e. (test item 5) (Touch under **a.**) What sound? (Signal.) *aaa.*
f. (test item 6) (Touch under **d.**) What sound? (Signal.) *d.*
g. (test item 7) (Touch under **o.**) What sound? (Signal.) *ooo.*
h. (test item 8) (Touch under **s.**) What sound? (Signal.) *sss.*
i. (test item 9) (Touch under **i.**) What sound? (Signal.) *iii.*
j. (test item 10) (Touch under **r.**) What sound? (Signal.) *rrr.*
k. (test item 11) (Touch under **ē.**) What sound? (Signal.) *ēēē.*
l. (test item 12) (Touch under **m.**) What sound? (Signal.) *mmm.*
m. (test item 13) (Touch under **f.**) What sound? (Signal.) *fff.*

Total number of test items: **13**

Part 2

a. (test item 1) Put your finger on the ball of the arrow. (The child responds.)
b. (test item 2) Touch the first word. (The child is to touch under **it.**)
c. (test item 3) Sound it out. Get ready. (Tap for each sound.) *iiit.*
d. (test item 4) Say it fast. (Signal.) *It.*
   (test item 5) What word? (Signal.) *It.*
e. Touch the next word. (The child responds.)
   (test item 6) Sound it out. Get ready. (Tap for each sound.) *iiisss.*
f. (test item 7) Say it fast. (Signal.) *Is. (Iz.)*
   (test item 8) What word? (Signal.) *Is.*
g. Touch the next word. (The child responds.)
   (test item 9) Sound it out. Get ready. (Tap for each sound.) *Fffaaat.*
h. (test item 10) Say it fast. (Signal.) *Fat.*
   (test item 11) What word? (Signal.) *Fat.*

Total number of test items: **11**

Reading Mastery Plus, **Level 1 Placement Test**

Student's Name _____

t

th

n

c

a   d   o   s

i   r   ē

m   f

it•is•fat.

Reading Mastery Plus, Level 2

For the *Reading Mastery Plus,* Level 2 placement test, each student reads a story aloud as you count the student's decoding errors.

Level 2 Placement Test Directions

You will need to make one copy of the story on page 77.

Use the child's copy to mark errors that the child makes. The simplest procedure is to give the child your copy of the placement test. Mark errors on the child's copy.

You should administer the test in a place that is somewhat removed from the other students so that they will not overhear the testing.

Use the following procedures to administer the placement test.

1. Give the student a copy of the story.
2. Point to the passage and say, I want you to read this story out loud. Take your time. Start with the title and read the story as well as you can.
3. Time the student and make one tally mark for each error. Use the following guidelines when tallying errors.

   - If the student misreads a word, tell the student the word and mark one error.
   - If the student reads a word incorrectly and then correctly, mark one error.
   - If the student sounds out a word instead of reading it normally, mark one error.
     (Note: Correct the student the first time the student sounds out a word. Ask the student, What word is that? If the student reads the word correctly, do not mark an error. If the student sounds out the word, mark an error. Do not correct the student on any subsequent sounding-outs.)
   - If the student does not identify a word within four seconds, tell the student the word and mark one error.
   - If the student skips a word, point to the word. If the student does not read the word correctly, mark one error.
   - If the student skips a line, point to the line. If the student does not read the line correctly, mark one error.

4. After two minutes, stop the student. Count every word not read as an error. For example, if the student is eight words from the end of the passage at the end of the time limit, count eight errors.
5. Total the student's errors.

Placement Guidelines

Place your students as follows:
- Students who made 0–8 errors should be placed in lesson 1 of *Reading Mastery Plus,* Level 2.
- Students who made more than 8 errors should be placed in *Reading Mastery Plus,* Level 1. To determine an appropriate placement for these students, give them the individual rate-and-accuracy checkouts from *Reading Mastery Plus,* Level 1. Start with the checkout for lesson 140. If the student passes this checkout, place the student in lesson 141. If the student does not pass this checkout, present the checkout for lesson 130. Continue working backward until the student passes a checkout. Place the student in the lesson that follows the checkout lesson.

Placement Test Summary Form				
Child's Name	Number of Errors	Time (min:sec)	Entry Lesson	Instructional Group

Copyright © SRA/McGraw-Hill. Permission is granted to reproduce this page for classroom use.

the cow on the rōₐd

lots of men went down the rōₐd in a littlₑ car.

a cow was sittīng on the rōₐd. sō the men ran to the cow. "wē will lift this cow," they said.

but the men did not lift the cow. "this cow is sō fat wē can not lift it."

the cow said, "I am not sō fat. I can lift mē." then the cow got in the car.

the men said, "now wē can not get in the car." sō the men sat on the rōₐd and the cow went hōmₑ in the car.

the end

Guidelines for Placement Tests, Levels 3, 4, 5, and 6

The placement tests for *Reading Mastery Plus*, Levels 3, 4, 5, and 6 are similar in many respects. In part 1 of each test, individual students read a passage aloud as you count decoding errors. You will need to make one copy of the appropriate test for each student and mark that copy. You should administer Part 1 in a place that is somewhat removed from the other students, so that they will not overhear the testing.

How to Count Decoding Errors

Use the following guidelines when counting decoding errors on Part 1.
- If the student misreads a word, count one error.
- If the student omits a word ending, such as *s* or *ed,* count one error.

- If the student reads a word incorrectly and then correctly, count one error.
- If the student sounds out a word instead of reading it normally, count one error.
- If the student does not identify a word within three seconds, tell the student the word and count one error.
- If the student skips a word, count one error.
- If the student skips a line, point to the line and count one error.
- If the student does not finish the passage within the given time limit, count every word not read as an error. For example, if the student is eight words from the end of the passage at the end of the time limit, count eight errors.

Reading Mastery Plus, Level 3

Level 3 Placement Test Directions

Instructions for Part 1

Reproduce the Placement Test that appears on page 80. Make one copy for each student that you are to test. Then follow these steps:

1. Call a student to a corner of the room, where the test will be given.

2. Show a copy of the test to the student.

Part 1 Vocabulary Reading

- (Teacher reference:)

1. expert	7. difference
2. clinic	8. mirror
3. interest	9. through
4. changes	10. practicing
5. themselves	11. questions
6. people	

3. Point to the column of words at the top of the test. Tell the student: Touch word 1. (Wait.) That word is **expert.**

4. Repeat step 3 for words 2–11.

5. Your turn to read those words.

6. Word 1. What word?

7. Repeat step 6 for words 2–11.

Part 1 Passage Reading

8. Point to the passage in Part 1.

9. Tell the student: You're going to read this passage out loud. I want you to read it as well as you can. Don't try to read it so fast that you make mistakes. But don't read it so slowly that it doesn't make any sense. You have two minutes to read the passage. Go.

10. Time the student. If the student takes more than three seconds on a word, say the word, count it as an error, and permit the student to continue reading. To record errors, make one tally mark for each error.

Use the guidelines detailed above when counting decoding errors in Part 1.

Also count each word not read by the end of the two-minute time limit as an error. For example, if the student is eight words from the end of the passage by the end of the time limit, count eight errors.

11. Collect the test sheet.

After you've administered Part 1 to all the students, present Part 2, which is a group test. Administer Part 2 no more than 2 hours after students complete Part 1. Here are the steps to follow:

1. Assemble the students.

2. Give each student a copy of the placement test.

3. Give the group these instructions: At the bottom of the page are questions about the passage that you read earlier. Write the answers. You have two minutes to finish.

4. Time the students. Collect the test sheets after two minutes.

Answer Key   Part 2

1. What was the first name of the man in the story? _____ Bill _____

2. Underline 4 things he did to try to be more interesting.

   - frown more
   - <u>smile more</u>
   - whisper
   - <u>ask questions</u>
   - answer questions
   - <u>talk louder</u>
   - talk softer
   - <u>talk faster</u>
   - talk slower

3. His problem was that he
   - was old
   - had five dogs
   - <u>put people to sleep</u>

4. He practiced in front of
   - his wife
   - <u>the mirror</u>
   - the TV

5. Who came over when he was practicing?
   - a sleeper
   - a dog expert
   - <u>a sleep expert</u>

6. Name the place where she worked.
   _____ Sleep More Clinic _____

Use the table below to determine placement for each student.

Errors	Placement
If a student makes 7 errors or more on Part 1 **OR** 2 errors or more on Part 2	Place the student in a reading-language program more elementary than *Reading Mastery Plus* Level 3, possibly *Reading Mastery Plus* Level 1 or Level 2.
If a student makes no more than 6 errors on Part 1 **AND** no more than 1 error on Part 2.	Place the student at *Reading Mastery Plus* Level 3, lesson 1.

Part 1

Bill tried to say things that would interest other people. He asked questions and tried to get people to talk about themselves. He said things that were funny. He talked faster and louder. He tried to smile more when he talked. But all those changes made no difference. After Bill was through speaking, everybody else was sleeping.

One day, Bill was at home. He was practicing in front of the mirror. He smiled, moved around a lot, and talked to the mirror.

Just then the door bell rang. Bill opened the door and saw a woman who said, "I am an expert at making people sleep. I work for the Sleep More Clinic. We help people who have trouble sleeping. I hear that you can make people sleep, too."

"Yes," Bill said. "If I speak for a while, people will sleep."

"That is interesting," the sleep expert said. "Can you explain why people sleep?"

"Yes, I can," Bill said.

1. expert
2. clinic
3. interest
4. changes
5. themselves
6. people
7. difference
8. mirror
9. through
10. practicing
11. questions

Part 2

1. What was the first name of the man in the story?

2. Underline 4 things he did to try to be more interesting.

- frown more
- smile more
- whisper
- ask questions
- answer questions

- talk louder
- talk softer
- talk faster
- talk slower

3. His problem was that he
   - was old • had five dogs • put people to sleep

4. He practiced in front of
   - his wife • the mirror • the TV

5. Who came over when he was practicing?
   - a sleeper • a dog expert • a sleep expert

6. Name the place where she worked.

Reading Mastery Plus, Level 4

Level 4 Placement Test Directions

Instructions for Part 1

Reproduce the one-page Placement Test that appears on page 82. Make one copy for each student that you are to test.

1. Call a student to a corner of the room, where the test will be given.

2. Give a copy of the test to the student.

3. Point to the column of words at the top of the test. Tell the student: "Touch word 1." (Wait.) "That word is California."

4. Repeat step 3 for words 2–5.

5. Point to the passage on part 1.

6. Tell the student: "You're going to read this passage out loud. I want you to read it as well as you can. Don't try to read it so fast that you make mistakes. But don't read it so slowly that it doesn't make any sense. You have two minutes to read the passage. Go."

7. Time the student. If the student takes more than three seconds on a word, say the word, count it as an error, and permit the student to continue reading. To record errors, make one tally mark for each error.

Count all the following behaviors as errors:

- Misreading a word (Count as one error.)

- Omitting a word part (Listen carefully for *s* and *ed*.) (Count as one error.)

- Sounding out a word but not saying the word at a normal speaking rate (Count as one error.)

- Skipping a word (Count as one error.)

- Skipping a line (Immediately show the student the correct line.) (Count as one error.)

- Not identifying a word within three seconds (Tell the word.) (Count as one error.)

- Reading a word incorrectly and then reading it correctly (Count as one error.)

Also count each word not read by the end of the two-minute time limit as an error. For example, if the student is eight words from the end of the passage by the end of the time limit, count eight errors.

Instructions for Part 2

After you've administered Part 1 to all the students, present Part 2 to those students who made no more than six errors on Part 1. (Part 2 is a group test.)

1. Assemble the students.

2. Give each student a copy of the placement test.

3. Make sure the students have pencils.

4. Give the group these instructions: "These are questions about the passage that you read earlier. Write the answers to the comprehension items at the bottom of your paper. You have five minutes to finish the questions."

5. Collect the test sheets after five minutes.

Answer Key Part 2

1. *Idea:* Because the ship was on fire
2. Linda, Kathy   3. lifeboats
4. Linda   5. 13   6. 10   7. hand
8. Idea: In a lifeboat   9. Japan
10. Idea: To see their father   11. 3 days

READING MASTERY PLUS LEVEL 4 PLACEMENT TEST

Part 1

"Fire! Fire!" a voice said over the loudspeaker. "The forward deck is on fire," the voice announced. "Everybody, leave the ship. Get into the lifeboats!"

Linda and her sister were on their way from the United States to Japan. Linda was thirteen years old, three years older than Kathy. Their father was in Japan, and they were on their way to visit him. Three days before, they had left California on a great ship called an ocean liner. They were now somewhere in the middle of the Pacific Ocean.

"Fire! Fire!" the voice shouted. "Everybody get into the lifeboats!"

People were running this way and that way on the deck of the ship. They were yelling and crying.

"Hold on to my hand," Linda said. The girls went to the lifeboats. People were all around them, shoving and yelling. Linda could not see much. She was afraid. Suddenly she was no longer holding Kathy's hand.

Suddenly a strong pair of arms grabbed Linda. "In you go," a voice said. A big man picked Linda up and put her in the lifeboat.

"Where's my sister?" Linda asked. Linda looked but she couldn't see her younger sister.

1. California
2. Pacific
3. lifeboat
4. Japan
5. loudspeaker

Part 2

1. Why was everybody trying to leave the ship? _____

2. Name the two sisters that were on the ship. _____

3. People were trying to get into the _____

4. Which sister was older? _____

5. How old was that girl? _____

6. How old was her sister? _____

7. Linda told Kathy, "Hold on to my _____"

8. When the big man picked up Linda, where did he put her? _____

9. What country were the girls going to? _____

10. Why were the girls going there? _____

11. How long had they been on the ship? _____

Placement Criteria

Use the table below to determine placement for each student.

Errors	Placement
If a student makes seven errors or more on Part 1 **OR** three errors or more on Part 2	Place the student in a reading-language program more elementary than *Reading Mastery Plus* Level 4
If a student makes no more than six errors on Part 1 **AND** no more than two errors on Part 2	Place the student at *Reading Mastery Plus* Level 4, lesson 1

If you suspect that some students are too advanced for the program (students who score 0 or 1 on the placement test and who exhibit good comprehension skills), present the main story from lesson 103 to them. Present the tasks specified for the main story oral reading, and assign items 1–10 (17 responses) from lesson 103 in the workbook.

If the student makes no more than eight story-reading errors and no more than two workbook errors on lesson 103, place the student in a higher-level program, *Reading Mastery Plus* Level 5.

Reading Mastery Plus, Level 5

Instructions for Part 1

Use the following procedures to administer part 1.

1. (Give the student a blank copy of the Level 5 placement test. Use the student's copy to mark errors that the student makes. The simplest procedure is to give the student your copy of the placement test. Mark errors on the student's copy.)
2. (Point to the passage and say:) You're going to read this passage aloud. I want you to read it as well as you can. Don't try to read it so fast that you make mistakes, but don't read it so slowly that it doesn't make any sense. You have two minutes to read the passage. Go.
3. (Time the student and make one tally mark for each error.)
4. (After two minutes, stop the student. Count every word not read as an error.)
5. (Total the student's errors.)

Instructions for Part 2

After all the students have finished part 1, administer part 2 to the entire group. Use the following procedure.

1. (Assemble the students.)
2. (Give each student a copy of the test, and make sure the students have pencils.)
3. (Say:) Here is the passage that you read earlier. Read the passage again silently; then answer the questions in part 2. You have seven minutes. Go.
4. (Collect the test papers after seven minutes.)
5. (Total each student's errors, using the answer key.)

Answer Key for Part 2

1. Idea: *The Bermuda Islands.*
2. Ideas: *To dive; to see the bottom of the ocean.*
3. Response: *Warm.*
4. Response: *The guide.*
5. Ideas: *Partner; person.*
6. Idea: *Signal the guide.*
7. Idea: *Go to the surface of the water.*
8. Idea: *The diver might get the bends.*
9. Response: *Pressure.*

Placement Guidelines

Place your students as follows:

- Students who made zero errors or one error should be given the placement test for *Reading Mastery Plus,* Level 6.
- Students who made zero to six errors on part 1 *and* zero to two errors on part 2 can be placed in *Reading Mastery Plus,* Level 5.
- Students who made more than six errors on part 1 *or* more than two errors on part 2 should be given the placement test for *Reading Mastery Plus,* Level 4.

Placement Test

Name _____

PART 1

An Underwater World

The diving boat was anchored in a place where the water changed from light green to dark, dark blue. One by one, the divers went down the ladder on the side of the boat and entered the warm water. The boat was about 1,600 kilometers east of Florida. They were south of the Bermuda Islands. Darla was the last diver to go down the ladder and enter the warm water.

"Now stick together," the guide said as he floated with his mask tilted back on his forehead. "You've got your partners. Stay with your partner. If you see something you want to look at, signal me. If one person stops, we all stop or somebody's going to get lost."

The guide continued, "If you get separated, go to the surface of the water. Don't try to look for the rest of us. Just go to the surface. And remember, don't go up too fast. Take at least two minutes to go up, or you may get the bends."

The bends. Darla had read about the bends. She knew that a person gets them because of the great pressure of the water.

PART 2

1. Near which islands does this story take place?

   _____

2. Why was the group in this place?

   _____

3. Was the water warm or cold?

   _____

4. Who led the group?

   _____

5. Each diver was supposed to stay with a

   _____.

6. What was a diver supposed to do if the diver wanted to stop to examine something?

   _____

7. What was a diver supposed to do if the diver got separated from the group?

   _____

8. What problem would the diver have if the diver went up to the surface too fast?

   _____

9. This problem was caused by the great

   _____ of the water.

Reading Mastery Plus, Level 6

Instructions for Part 1

Use the following procedures to administer Part 1.

1. (Give the student a blank copy of the Level 6 placement test. Use the student's copy to mark errors that the student makes. The simplest procedure is to give the student your copy of the placement test. Mark errors on the student's copy.)
2. (Point to the passage and say:) You're going to read this passage aloud. I want you to read it as well as you can. Don't try to read it so fast that you make mistakes, but don't read it so slowly that it doesn't make any sense. You have two minutes to read the passage. Go.
3. (Time the student and make one tally mark for each error.)
4. (After two minutes, stop the student. Count every word not read as an error.)
5. (Total the student's errors.)

Instructions for Part 2

After all the students have finished part 1, administer part 2 to the entire group. Use the following procedure.

1. (Assemble the students.)
2. (Give each student a copy of the placement test.)
3. (Say:) Here is the passage that you read earlier. Read the passage again silently; then answer the questions in part 2. You have seven minutes. Go.
6. (Collect the test papers after seven minutes.)
7. (Total each student's errors, using the answer key that follows.)

Answer Key for Part 2

1. Response: *A king.*
2. Response: *A princess.*
3. Ideas: *His daughter; Marygold.*
4. Response: *Gold.*
5. Ideas: *His daughter; gold.*
6. Idea: *They weren't gold.*
7. Response: *Roses.*
8. Response: *Perfume.*
9. Idea: *How much it would be worth if the roses were gold.*

Placement Guidelines

Place your students as follows:

- Students who made zero to six errors on part 1 *and* zero to two errors on part 2 can be placed in *Reading Mastery Plus*, Level 6.
- Students who made more than six errors on part 1 *or* more than two errors on part 2 should be given the placement test for *Reading Mastery Plus*, Level 5.

Placement Test

Name _____

PART 1

The Golden Touch

Once upon a time in ancient Turkey there lived a rich king named Midas, who had a daughter named Marygold.

King Midas was very fond of gold. The only thing he loved more was his daughter. But the more Midas loved his daughter, the more he desired gold. He thought the best thing he could possibly do for his child would be to give her the largest pile of yellow, glistening coins that had ever been heaped together since the world began. So Midas gave all his thoughts and all his time to collecting gold.

When Midas gazed at the gold-tinted clouds of sunset, he wished they were real gold and that they could be herded into his strong box. When little Marygold ran to meet him with a bunch of buttercups and dandelions, he used to say, "Pooh, pooh, child. If these flowers were as golden as they look, they would be worth picking."

And yet, in his earlier days, before he had this insane desire for gold, Midas had shown a great love for flowers. He had planted a garden with the biggest and sweetest roses any person ever saw or smelled. These roses were still growing in the garden, as large, as lovely, and as fragrant as they were when Midas used to pass whole hours looking at them and inhaling their perfume. But now, if he looked at the flowers at all, it was only to calculate how much the garden would be worth if each of the rose petals was a thin plate of gold.

PART 2

1. *Circle the answer.* What kind of royal person was Midas?

   • an emperor   • a king   • a prince

2. *Circle the answer.* So his daughter was __.

   • an empress   • a queen   • a princess

3. What did Midas love most of all?

   _____

4. What did he love almost as much?

   _____

5. The more Midas loved _____,
   the more he desired _____.

6. Why did Midas think that dandelions were not worth picking?

   _____

7. What kind of flowers had Midas planted in his earlier days?

   _____

8. Midas used to inhale the _____
   of those flowers.

9. What did Midas think about his garden now?

   _____

Sample Lessons

This section contains complete sample lessons from every level of *Reading Mastery Plus*. The lessons are reproduced here in their entirety so that you can practice the skills discussed in this guide before presenting *Reading Mastery Plus* to your students.

Level K

Lesson 55 and Lesson 144 from *Reading Mastery Plus*, Level K:

Lesson 55 - Language Presentation Book B

Students begin Lesson 55 by completing 8 language exercises with the teacher in the *Language Presentation Book*. Language Exercise 8 is followed by a plain-paper activity and four *Workbook* exercises on Side 1 and Side 2.

Lesson 55 - Workbook B: Side 1 and Side 2
Lesson 55 - Pre-Reading Presentation Book

The *Pre-Reading Presentation Book* activities involve the remaining Side 2 exercises from Worksheet 55.

Lesson 144 - Workbook C: Side 2
Lesson 144 - Reading Presentation Book

Reading lessons begin at lesson 101. Lesson 144 begins with sound-practice activities from the *Reading Presentation Book* and includes the completion of several Workbook activities from Side 2 of Worksheet 144.

Level 1

Lesson 54 from *Reading Mastery Plus*, Level 1:

Lesson 54 - Storybook
Lesson 54 - Reading Workbook B: Side 1 and Side 2
Lesson 54 - Reading Presentation Book B

Reading Lesson 54 begins with sound-reading activities in the *Reading Presentation Book*, which includes the *Storybook* reading and comprehension activities. Then students complete all *Reading Workbook* activities on Side 1 and Side 2.

Level 1, continued

Lesson 54 - Language Workbook: Worksheet 54
Lesson 54 - Language Presentation Book

In addition to reading activities, students complete language activities from the *Language Presentation Book* and *Language Workbook*, Worksheet 54.

Lesson 54 - Spelling Book

Teachers present spelling exercises from the *Spelling Book*. The students use lined paper.

Level 2

Lesson 11 and Lesson 141 from *Reading Mastery Plus*, Level 2:

Lesson 11 - Storybook
Lesson 11 - Workbook A
Lesson 11 - Reading Presentation Book A

Reading Lesson 11 begins with word-reading exercises in the *Reading Presentation Book*, followed by the *Storybook* reading, and ends with various activities in the *Workbook*.

Lesson 141 - Textbook
Lesson 141 - Workbook C
Lesson 141 - Reading Presentation Book C

Lesson 141 reading activities begin with *Textbook* word-reading exercises, followed by the *Textbook* reading and comprehension activities, and end with various *Workbook* activities.

Language Lesson 141–145 - Workbook C
Language Lesson 141–145 - Language Presentation Book

Sometime between reading lessons 141 and 145, teachers lead students through the language exercises in the *Language Presentation Book*. These exercises include activities in the *Workbook* for Language Lesson 141–145.

Level 3

Lesson 71 from *Reading Mastery Plus*, Level 3:

Lesson 71 - Textbook B

Lesson 71 - Workbook B

Lesson 71 - Presentation Book B

Students begin this lesson by reading word lists and a comprehension passage, followed by story reading in the *Textbook*. The students then work independently on the remaining *Workbook* and *Textbook* activities.

Lesson 71 - Writing and Spelling Guide

During writing and spelling, students use lined paper as the teacher leads them through *Writing and Spelling Guide* activities.

Lesson 71 - Language Arts Guide
>**Blackline masters 17 and 18;**
>**Teacher Presentation Script 71**

The *Language Arts Guide* exercises end with the students independently completing blackline masters 17 and 18.

Level 4

Lesson 21 from *Reading Mastery Plus*, Level 4:

Lesson 21 - Textbook A

Lesson 21 - Workbook A

Lesson 21 - Presentation Book A

Students begin Lesson 21 by reading word lists and a comprehension passage, followed by story reading in the *Textbook*. The students then work independently on the remaining *Workbook* and *Textbook* activities.

Lesson 21 - Language Arts Guide:
>**Blackline master 17;**
>**Teacher Presentation Script 21**

The *Language Arts Guide* exercise ends with the students independently completing the top of blackline master 17.

Lesson 21 - Activities Across the
>**Curriculum**
>**Blackline master 2;**
>**Teacher Presentation Script 2**

Students work to complete Activity 2 from *Activities Across the Curriculum*.

Level 5

Lesson 76 from *Reading Mastery Plus*, Level 5:

Lesson 76 - Textbook B

Lesson 76 - Workbook

Lesson 76 - Presentation Book B

Students begin this lesson by reading word lists and completing vocabulary activities. They then read a story-background passage and the first chapter of "Beauty and the Beast." After the reading, the students work independently on *Workbook* and *Textbook* activities.

Lesson 76 - Language Arts Guide:
>**Blackline master 76;**
>**Teacher Presentation Script 76**

For the *Language Arts Guide*, exercises end with the students completing blackline master 76. (Students also have the option of reading from the *Literature Anthology* or completing *Activities across the Curriculum* materials.)

Level 6

Lesson 57 from *Reading Mastery Plus*, Level 6:

Lesson 57 - Textbook A

Lesson 57 - Workbook

Lesson 57 - Presentation Book A

Students begin this lesson by reading word lists and vocabulary definitions. They then complete a skill exercise on making inferences. Afterward, the students read the first part of the classic short story "A White Heron." Following the reading, they work independently on *Workbook* and *Textbook* activities.

Lesson 57 - Language Arts Guide:
>**Blackline master 57;**
>**Teacher Presentation Script 57**

Students complete two *Language Arts Guide* exercises with the teacher and independently complete blackline master 57. (Students also have the option of reading from the *Literature Anthology* or completing *Activities across the Curriculum* materials.)

Lesson 55

EXERCISE 1   Rhyming

a. I'm going to say three words. These words rhyme. What do they do? (Signal.) *Rhyme.*
Listen: **cake, lake, steak.**

b. Listen again: **cake, lake, steak.**
Say those words. (Signal.) *Cake, lake, steak.*

c. (Repeat step b until firm.)

d. I'll say the first two words. See if **you** can say the last word. **Cake, lake** . . . Your turn. (Signal.) *Steak.*
I'll say the first word. See if you can say the other words. Listen: **cake** . . . Your turn. (Signal.) *Lake, steak.*

e. I'll say things. When I stop, see if you can say the right rhyming word.
Listen. The girl had a piece of chocolate . . . (signal) *cake.*
Say the whole thing. (Signal.) *The girl had a piece of chocolate cake.*

f. Her dad was cooking a great big . . . (Signal.) *Her dad was cooking a great big steak.*
Say the whole thing. (Signal.) *Her dad was cooking a great big steak.*

g. That girl went swimming in a . . . (signal) *lake.*
Say the whole thing. (Signal.) *That girl went swimming in a lake.*

h. Let's do those again.
Her dad was cooking a great big . . . (signal) *steak.*
Say the whole thing. (Signal.) *Her dad was cooking a great big steak.*
That girl went swimming in a . . . (signal) *lake.*
Say the whole thing. (Signal.) *That girl went swimming in a lake.*
The girl had a piece of chocolate . . . (signal) *cake.*
Say the whole thing. (Signal.) *The girl had a piece of chocolate cake.*

i. (Repeat step h, calling on different children for each sentence.)

j. You're using words that rhyme. Good for you.

EXERCISE 2   Actions—Review

1. It's time for an action game.

a. Everybody, hold your hand **in front of** your head. (Signal. Wait.) Where is your hand? (Signal.) *In front of my head.*

b. Hold your hand **in back of** your head. (Signal. Wait.) Where is your hand? (Signal.) *In back of my head.*
Keep it there.

c. Listen carefully. Where **was** your hand? (Signal.) *In front of my head.*
Say the whole thing about where your hand **was.** (Signal.) *My hand was in front of my head.*

d. Again. (Signal.) *My hand was in front of my head.*
(Repeat step d until all children's responses are firm.)
Hands down.

e. (Repeat steps a through d until all children's responses are firm.)

2. Let's do another one.

a. Everybody, put your hand **over** your knee. (Signal. Wait.) Where is your hand? (Signal.) *Over my knee.*
Say the whole thing. (Signal.) *My hand is over my knee.*

b. Everybody, put your hand **on** your knee. (Signal. Wait.) Where is your hand now? (Signal.) *On my knee.*
Keep it there.

c. Where **was** your hand? (Signal.) *Over my knee.*
Say the whole thing. (Signal.) *My hand was over my knee.*

d. (Repeat steps a through c until all children's responses are firm.)

32

EXERCISE 3   Actions—Plurals

1. Listen carefully.
a. Everybody, touch your knees. (Pause. Signal. Wait.)
What are you touching? (Signal.) ●
My knees.
Say the whole thing about what you are doing. (Signal.) *I am touching my knees.*
b. Again. (Signal.) *I am touching my knees.*
(Repeat step b until all children's responses are firm.)
c. Everybody, touch your knee. (Pause. Signal. Wait.)
What are you touching? (Signal.) *My knee.*
Say the whole thing. (Signal.) *I am touching my knee.*
d. Everybody, touch your knees. (Pause. Signal. Wait.) What are you touching? (Signal.) *My knees.*
Say the whole thing. (Signal.) *I am touching my knees.*
e. Everybody, touch your shoes. (Pause. Signal. Wait.) What are you touching? (Signal.) *My shoes.*
Say the whole thing. (Signal.) *I am touching my shoes.*
f. Everybody, touch your shoe. (Pause. Signal. Wait.)
What are you touching? (Signal.) *My shoe.*
Say the whole thing. (Signal.) *I am touching my shoe.*

2. (Repeat steps c through f until all children's responses are firm.)

EXERCISE 4   Actions—And

1. It's time for some actions.
a. Everybody, stand up. (Signal. Wait.)
What are you doing? (Signal.) *Standing up.*
Say the whole thing. (Signal.) *I am standing up.*
Sit down.
b. Everybody, stand up **and** touch your head.
Get ready. (Signal. Wait.)
What are you doing? (Signal.) *Standing up and touching my head.*
(Repeat step b until all children can make the statement.)
c. Say the whole thing with me. (Signal. Respond with the children.)
I am standing up and touching my head.
(Repeat step c until all children's responses are firm.)
d. All by yourselves. Say the whole thing. (Signal. Do not respond with the children.)
I am standing up and touching my head.
e. Again. (Signal.) *I am standing up and touching my head.*
(Repeat step e until all children can make the statement.)
Sit down.

2. Let's do that again.
a. Everybody, stand up and touch your head.
Get ready. (Signal.) *Standing up and touching my head.*
b. Say the whole thing. (Signal.) *I am standing up and touching my head.*

3. Here's another one.
a. Everybody, sit down and touch your nose.
Get ready. (Signal. Wait.)
What are you doing? (Signal.) *Sitting down and touching my nose.*
Say the whole thing. (Signal.) *I am sitting down and touching my nose.*
b. (Repeat step a until all children's responses are firm.)

Corrections

EXERCISE 3

● **Error**
(Children say *knee.*)

Correction
1. Say it with me. (Signal. Respond with the children.) My kneessss.
Again. (Signal.) My kneessss.
2. All by yourselves. Say it. (Signal. Do not respond with the children.) *My knees.*
Again. (Signal.) *My knees.*
3. (Repeat step a.)

Lesson 55

33

b

a

EXERCISE 5   Tense

1. Look at these pictures. They show what a bird did.

a. (Point to a.)
Where is the bird in this picture? (Touch.)
In the cage.
Yes, the bird is in the cage.
Say the whole thing. (Touch.) *The bird is in the cage.*

b. (Point to b.)
Now look at where the bird is.
Where is it? (Touch.) *On the cage.*
Yes, the bird is on the cage. Say the whole thing. (Touch.) *The bird is on the cage.*

2. Listen. Where was the bird before it got on the cage? (Signal. Do not touch the picture.) *In the cage.*
Say the whole thing about where the bird was. (Touch.) *The bird was in the cage.*

3. (Repeat parts 1 and 2 until all children's responses are firm.)

Individual Turns
(Repeat parts 1 and 2, calling on different children for each step.)

Corrections

EXERCISE 5

(Correct all mistakes immediately, then return to the beginning of the exercise.)

34

a

c

b

EXERCISE 6   Prepositions—In Back Of, Over, On

1. One of these footballs is **in back of** the bike.
One of these footballs is **over** the bike.
One of these footballs is **on** the bike.
(Point to each football and ask:)
Is this football in back of the bike?
(The children are to answer *yes* or *no*.)

2. We'll talk about each football.
a. (Point to a.)
What is this? (Touch.) *A football.*
Where is this football? (Touch.) *Over the bike.*
Say the whole thing about where this football is. (Touch.) *This football is over the bike.*
(Repeat step a until all children can make the statement.)
b. (Point to b.)
What is this? (Touch.) *A football.*
Where is this football? (Touch.) *In back of the bike.*
Say the whole thing about where this football is. (Touch.) *This football is in back of the bike.*
(Repeat step b until all children can make the statement.)
c. (Point to c.)
What is this? (Touch.) *A football.*
Where is this football? (Touch.) *On the bike.*
Say the whole thing about where this football is. (Touch.) *This football is on the bike.*
(Repeat step c until all children can make the statement.)

3. Look at this football again.
a. (Point to c.)
Is this football in back of the bike? (Touch.) *No.*

b. Say the whole thing. (Touch.) *This football is not in back of the bike.*
(Repeat part 3 until all children can make the statement.)

Individual Turns
(Repeat parts 2 and 3, calling on different children for each step.)

Lesson 55

35

Lesson 55

EXERCISE 7   Part/Whole

1. Today we're going to do the parts of an umbrella again.

a. (Circle the umbrella.) Everybody, what is this? (Touch.) *An umbrella.*

b. Get ready to tell me the parts of an umbrella.
(Point to the frame.) What is this part called? (Touch.) *A frame.*
(Point to the handle.) What is this part called? (Touch.) *A handle.*
(Point to the covering.) What is this part called? (Touch.) *A covering.*

c. (Repeat step b until all children's responses are firm.)

2. Listen.

a. (Point to the handle.)
An umbrella has . . . (touch) *a handle.*
(Point to the covering.) An umbrella has . (touch) *a covering.*
(Point to the frame.) An umbrella has . . . (touch) *a frame.*
(Circle the umbrella.) And what's the whc object called? (Touch.) *An umbrella.*

b. (Repeat step a until all children's responses are firm.)

c. Get ready to tell me the parts of an umbrella. Say the whole thing.
(Point to the handle. Pause. Touch.)
An umbrella has a handle.
(Point to the covering. Pause. Touch.)
An umbrella has a covering.
(Point to the frame. Pause. Touch.)
An umbrella has a frame.
(Repeat step c until all children can make the statements.)

3. (Circle the umbrella.) And what's the whole object called? (Touch.) *An umbrella.*
What do we usually do with an umbrella? (Praise reasonable responses.)

36

EXERCISE 8   Classification

1. We're going to play a game about vehicles.
What's the rule about vehicles? (Signal.) *If it is made to take you places, it is a vehicle.*

2. Listen. I'm going to name some vehicles, but don't let me fool you.

a. If I name something that is a vehicle, you say **yes**.
If I name something that is **not** a vehicle, you say **no**.

b. What are you going to say if it is a vehicle? (Signal.) *Yes.*
What are you going to say if it is not a vehicle? (Signal.) *No.*

3. Remember, I'm going to name some vehicles, but I may fool you.

a. Listen. (Pause.) Airplane. (Signal.) *Yes.*
Bus. (Signal.) *Yes.*
Canoe. (Signal.) *Yes.*
Shovel. (Signal.) *No.* ●
Why did you say no? (Signal.) *Because a shovel is not a vehicle.*

b. Listen. (Pause.) Ship. (Signal.) *Yes.*
Truck. (Signal.) *Yes.*
Motorboat. (Signal.) *Yes.*
Taxi. (Signal.) *Yes.*
Cat. (Signal.) *No.*
Why did you say no? (Signal.) *Because a cat is not a vehicle.*

c. Listen. (Pause.) Sailboat. (Signal.) *Yes.*
Car. (Signal.) *Yes.*
Motorcycle. (Signal.) *Yes.*
Bike. (Signal.) *Yes.*
Table. (Signal.) *No.*
Why did you say no? (Signal.) *Because a table is not a vehicle.*

d. Listen. (Pause.) Tricycle. (Signal.) *Yes.*
Rowboat. (Signal.) *Yes.*
Hat. (Signal.) *No.*
Why did you say no? (Signal.) *Because a hat is not a vehicle.*

e. (Repeat part 3 until all children's responses are firm.)

Individual Turns
(Repeat the exercise, calling on different children for each step.)

Corrections

EXERCISE 8

● **Error**
(Children don't say *No.*)

Correction

1. What's the rule about vehicles? (Signal.) *If it is made to take you places, it is a vehicle.*

2. Does a shovel take you places? (Signal.) *No.*

3. So is it a vehicle? (Signal.) *No.*

4. So you should have said no.

5. (Repeat step a until all children's responses are firm.)

37

Lesson 55

Worksheet 55

[Note: Each child will need a piece of paper.]

Front/Back

1. (Pass out a piece of paper to each child.)

a. Listen. Make a cross-out mark at the bottom of your paper. ✓

b. The cross-out mark is on the front of your paper.
What side? (Signal.) *Front.*

2. Turn your paper over so you are looking at the back. ✓

a. What's on the back? (Signal.) *Nothing.*
Listen. Make a circle in the **middle** of the back. A circle in the middle. ✓

b. Everybody, what's on the back of your paper? (Signal.) *A circle.*

3. Turn your paper so you are looking at the front. ✓

a. What's on the front of your paper?
(Signal.) *A cross-out mark.*
Is the cross-out mark at the top or the bottom of that side? (Signal.) *The bottom.*

b. Turn your paper so the cross-out mark is at the top of the front. ✓

SIDE 1

Matching

1. (Hold up worksheet. Point to each object in the left column, one at a time.) What is this?

2. Draw lines to show the objects that are the same. ✓

Then draw a line to the empty box. ✓
Draw a pencil in the empty box. Be sure to draw all the parts of the pencil. Remember—a pencil has an eraser, a shaft, and a point. ✓

3. Later you may color all the objects on your worksheet.

Coloring

1. When I tap, hold up your blue crayon. (Pause.) Get ready. (Tap.)
Everybody, touch the umbrella. ✓
You're going to color the umbrella blue.
Everybody, put a little blue mark on the umbrella. ✓
Everybody, what color did you mark on the umbrella? (Signal.) *Blue.*

2. Now, when I tap, hold up your green crayon. (Pause.) Get ready. (Tap.)
Everybody, touch the tree. ✓
You're going to color the tree green.
Everybody, put a little green mark on the tree. ✓

3. Now when I tap, hold up your yellow crayon. (Pause.) Get ready. (Tap.)
You're going to color the rabbit yellow.
Everybody, put a little yellow mark on the rabbit. ✓
Later you may color the umbrella blue, the tree green, and the rabbit yellow.

Spatial First, Next, Last

1. We're going to talk about the birds on your worksheet.

a. Touch the birds. ✓
You're going to make colored marks on these birds.

b. Listen. The bird that is first in line should be blue.
What color should the first bird be? (Signal.) *Blue.*
Make a blue mark on that bird. ✓

c. Listen. The bird that is next in line should be yellow.
What color should the bird next in line be? (Signal.) *Yellow.*
Make a yellow mark on that bird. ✓

d. The bird that does not have a mark on it is last in line.
Where is that bird? (Signal.) *Last in line.*

e. Listen. The bird that is last in line should be red.
What color should the last bird be? (Signal.) *Red.*
Make a red mark on that bird. ✓

2. Listen.

a. One of the birds has a red mark.
Is that bird first in line, next in line, or last in line? (Signal.) *Last in line.*

b. Listen. One of the birds has a yellow mark.
Is that bird first in line, next in line, or last in line? (Signal.) *Next in line.*

c. What color is the mark on the bird that is first in line? (Signal.) *Blue.*

d. Later you may color those birds.

Lesson 55

38

Worksheet 55 continued

SIDE 2

Pair Relations

1. (Hold up worksheet.) Find the first box with a line and a ball. ✓
Here's a circling rule: Circle each box with a line and a ball.
Do it. ✓

2. You should have circled two boxes. All the other boxes have something missing. Some have the line missing, and some have the ball missing.

a. Touch the first box. ✓
What's missing, the line or the ball? (Signal.) *The ball.*
Fix up the box so it has a line and a ball. ✓

b. Touch the next box. ✓
What's missing in the box? (Signal.) *The line.*
Fix up the box so it has a line and a ball. ✓

c. Touch the next box. ✓
Is anything missing in that box? (Signal.) *No.*

d. Touch the next box. ✓
Is anything missing in that box? (Signal.) *Yes.*
What's missing? (Signal.) *The line.*
Fix up the box so it has a line and a ball. ✓

e. Touch the next box. ✓
Is anything missing in that box? (Signal.) *Yes.*
What's missing? (Signal.) *The ball.*
Fix up the box so it has a line and a ball. ✓

f. Touch the next box. ✓
Is anything missing in that box? (Signal.) *No.*

g. Touch the last box. ✓
Is anything missing in that box? (Signal.) *Yes.*
What's missing? (Signal.) *The ball.*
Fix up the box so it has a line and a ball. ✓

> Reread "Polly and the Lion," Storybook 1, page 1.

[**Note:** Present the Pre-Reading exercises for lesson 55.]

Lesson 55

39

Lesson 55

ALPHABET

a. You've learned the whole alphabet.
b. Start with the letter **A** and say the whole alphabet. Get ready. **(Tap for each letter.)** *A, B, C, D, E, F, G, H, I, J, K, L, M, N, O, P, Q, R, S, T, U, V, W, X, Y, Z.*

Individual Turns

• (Call on individual children to say the alphabet. Praise good performers.)

LETTER IDENTIFICATION

a. (Write on the board:)

p m c o	

• (Point to **p.**)
• You've learned all these letters. I'll touch each letter. You'll tell me the name.
b. (Touch under **p.**) What letter? (Touch.) *P.*
• (Touch under **m.**) What letter? (Touch.) *M.*
• (Touch under **c.**) What letter? (Touch.) *C.*
• (Touch under **o.**) What letter? (Touch.) *O.*
c. (Repeat step b until firm.)

Worksheet **55**

SIDE 2

d. (Hold up worksheet.) Find the pencil. ✓
• (Teacher reference:)

p j g d c a d q p	

e. Some of the letters are **P.** Some are not **P.**
• Listen. Circle all the **P**s. There are two **P**s.
  (Observe children and give feedback.)
• Everybody, what letter did you just circle? (Signal.) *P.*
f. Some of the letters that you didn't circle are **D.**
• Listen. Make a line under all the **D**s. There are two **D**s.
  (Observe children and give feedback.)
• Everybody, what letter did you make a line under? (Signal.) *D.*

LETTER WRITING

a. Touch the first row of dotted letters. ✓
• Everybody, what letter is that? (Signal.) *O.*
• Touch the big dot on the first **O.** ✓
b. The **O** is just like a **C,** except you go all the way around.
• I'll show you how to write **O.**
• (Hold up worksheet and pencil.)
• I'll start the same way I start with a **C** and go **all** the way around. Watch.
• (Trace first three **o**s.)

c. Your turn. Trace the first **O**. Pencils down when you've done that much.
(Observe children and give feedback.)

• Now complete the row of **O**s. Pencils down when you're finished.
(Observe children and give feedback.)

• Everybody, what letter did you write? (Signal.) *O.*

d. Touch the next row. ✓

• Everybody, what letter is that? (Signal.) *F.*

e. The first letters have dotted lines for the line that goes around and down and for the line that goes across. But the rest of the letters don't have all the dotted lines. Trace the **F**s that have all the dotted lines. Pencils down when you've done that much.
(Observe children and give feedback.)

f. Now make the next **F**. Start at the big dot and make the line around and down. Then start at the little dot and make the line across. Pencils down when you've done that much.
(Observe children and give feedback.)

• Complete the rest of the **F**s. Pencils down when you're finished.
(Observe children and give feedback.)

• Everybody, what letter did you write? (Signal.) *F.*

144 Side 2   Name _____

.tha̲t̲ ■ i̲s̲ ■ me̅.

i̲s̲ ■ me

th• •f
f•   •n
d•   •a
n•   •d
t•   •th
a•   •t

n ___
i f ___
f ___
s ___
a ___

s t

i
t   n   s
s   i
th   t   t
t   n
d   f   s
     s

| | e | | | i | | | i | e | | | | |
| d | m | | | | | | | d | | | | m |

Lesson 144

SAYING SOUNDS

EXERCISE 1

Children say the sounds

a. You're going to say some sounds. When I hold up my finger, say (pause) **c.** Get ready. (Hold up one finger.) c.

b. Next sound. Say (pause) **vvv.** Get ready. (Hold up one finger.) vvv.

c. Next sound. Say (pause) **ŭ ŭ ŭ.** Get ready. (Hold up one finger.) ŭ ŭ ŭ.

d. (Repeat c for sounds **c, vvv,** and **ŭ ŭ ŭ.**)

e. (Call on different children to do a, b, or c.)

f. Good saying the sounds.

LETTER SOUNDS

EXERCISE 2

Introducing c as in cat

a. (Point to **c.**) My turn to say the sound for the letter **c.** It's a quick sound.

b. My turn. (Pause. Touch **c** for an instant, saying:) **c.** (Do not say **cuuh.**)

c. Again. (Touch **c** and say:) **c.**

d. (Point to **c.**) Your turn. When I touch the letter, you say the sound. (Pause.) Get ready. (Touch **c.**) c.

e. Again. (Touch **c.**) c.

f. (Repeat e until firm.)

EXERCISE 3

Individual test

(Call on different children to identify **c.**)

EXERCISE 4

Sounds firm-up

a. Get ready to say the sounds when I touch them.

b. (Alternate touching **c** and **d.** Point to the sound. Pause one second. Say:) Get ready. (Touch the sound.) *The children respond.*

c. (When **c** and **d** are firm, alternate touching **c, s, d,** and **n** until all four sounds are firm.)

EXERCISE 5

Individual test

(Call on different children to identify **c, s, d,** or **n.**)

287   Lesson 144

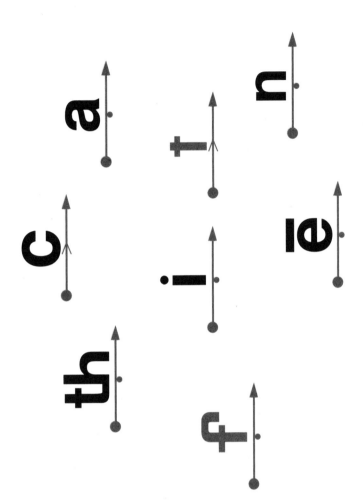

EXERCISE 6

Sounds firm-up

a. (Point to **c.**) When I touch the letter, you say the sound.

b. (Pause.) Get ready. (Touch **c.**) c.

c. Again. (Repeat *b* until firm.)

d. Get ready to say the sounds for all these letters.

e. (Alternate touching **th, c, a, f, i, t, ē,** and **n** three or four times. Point to the sound. Pause one second. Say:) Get ready. (Touch the sound.) *The children respond.*

EXERCISE 7

Individual test

(Call on different children to identify one or more sounds in exercise 6.)

READING VOCABULARY

As soon as you read all the words on this page without making a mistake, we'll go on to the next page.

EXERCISE 8

Children sound out the word and say it fast

a. (Touch the first ball of the arrow for **an.**) Sound it out. Get ready. (Move quickly under each sound.) *Aaannn.*

b. (Return to the first ball.) Again, sound it out. Get ready. (Move quickly under each sound.) *Aaannn.*

c. (Repeat *b* until firm.)

d. (Return to the first ball.) Say it fast. (Slash.) *An.* Yes, what word? (Signal.) *An.* A dog is (pause) **an** (pause) animal.

EXERCISE 9

Children sound out the word and say it fast

a. (Touch the first ball of the arrow for **in.**) Sound it out. Get ready. (Move quickly under each sound.) *iiinnn.*

b. (Return to the first ball.) Again, sound it out. Get ready. (Move quickly under each sound.) *iiinnn.*

c. (Repeat *b* until firm.)

d. (Return to the first ball.) Say it fast. (Slash.) *In.* Yes, what word? (Signal.) *In.*

EXERCISE 10

Children sound out the word and say it fast

a. (Touch the first ball of the arrow for **mē.**) Sound it out. Get ready. (Move quickly under each sound.) *Mmmēēē.*

b. (Return to the first ball.) Again, sound it out. Get ready. (Move quickly under each sound.) *Mmmēēē.*

c. (Repeat *b* until firm.)

d. (Return to the first ball.) Say it fast. (Signal.) *Me.* Yes, what word? (Signal.) *Me.*

EXERCISE 11

Children sound out the word and say it fast

a. (Touch the first ball of the arrow for **it.**) Sound it out. Get ready. (Move quickly under each sound.) *iiit.*

b. (Return to the first ball.) Again, sound it out. Get ready. (Move quickly under each sound.) *iiit.*

c. (Repeat *b* until firm.)

d. (Return to the first ball.) Say it fast. (Slash.) *It.* Yes, what word? (Signal.) *It.* Where is (pause) **it?**

EXERCISE 12

Children sound out the word and say it fast

a. (Touch the first ball of the arrow for **is.**) Sound it out. Get ready. (Move quickly under each sound.) *iiisss.* (Children should not say **iiizzz.**)

b. (Return to the first ball.) Again, sound it out. Get ready. (Move quickly under each sound.) *iiisss.*

c. (Repeat *b* until firm.)

d. (Return to the first ball.) How do we say the word? (Slash.) *Iz.* Yes, **iz.** My candy (pause) **is** (pause) sweet.

Criterion

(If the children read the words in exercises 8, 9, 10, 11, and 12 without making any mistakes, present individual turns.)

(If the children made mistakes, say:) That was pretty good. Let's read the words again. See if you can read them without making a mistake.

EXERCISE 13

Individual test

(Call on different children. Each child is to do exercise 8, 9, 10, 11, or 12.)

READING VOCABULARY—RHYMING

EXERCISE 14

Children rhyme with an

a. (Point to **an** and **ran**.) These words rhyme.

b. (Touch the first ball of the arrow for **an.** Pause.) Sound it out. Get ready. (Move quickly under each sound.) *Aaannn.*

c. (Return to the first ball.) Again sound it out. Get ready. (Move quickly under each sound.) *Aaannn.*

d. (Return to the first ball.) Say it fast. (Slash.) *An.* Yes, **an.**

e. (Touch the first ball of the arrow for **ran.**) The red part of this word is (pause) **an.** So what does this word rhyme with? (Tap the ball.) *An.* Yes, **an.** Rhyme with (pause) **an.** Get ready. (Move quickly to the second ball. Hold.) *rrr.* (Slash.) *Rrran.* (Return to the first ball.) What word? (Slash.) *Ran.* Yes, **ran.** They (pause) **ran.**

f. (Call on different children to do e.)

EXERCISE 15

Children rhyme with an

a. (Point to **an** and **dan.**) These words rhyme.

b. (Touch the first ball of the arrow for **an.** Pause.) Sound it out. Get ready. (Move quickly under each sound.) *Aaannn.*

c. (Return to the first ball.) Again, sound it out. Get ready. (Move quickly under each sound.) *Aaannn.*

d. (Return to the first ball.) Say it fast. (Slash.) *An.* Yes, **an.**

e. (Touch the first ball of the arrow for **dan.**) This word rhymes with (pause) **an.** Say it fast and rhyme with (pause) **an.** (Pause.) Get ready. (Slash.) *Dan.* Yes, **dan.**

f. (Return to the first ball for **dan.**) Again, rhyme with (pause) **an.** Get ready. (Slash.) *Dan.* Yes, **dan.**

g. (Repeat f until firm.)

h. (Call on different children to do f.)

Worksheet 144 Side 2

STORY READING
EXERCISE 16

First reading—children sound out each word and say it fast

a. (Hold up worksheet. Point to *that is mē.*) This is a story. You're going to read the story. Then we'll talk about the picture for this story. The first word in the story has a ball. The other words in the story have boxes.

b. Everybody, touch the ball for the first word. ✔
Touch the box for the next word. ✔
Touch the box for the next word. ✔

c. Again. (Repeat b until firm.)

d. Touch the ball for the first word again. ✔
Sound it out. Get ready. (Tap for each sound, pausing about two seconds between taps. Children move their finger under each sound as they say *ththththaaat.*)

e. Again, finger on the ball. ✔
First you'll sound it out and then you'll say it fast.
Sound it out. Get ready. (Tap for each sound.) *Ththththaaat.*
Say it fast. (Signal.) *That.*
Yes, what word? (Signal.) *That.*

f. Touch the box for the next word. ✔
Sound it out. Get ready. (Tap for each sound, pausing about two seconds between taps. Children move their finger under each sound as they say *iiisss.* Children should not say **iiizzz.**)

g. Again, back to the box. ✔
Sound it out. Get ready. (Tap for each sound.) *iiisss.*
How do we say the word? (Signal.) *Iz.*
Yes, what word? (Signal.) *Is.*

h. Touch the box for the next word. ✔
Sound it out. Get ready. (Tap for each sound, pausing about two seconds between taps. Children move their finger under each sound as they say *mmmēēē.*)

i. Again, back to the box. ✔
Sound it out. Get ready. (Tap for each sound.) *Mmmēēē.*
Say it fast. (Signal.) *Me.*
Yes, what word? (Signal.) *Me.*

EXERCISE 17

Second reading—children sound out each word and say it fast

a. Get ready to read the story again.
Everybody, finger on the first ball. ✔
Sound it out. Get ready. (Tap for each sound.) *Ththththaaat.*

b. Again, finger on the first ball. ✔
Sound it out. Get ready. (Tap for each sound.) *Ththththaaat.*
Say it fast. (Signal.) *That.*
Yes, what word? (Signal.) *That.*

c. Touch the box for the next word. ✔
Sound it out. Get ready. (Tap for each sound.) *iiisss.* (Children should not say **iiizzz.**)

d. Again, back to the box. ✔
Sound it out. Get ready. (Tap for each sound.) *iiisss.*
How do we say the word? (Signal.) *Iz.*
Yes, **iz.**

e. Touch the box for the next word. ✔
Sound it out. Get ready. (Tap for each sound.) *Mmmēēē.*

f. Again, back to the box. ✔
Sound it out. Get ready. (Tap for each sound.) *Mmmēēē.*
Say it fast. (Signal.) *Me.*
Yes, what word? (Signal.) *Me.*

EXERCISE 18

Individual test

a. Everybody, follow along with your finger as I call on different children to read one of the words.

b. Everybody, touch the ball for the first word. ✔
(Call on a child.) Sound it out. Get ready. (Tap for each sound, pausing about two seconds between taps.) *Ththththaaat.*
Say it fast. (Signal.) *That.* Yes, **that.**

c. Everybody, touch the box for the next word. ✔
(Call on a child.) Sound it out. Get ready. (Tap for each sound, pausing about two seconds between taps.) *iiisss.* (The child should not say **iiizzz.**)
How do we say the word? (Signal.) *Iz.*
Yes, **iz.**

d. Everybody, touch the box for the next word. ✔
(Call on a child.) Sound it out. Get ready. (Tap for each sound, pausing about two seconds between taps.) *Mmmēēē.*
Say it fast. (Signal.) *Me.* Yes, **me.**

e. (Call on different children. Each child reads one word from *b, c,* or *d.*)

291   Lesson 144

EXERCISE 19
Teacher reads the fast way

a. (Hold up worksheet and point to the story.)
b. Everybody, I'm going to read this story the fast way.
c. (Move your finger quickly under **that** and say:) **that.** (Pause. Then move your finger quickly under **is** and say:) **is.** (Pause.) (Then move your finger quickly under **mē** and say:) **me.**
d. I'll read it again. (Repeat c.)

COMPREHENSION
EXERCISE 20
Picture comprehension

a. You will see a picture . . . . (Signal.) *That is me.*
Yes, you will see a picture . . . . (Signal.) *That is me.*
b. (Repeat a until firm.)
c. Look at the picture.
d. (Ask these questions:)
 1. Is that really me? (Signal.) *No.* No, that's not me.
 2. Who is that? (Call on a child. Idea: *A cowboy.*)
 Yes, a cowboy.
 3. Have you ever seen a cowboy? (Call on a child. Accept reasonable responses.)

STORY COPYING
EXERCISE 21
Children copy the story

a. (Point to the dotted **is mē**.) You're going to write **is me** on this line. What are you going to write? (Signal.) *Is me.*
b. Everybody, follow the dotted lines and write **is me.** (Observe children and give feedback.)
c. (Point to the next line.) What are you going to write on this line? (Signal.) *Is me.*
d. (Point to the bottom line.) What are you going to write on this line? (Signal.) *Is me.*
e. You will write **is me** on these lines later.

SUMMARY OF INDEPENDENT WORK
EXERCISE 22
Introduction to independent activity

a. (Hold up worksheet.)
b. Everybody, you're going to finish this worksheet on your own. (Tell the children when they will work the remaining items.)
 • Let's go over the things you're going to do.

Story copying

(Point to the writing space below the story.) You're going to write **is me** on each line.

Matching

(Point to the first column of sounds in the Matching Game.) You're going to draw lines for every sound over here.

Sound writing

a. (Point to the letter-writing exercise.) Here are the letters you're going to write today. I'll touch the letters. You say the sounds.
b. (Touch each sound.) *The children respond.*
c. (Repeat the series until firm.)

Cross-out game

(Point to the boxed sounds in the Cross-out Game.) Everybody, what sound are you going to circle today? (Signal.) *t.*
What sound are you going to cross out? (Signal.) *sss.*

Pair relations

(Point to the pair-relations exercise.) You're going to fix up each row. First you find the box in each row that's fixed up. Then you fix up the other boxes.

Story picture

(Point to the story picture.) After you finish your worksheet, you can color the story picture.

Note: Before presenting lesson 145, present language lesson 144.

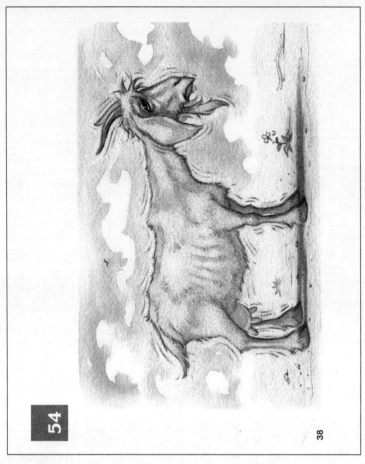

54

38

54

thē ōld gōₐt had an ōld cōₐt.

thē ōld gōₐt said, "I will ēₐt this

ōld cōₐt." sō shē did.

"that was fun," shē said. "I āte

thē ōld cōₐt. and now I am cōld."

now thē ōld gōₐt is sad.

37

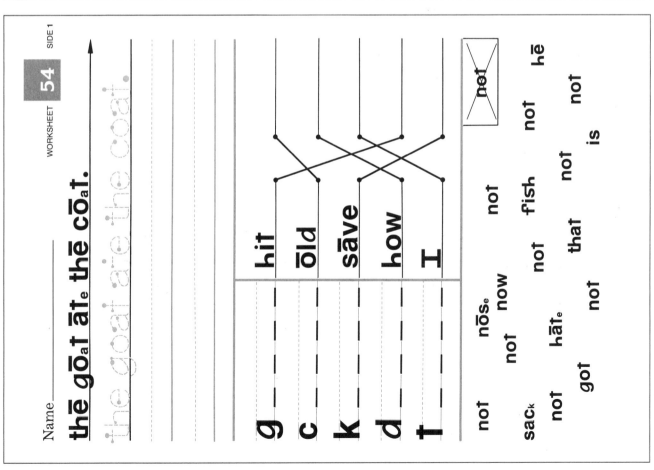

Lesson 54

p

d   t

g

SOUNDS

EXERCISE 1

Teaching p as in pat

a. (Point to **p.**) My turn to say the sound for the letter **p.** It's a quick sound.

b. My turn. (Pause. Touch **p** for an instant, saying:) **p.** (Do not say **puuh.**)

c. Again. (Touch **p** and say:) **p.**

d. (Point to **p.**) Your turn. When I touch the letter, you say the sound. (Pause.) Get ready. (Touch **p.**) *p.*

e. Again. (Touch **p.**) *p.*

f. (Repeat *e* until firm.)

EXERCISE 2

Individual test

(Call on different children to identify **p.**)

EXERCISE 3

Sounds firm-up

a. Get ready to say the sounds when I touch them.

b. (Alternate touching **p** and **d.** Point to the sound. Pause one second. Say:) Get ready. (Touch the sound.) *The children respond.*

c. (When **p** and **d** are firm, alternate touching **p, g, d,** and **t** until all four sounds are firm.)

EXERCISE 4

Individual test

(Call on different children to identify **p, g, d,** or **t.**)

EXERCISE 5

Sounds firm-up

a. (Point to **p.**) When I touch the sound, you say it.

b. (Pause.) Get ready. (Touch **p.**) *p.*

c. Again. (Repeat *b* until firm.)

d. Get ready to say all the sounds when I touch them.

e. (Alternate touching **k, v, u, ō, p, sh, h,** and **n** three or four times. Point to the sound.) (Pause one second. Say:) Get ready. (Touch the sound.) *The children respond.*

p   k

v   ō   sh

m   h   n

EXERCISE 6

Individual test

(Call on different children to identify one or more sounds in exercise 5.)

mop

cop

top

was

ōld

READING VOCABULARY

EXERCISE 7

Children rhyme with mop

a. (Touch the ball for **mop.**) You're going to read this word the fast way. (Pause three seconds.) Get ready. (Move your finger quickly along the arrow.) *Mop.*

b. (Touch the ball for **cop.**) This word rhymes with (pause) **mop.** (Move to **c,** then quickly along the arrow.) *Cop.* Yes, what word? (Signal.) *Cop.*

c. (Touch the ball for **top.**) This word rhymes with (pause) **mop.** (Move to **t,** then quickly along the arrow.) *Top.* Yes, what word? (Signal.) *Top.*

EXERCISE 8

Children identify, then sound out an irregular word (was)

a. (Touch the ball for **was.**) Everybody, you're going to read this word the fast way. (Pause three seconds.) Get ready. (Move your finger quickly along the arrow.) *Was.* Yes, **was.**

b. Now you're going to sound out the word. Get ready. (Quickly touch **w, a, s** as the children say *wwwaaasss.*)

c. Again. (Repeat *b.*)

d. How do we say the word? (Signal.) *Was.* Yes, **was.**

e. (Repeat *b* and *d* until firm.)

EXERCISE 9

Individual test

(Call on different children to do *b* and *d* in exercise 8.)

EXERCISE 10

Children read the fast way

(Touch the ball for **ōld.**) Get ready to read this word the fast way. (Pause three seconds.) Get ready. (Signal.) *Old.*

EXERCISE 11

Children read the words the fast way

(Have the children read the words on this page the fast way.)

EXERCISE 12

Individual test

(Call on different children to read one word the fast way.)

23   Lesson 54

Do not touch any small letters.

of

to

that

cōat

gōat

EXERCISE 13

Children identify, then sound out an irregular word (of)

a. (Touch the ball for **of.**) Everybody, you're going to read this word the fast way. (Pause three seconds.) Get ready. (Move your finger quickly along the arrow.) *Of.* Yes, **of.**

b. Now you're going to sound out the word. Get ready. (Quickly touch **o, f** as the children say *ooofff.*)

c. Again. (Repeat *b.*)

d. How do we say the word? (Signal.) *Of.* Yes, **of.**

e. (Repeat *b* and *d* until firm.)

f. (Call on different children to do *b* and *d.*)

EXERCISE 14

Children identify, then sound out an irregular word (to)

(Repeat the procedures in exercise 13 for **to.**)

EXERCISE 15

Children read the fast way

(Touch the ball for **that.**) Get ready to read this word the fast way. (Pause three seconds.) Get ready. (Signal.) *That.*

EXERCISE 16

Children sound out the word and tell what word

a. (Touch the ball for **cōat.**) Sound it out.

b. Get ready. (Touch **c, ō, t** as the children say *cōōōt.*)

• (If sounding out is not firm, repeat *b.*)

c. What word? (Signal.) *Coat.* Yes, **coat.**

EXERCISE 17

Children sound out the word and tell what word

a. (Touch the ball for **gōat.**) Sound it out.

b. Get ready. (Touch **g, ō, t** as the children say *gōōōt.*)

• (If sounding out is not firm, repeat *b.*)

c. What word? (Signal.) *Goat.* Yes, **goat.**

EXERCISE 18

Children read the words the fast way

(Have the children read the words on this page the fast way.)

EXERCISE 19

Individual test

(Call on different children to read one word the fast way.)

24   Lesson 54

Storybook

STORY 54

EXERCISE 20

First reading—children read the story the fast way

(Have the children reread any sentences containing words that give them trouble. Keep a list of these words.)

a. (Pass out Storybook.)

b. Open your book to page 37 and get ready to read. ✓

c. We're going to read this story the fast way.

d. Touch the first word. ✓

e. Reading the fast way. First word. (Pause three seconds.) Get ready. (Tap.) *Thē.*

f. Next word. ✓
(Pause three seconds.) Get ready. (Tap.) *Old.*

g. (Repeat *f* for the remaining words in the first sentence. Pause at least three seconds between taps. The children are to identify each word without sounding it out.)

h. (Repeat *d* through *g* for the next two sentences. Have the children reread the first three sentences until firm.)

i. (The children are to read the remainder of the story the fast way, stopping at the end of each sentence.)

j. (After the first reading of the story, print on the board the words that the children missed more than one time. Have the children sound out each word one time and tell what word.)

k. (After the group's responses are firm, call on individual children to read the words.)

Individual test

a. I'm going to call on different children to read a whole sentence the fast way.

b. (Call on different children to read a sentence. Do not tap for each word.)

EXERCISE 21

EXERCISE 22

Second reading—children read the story the fast way and answer questions

a. You're going to read the story again the fast way and I'll ask questions.

b. First word. ✓
Get ready. (Tap.) *Thē.*

c. (Tap for each remaining word. Pause at least three seconds between taps. Pause longer before words that gave the children trouble during the first reading.)

d. (Ask the comprehension questions below as the children read.)

After the children read:

The old goat had an old coat.

The old goat said, "I will eat this old coat."

So she did.

"That was fun," she said.

"I ate the old coat."

"And now I am cold."

Now the old goat is sad.

You ask:

What did she have? (Signal.)
An old coat.

What did she say? (Signal.)
I will eat this old coat.

What did she do? (Signal.)
She ate the old coat.

What did she say? (Signal.)
That was fun.

What did the goat say? (Signal.)
I ate the old coat.

What did she say? (Signal.)
And now I am cold.

How does she feel? (Signal.) *Sad.*
Why? (Signal.) *The children respond.*

EXERCISE 23

Picture comprehension

a. What do you think you'll see in the picture? (Call on a child. Accept appropriate responses.)

b. Turn the page and look at the picture. ✓

c. (Ask these questions:)

1. How does that goat feel? (Call on a child. Idea: *Cold and sad.*)

2. Why is she out in the cold without a coat? (Call on a child. Idea: *Because she ate her coat.*)

3. Did you ever go outside without a coat when it was cold? (Call on a child. Accept appropriate responses.)

25   Lesson 54

Worksheet 54

SUMMARY OF INDEPENDENT WORK

EXERCISE 24

Introduction to independent activity

a. (Hold up worksheet 54.)

b. Everybody, you're going to do this worksheet on your own. (Tell the children when they will work the items.) Let's go over the things you're going to do.

Sentence copying

a. (Hold up side 1 of your worksheet and point to the first line in the sentence-copying exercise.)

b. Everybody, here's the sentence you're going to write on the lines below.

c. Get ready to read the words in this sentence the fast way. First word. ✓
Get ready. (Tap.) *Thē.*

d. Next word. ✓
Get ready. (Tap.) *Goat.*

e. (Repeat *d* for the remaining words.)

f. After you finish your worksheet, you get to draw a picture about the sentence, **thē gōat āte thē cōat.**

Sound writing

a. (Point to the sound-writing exercise.) Here are the sounds you're going to write today. I'll touch the sounds. You say them.

b. (Touch each sound.) *The children respond.*

c. (Repeat the series until firm.)

Matching

a. (Point to the column of words in the Matching Game.)

b. Everybody, you're going to follow the lines and write these words.

c. Reading the fast way.

d. (Point to the first word. Pause.) Get ready. (Signal.) *The children respond.*

e. (Repeat *d* for the remaining words.)

f. (Repeat *d* and *e* until firm.)

Cross-out game

(Point to the boxed word in the Cross-out Game.) Everybody, here's the word you're going to cross out today. What word? (Signal.) *Not.* Yes, **not.**

Pair relations

a. (Point to the pair-relations exercise on side 2.) You're going to circle the picture in each box that shows what the words say.

b. (Point to the space at the top of the page.) After you finish, remember to draw a picture that shows **thē gōat āte thē cōat.**

Reading Checkout

(Make a permanent chart for recording results of individual checkouts. See Teacher's Guide for sample chart.)

EXERCISE 25

2½-minute individual checkout: rate and accuracy

a. As you are doing your worksheet, I'll call on children one at a time to read the **whole story.** If you can read the whole story the fast way in less than two and a half minutes and if you make no more than three errors, I'll put two stars after your name on the chart for lesson 54.

b. If you make too many errors or don't read the story in less than two and a half minutes, you'll have to practice it and do it again. When you do read it in under two and a half minutes with no more than three errors, you'll get one star. Remember, two stars if you can do it the first time, one star if you do it the second or third time you try.

c. (Call on a child. Tell the child:) Read the whole story very carefully the fast way. Go. (Time the child. If the child makes a mistake, quickly tell the child the correct word and permit the child to continue reading. As soon as the child makes more than three errors or exceeds the time limit, tell the child to stop.) You'll have to read the story to yourself and try again later. (Plan to monitor the child's practice.)

d. (Record two stars for each child who reads appropriately. Congratulate those children.)

e. (Give children who do not earn two stars a chance to read the story again before the next lesson is presented. Award one star to each of those children who meet the rate and accuracy criterion.)

END OF LESSON 54

Present Language lesson 54 and Spelling lesson 54 before presenting lesson 55.

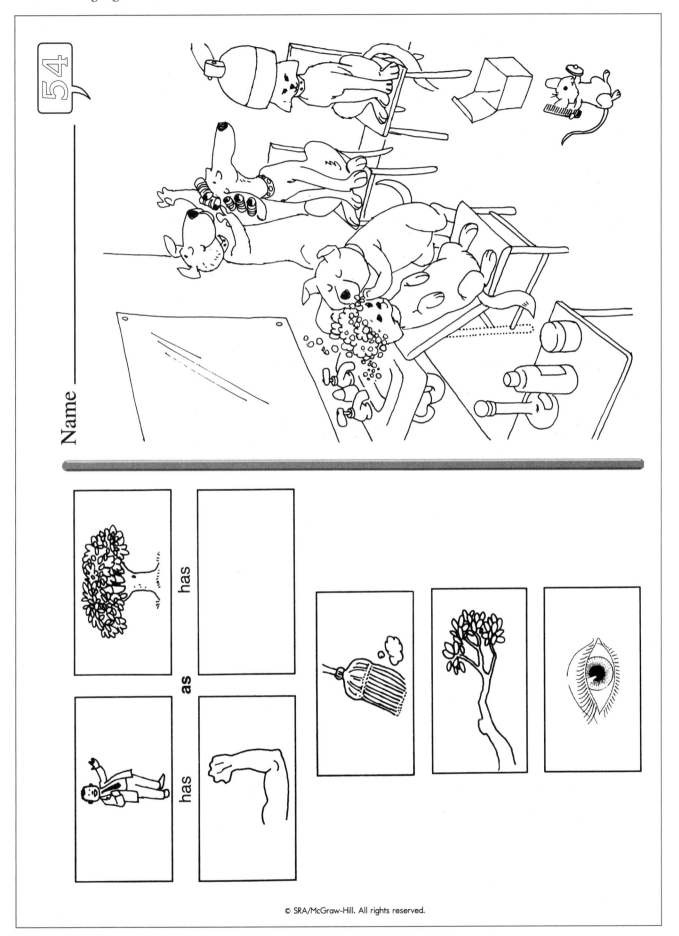

54

Name

has

as

has

Lesson 54

EXERCISE 1

ACTIONS

a. Everybody, you're going to move your finger from your elbow to your ear. How are you going to move your finger? (Signal.) *From my elbow to my ear.*

b. (Repeat step a until firm.)

c. Move your finger from your elbow to your ear. Get ready. (Signal.) ✓ (Every child is to move a finger from an elbow to an ear.)

d. (Repeat step c until firm.)

e. How did you move your finger? (Signal.) *From my elbow to my ear.*

f. (Repeat step e until firm.)

EXERCISE 2

CLASSIFICATION

a. Now we're going to talk about **living things, cats, pets,** and **animals.** What are we going to talk about? (Signal.) *Living things, cats, pets, and animals.*

b. You're going to name four classes a cat is in.
   - (Make a small circle with your hands.) What's the smallest class for a cat? (Signal.) *Cats.*
   - (Make a wider circle.) What's the next bigger class? (Signal.) *Pets.*
   - (Make a still wider circle.) What's the next bigger class? (Signal.) *Animals.*
   - (Make an even wider circle.) What's a really big class? (Signal.) *Living things.*

c. (Repeat step b until firm.)

d. There is one kind of object you would find in all of those classes. Everybody, name the kind of object you would find in all of those classes. Get ready. (Signal.) *A cat.*

EXERCISE 3

CALENDAR

a. (Present calendar.)
   - We're going to talk about today, tomorrow, and one week from today.

b. Tell me the day of the week it is today. Get ready. (Signal.)
   - Tell me the day of the week it will be tomorrow. Get ready. (Signal.)
   - Tell me the day of the week it will be one week from today. Get ready. (Signal.)

c. (Repeat step b until firm.)

d. Now the dates.
   - Tell me today's date. Get ready. (Signal.)
   - Look at the calendar. ✓
   - Tell me the date it will be one week from today. Get ready. (Signal.)

e. Once more.
   - Listen. Tell me today's date. Get ready. (Signal.)
   - Tell me tomorrow's date. Get ready. (Signal.)
   - Tell me the date it will be one week from today. Get ready. (Signal.)

f. (Repeat step e until firm.)

EXERCISE 4

DESCRIPTION

a. I'm thinking of an object. See if you can figure out what object I'm thinking of. I'll tell you something about the object.

b. Listen. It's made of wood. Everybody, what do you know about the object? (Signal.) *It's made of wood.*
   - Could I be thinking of a dress? (Signal.) *No.*
   - Could I be thinking of a ruler? (Signal.) *Yes.*
   - Could I be thinking of a suitcase? (Signal.) *No.*
   - Could I be thinking of a table? (Signal.) *Yes.*

c. Listen. The object I'm thinking of is (hold up one finger) made of wood **and** (hold up two fingers) it's found in a classroom.

d. Everybody, what do you know about the object? (Hold up one finger.) (Signal.) *It's made of wood* **and** (hold up two fingers) *it's found in a classroom.*

e. (Repeat step d until firm.)

Lesson 54   201

---

f. Is a boat made of wood and is it found in the classroom? (Signal.) *No.*
• Could I be thinking of a boat? (Signal.) *No.*
  Why not? (Signal.) *It's not found in the classroom.*
• Is a ruler made of wood and is it found in the classroom? (Signal.) *Yes.*
• Could I be thinking of a ruler? (Signal.) *Yes.*
• Could I be thinking of a pencil? (Signal.) *Yes.*
g. (Repeat step f until firm.)
h. Listen. The object I'm thinking of is (hold up one finger) made of wood **and** (hold up two fingers) it's found in a classroom **and** (hold up three fingers) you use it to write with.
i. Everybody, name the object I am thinking of. (Pause two seconds.) Get ready. (Signal.) *A pencil.*
   Yes, a pencil.

EXERCISE 5

CAN DO

a. I'm going to ask questions about a man and a spoon.
b. Everybody, can a man put a spoon on the table? (Signal.) *Yes.*
• Say the statement. Get ready. (Signal.) *A man can put a spoon on the table.*
c. Everybody, can a man hide in a spoon? (Signal.) *No.*
• Say the statement. Get ready. (Signal.) *A man cannot hide in a spoon.*
d. (Call on one child.)
   Your turn. Make up another statement that tells something a man can do with a spoon. (After the child makes the statement, call on the group.) Everyone, say that statement about what a man can do with a spoon. Get ready. (Signal.) (The group repeats the child's statement.)
e. (Call on a different child.)
   Your turn. Make up a statement that tells something a man can**not** do with a spoon. (After the child makes the statement, call on the group.) Everyone, say that statement about what a man cannot do with a spoon. (Signal.) (The group repeats the child's statement.)
f. (Repeat steps d and e until firm.)

EXERCISE 6

MATERIALS

a. A woman is going to make some objects.
b. A woman is going to make some objects from plastic. What will the objects be made of? (Signal.) *Plastic.*
c. (Write on the board:)

| true | false |

• (Point to each word.) This word says **true.** This word says **false.** See if you can name objects she could make. Every time you name an object that she could make, I'll put a mark by the word **true.** If you name something that is not made of plastic, I'll put a mark by the word **false.**
• Your turn. Name things the woman could make. (Call on several different children. Keep a tally. The children should name a number of objects that can be made of plastic. When they have finished, add up the number of marks by the word **true.**)
• You made ___ statements that are true.

EXERCISE 7

TRUE–FALSE

a. I'm going to say statements. Some of these statements are true and some are false. You tell me about each statement.
b. You use an umbrella to sweep with. True or false? (Signal.) *False.*
   A hammer is a tool. True or false? (Signal.) *True.*
   An umbrella does not have petals. True or false? (Signal.) *True.*
   Ice cream is not food. True or false? (Signal.) *False.*
   Umbrellas have feathers. True or false? (Signal.) *False.*
c. (Repeat step b until firm.)
d. Your turn. Make up a statement about an umbrella that is true. (Call on three children. Praise each acceptable statement and have the group repeat it. Then say:) Everybody, that statement is . . . (Signal.) *true.*
e. Your turn. Now make up a statement about an umbrella that is false. (Call on three children. Praise each acceptable statement and have the group repeat it. Then say:) Everybody, that statement is . . . (Signal.) *false.*

EXERCISE 8
MAP READING

a. I'll point in different directions. You tell me the directions.

b. (Point north.) Which direction is this? (Signal.) *North.*
(Point south.) Which direction is this? (Signal.) *South.*
(Point east.) Which direction is this? (Signal.) *East.*
(Point west.) Which direction is this? (Signal.) *West.*

c. Watch me. I'm going to walk. You point to the wall I'm walking to. That's the **direction** I'm walking.

d. Watch. (Walk toward the south wall.) Everybody, which direction? (Signal.) *South.* Yes, I walked south.

e. Watch. (Walk toward the east wall.) Everybody, which direction? (Signal.) *East.* Yes, I walked east.

f. Watch. (Walk toward the north wall.) Everybody, which direction? (Signal.) *North.* Yes, I walked north.

g. Watch. (Walk toward the west wall.) Everybody, which direction? (Signal.) *West.* Yes, I walked west.

h. Watch. (Walk toward the south wall.) Everybody, which direction? (Signal.) *South.* Yes, I walked south.

i. Watch. (Walk toward the east wall.) Everybody, which direction? (Signal.) *East.* Yes, I walked east.

j. (Repeat steps d through i until firm.)

Worksheet 54

EXERCISE 9
ANALOGIES

a. (Hold up worksheet. Point to first half.)
• The pictures show something and part of the thing.
b. Touch the man. ✓
c. Now touch the picture that's right below the man. It shows part of the man. Everybody, what part? (Signal.) *An arm.*
• Yes, those pictures show that a man has an arm.
d. Touch the tree. ✓
• One of the pictures below the tree shows the part it has. Touch the picture that shows the part a tree has. ✓

• Everybody, what part does a tree have? (Signal.) *A branch.*
e. Listen: A man has an arm **as** a tree has a branch.
• Tell me about a man. Get ready. (Signal.) *A man has an arm.*
• Tell me about a tree. Get ready. (Signal.) *A tree has a branch.*
f. Draw a line from the tree to the part it has. (Observe children and give feedback.)

EXERCISE 10
LOCATION

a. (Hold up worksheet. Point to second half.)
b. What place do you see in this picture? (Call on a child. Idea: *a beauty parlor or barbershop.*)
c. Here's a coloring rule for this picture. Listen. Color the furniture brown. What's the rule? (Signal.) *Color the furniture brown.*
d. (Repeat step c until firm.)
e. Put a brown mark on **one** piece of furniture. ✓
f. Here's another coloring rule for this picture. Listen. Color the containers red. What's the rule? (Signal.) *Color the containers red.*
g. (Repeat step f until firm.)
h. Put a red mark on **one** container. ✓
i. There's one more thing to do.
j. One piece of furniture has a missing part. What piece of furniture is that? (Signal.) *A chair.*
Yes, a chair.
k. What part of the chair is missing? (Signal.) *The leg.*
• Yes, the leg. Before you color the chair, follow the dots and make the leg.

Note: Before presenting lesson 55, present Reading lesson 54.

Lesson 54   203

Lesson 54

WORD WRITING

EXERCISE 1

Children write me, he

a. You're going to write the word **me.** Listen. **Me.** Saying the sounds in (pause) **me** the hard way. Get ready. (Signal for each sound as the children say) *mmm* (pause) *ēēē.* (The children are to pause between the sounds. Repeat until firm.)

b. Everybody, write the word (pause) **me.** ✓

c. (Repeat *a* and *b* for **he.**)

EXERCISE 2

Children write tan, fit, mad, rid, sad, mud

a. You're going to write the word **tan.** Think about the sounds in (pause) **tan** and write the word. ✓

To correct
1. Say the sounds in **tan.** (Signal.) *Taaannn.*
2. Say the sounds the hard way. (Signal.) *T* (pause) *aaa* (pause) *nnn.*
3. Write the word **tan.** ✓

b. (Repeat *a* for **fit, rid, sad, mud.**)

EXERCISE 3

Children write and

a. You're going to write the word **and.** Listen. **And.** Saying the sounds in (pause) **and** the hard way. Get ready. (Signal for each sound as the children say) *aaa* (pause) *nnn* (pause) *d.* (The children are to pause between the sounds. Repeat until firm.)

b. Everybody, write the word (pause) **and.** ✓

EXERCISE 4

Children write hand

a. You're going to write the word (pause) **hand.** This word rhymes with **and.** I'll say the sounds in (pause) **hand** the hard way. Listen. **H** (pause) *aaa* (pause) *nnn* (pause) **d.**

b. Your turn. Say the sounds in (pause) **hand.** Get ready. (Signal for each sound as the children say) *h* (pause) *aaa* (pause) *nnn* (pause) *d.* (The children are to pause between the sounds. Repeat until firm.)

c. Everybody, write the word (pause) **hand.** ✓

EXERCISE 5

Children write fan, sin

a. You're going to write the word **fan.** Think about the sounds in (pause) **fan** and write the word. ✓

b. (Repeat *a* for **sin.**)

END OF SPELLING LESSON 54

sam gets a kite kit

sam liked to make things. he liked to make toy cars. so he went to the store and got a toy car kit. his mom said, "that kit has the parts of a car. you have to read and find out how to fit the parts so that they make a car."

sam said, "I will do that."

so sam began to read the paper that came with the car kit. then he began to fit the parts to make a car. soon he had a toy car.

his mom said, "that is a fine car. you are good at reading and at making things."

sam did not like to make the same thing again. he said, "I will not make

32

other cars. I will make something else."

so he went to the store and got a kite kit. when he got home, he showed his mom the kite kit. his mom said, "that kit has a lot of parts in it. you will have to read the paper that comes with the kit to find out how to make the kite."

sam looked inside the kit. then he said, "what paper? there is no paper in this kit."

sam's mom said, "that is too bad. how will you make the kite if there is no paper in the kit?"

sam said, "I will go back to the store and get a paper that tells how to make a kite from these parts."

33

11

35

when sam got to the store, the man in
the store said, "I dōn't have other pāpers
that tell how to make kites."
sam askₑd, "how can I make a kite if
I dōn't have the pāper?"
the man said, "you will havₑ to do the
best you can."
sam was not happy. he went home
and lookₑd at all the parts in the kite kit.

more to come

34

Worksheet 11

Side 2

look at the picture on page 35 of your rēader.

1. is sam rēading a pāper? _____

2. do you see sam's toy car? _____

bob got a kit for making a toy duck. the kit had a lot of parts. bob worked hard. at last, he said, "that duck looks rēal." the duck ate a hole in the wall. then he ate some grass. the duck went to the pond and swam awāy.

1. who got a kit for making a toy duck? _____

2. the duck ate a hole in the _____ .

3. then he ate some _____ .

4. where did he go for a swim? _____

Worksheet 11

Side 1

Name _____

1. who made a toy car from a car kit? _____

2. who said, "you are good at rēading and at making things"? his _____

3. what kit did sam get after he made a car? a
   • car kit   • cat kit   • kite kit   • log kit

4. what was missing from the kit? a
   • pāper   • kite part   • car part   • kit

5. where did sam go to get a pāper? _____
   • to the lake   • to the store
   • bēcause he nēēded it   • tōld him

6. did the man at the store have another pāper? _____

tim went to the park.

1. circle the word that tells who went to the park.

2. make a line ōver the words that tell where tim went.

3. make a line ōver the circle.

Lesson 11

READING VOCABULARY

Do not touch small letters.

Get ready to read all the words on this page without making a mistake.

EXERCISE 1

Sound out first

a. (Touch the ball for **best**.) Sound it out. Get ready. (Quickly touch **b, e, s, t** as the children say) *beeesssst.*
b. What word? (Signal.) *Best.* Yes, **best.**
c. (Repeat exercise until firm.)

ing

EXERCISE 2

ing words

a. (Point to **ing**.) When these letters are together, they usually say **ing**.
b. What do these letters usually say? (Signal.) *ing.* Yes, **ing**. (Repeat until firm.)
c. (Point to the words.) These are words you already know. See if you can read them when they look this way.
d. (Point to **ing** in **something**.) What do these letters say? (Signal.) *ing.*
e. (Touch the ball for **something**.) Read the fast way. Get ready. (Signal.) *Something.* Yes, **something.**
f. (Repeat d and e for **looking** and **rēading**.)
g. (Repeat the series of words until firm.)

something

looking

rēading

EXERCISE 3

ar word

a. (Touch the ball for **parts**.) Read this word the fast way. (Pause two seconds.) Get ready. (Signal.) *Parts.* Yes, **parts.**
b. (Point to **ar** in **parts**.) Everybody, what do these letters say? (Signal.) *Are.* Yes, **are.**
c. (Touch the ball for **parts**.) Sound it out. Get ready. (Quickly touch **p, ar, t, s** as the children say) *partsss.*
d. What word? (Signal.) *Parts.* Yes, **parts.**
e. (Repeat c and d until firm.)

parts

EXERCISE 4

Practice final-e rule

a. Read this word the fast way. Remember to look at the end of the word.
b. (Touch the ball for **kites**.) (Pause two seconds.) Get ready. (Signal.) *Kites.* Yes, **kites.**
c. (Touch the ball for **kites**.) Sound it out. Get ready. (Quickly touch **k, i, t, s** as the children say) *kiiitsss.*
d. What word? (Signal.) *Kites.* Yes, **kites.**
e. (Repeat b through d until firm.)

kites

Repeat any troublesome words.

Individual test

(Call on different children. Each child reads a different word.)

Do not touch small letters.

Get ready to read all the words on this page without making a mistake.

EXERCISE 5

Read the fast way

a. Read these words the fast way.

b. (Touch the ball for **store**.) (Pause two seconds.) Get ready. (Signal.) Store. Yes, **store**.

c. (Repeat b for **make, makes, making, home, pāper, what, when, then, who, how, from, began, other, else,** and **next**.)

how

from

began

other

else

next

home

pāper

what

when

then

who

store

make

makes

making

Individual test

(Call on different children. Each child reads a different wor

Repeat any troublesome words.

Get ready to read all the words on this page without making a mistake.

EXERCISE 6

Long and short vowel words

a. Read these words the fast way. Remember to look at the end of the word.

b. (Touch the ball for **rode**.) (Pause two seconds.) Get ready. (Signal.) *Rode*. Yes, **rode**.

c. (Repeat b for **kite, sam, not, same, rod, note,** and **kit.**)

not

same

rod

note

kit

rode

kite

sam

Storybook

STORY 11

EXERCISE 7

First reading—title and three sentences

a. (Pass out Storybook).

b. Everybody, open your reader to story 11. ✓

c. Everybody, touch the title of the story and get ready to read the words in the title.

d. First word. ✓
Get ready. (Tap.) *Sam.*

e. (Tap for each remaining word in the title.)

f. Everybody, say the title. (Signal.) *Sam gets a kite kit.*

g. Everybody, get ready to read this story.

h. First word. ✓
Get ready. (Tap.) *Sam.*

i. Next word. ✓
Get ready. (Tap.) *Liked.*

j. (Repeat i for the remaining words in the first three sentences. Have the children reread the first three sentences until firm.)

Individual test

(Call on individual children to read a column of words from this lesson. If the column contains only one or two words, direct the child to read additional words from an adjacent column.)

EXERCISE 8

Remaining sentences

a. I'm going to call on different children to read a sentence. Everybody, follow along and point to the words. If you hear a mistake, raise your hand.

b. (Call on a child.) Read the next sentence.

To correct word-identification errors (**from**, for example)
1. That word is **from**. What word? *From.*
2. Go back to the beginning of the sentence and read the sentence again.

c. (Call on a different child.) Read the next sentence.

d. (Repeat c for most of the remaining sentences in the story.)

e. (Occasionally have the group read a sentence.)
(When the group is to read, say) Everybody, read the next sentence. (Tap for each word in the sentence.)

---

sam gets a kite kit[1]

sam liked to make things. he liked to make toy cars. so he went to the store and got a toy car kit.[2] his mom said, "that kit has the parts of a car. you have to rēad and fīnd out how to fit the parts so that they make a car."

sam said, "I will do that."

so sam began to rēad the pāper that came with the car kit.[3] then he began to fīt the parts to make a car. soon he had a toy car.

his mom said, "that is a fīne car. you are good at rēading and at making things."[4]

sam did not like to make the same thing again. he said, "I will not make other cars. I will make something else."

so he went to the store and got a kite kit.[5] when he got home, he shōwed his mom the kite kit. his mom said, "that kit has a lot of parts in it. you will have to rēad the pāper that comes with the kit to fīnd out how to make the kite."[6]

EXERCISE 9

Second reading—sentences and questions

a. You're going to read the story again. This time I'm going to ask questions.

b. Starting with the first word of the title. ✓ Get ready. (Tap as the children read the title.)

c. (Call on a child.) Read the first sentence.

To correct word-identification errors (**from**, for example)
1. That word is **from**. What word? *From.*
2. Go back to the beginning of the sentence and read the sentence again.

d. (Call on a different child.) Read the next sentence.

e. (Repeat d for most of the remaining sentences in the story.)

f. (Occasionally have the group read a sentence.)

g. (After each underlined sentence has been read, present each comprehension question specified below to the entire group.)

[1] What will Sam get? (Signal.) *A kite kit.* What is a kite kit? *The children respond.* Yes, in a kite kit you get all the parts to build a kite.

[2] What kind of kit did he get? (Signal.) *A toy car kit.* What is he going to make? (Signal.) *A toy car.*

[3] Why does he have to read the paper? *The children respond.* Right, the paper tells him how to make the car.

[4] Everybody, say that. (Signal.) *You are good at reading and at making things.*

[5] What did he get this time? (Signal.) *A kite kit.*

[6] Why does he have to read the paper? *The children respond.* Right, the paper tells him how to make the kite.

sam looked inside the kit. then he
said, "what pāper? thêre is no pāper
in this kit."[7]

sam's mom said, "that is too bad.
how will you make the kite if thêre
is no pāper in the kit?"

sam said, "I will go back to the
store and get a pāper that tells how
to make a kite from these parts."

when sam got to the store, the
man in the store said, "I dõn't have
other pāpers that tell how to make
kites."

sam asked, "how can I make a
kite if I dõn't have the pāper?"[8]
The man said, "you will have to
do the best you can."[9]

sam was not happy. he went
home and looked at all the parts in
the kite kit.

more to come[10]

[7] Was there a paper in the kit? (Signal.) *No.* I
wonder how he'll make the kite without that
paper. *The children respond. Let's read and
find out.*
[8] Everybody, say that question. (Signal.) *How
can I make a kite if I don't have the paper?*
[9] Everybody, say the man's answer. (Signal.)
You will have to do the best you can.
[10] We'll read more next time.

EXERCISE 10

Picture comprehension

a. Look at the picture.
b. (Ask these questions:)
 1. (Point to the toy car. Who made that
  car? (Signal.) *Sam.*
 2. Why did Sam make that car? (Signal.)
  He likes to make things.
 3. (Point to the kite parts.) What is that
  stuff on the floor? *The children
  respond.* Yes, those are the kite parts.
 4. Can you see a paper telling Sam how to
  make the kite? (Signal.) *No.* Why not?
  The children respond. Right, the paper
  is missing. I hope he can put all those
  parts together.

Worksheet 11

SUMMARY OF INDEPENDENT WORK

Introduction to independent activity

(Hold up side 1 of your worksheet.)
Everybody, you're going to do this worksheet
on your own. (Tell the children when they will
work the items.) Let's go over the things
you're going to do.

EXERCISE 11

EXERCISE 12

Story items

(Point to the story-items exercise.) Everybody,
remember to write your answers in the blanks.

EXERCISE 13

Following instructions

a. (Touch the sentence in the box.)
b. Everybody, first you're going to read the
 sentence in the box. Then you're going to
 read the instructions below the box and do
 what the instructions tell you to do.

EXERCISE 14

Story-picture items

(Point to the story-picture items on side 2.)
Remember to follow these instructions and
look at the picture when you work these items.

EXERCISE 15

Reading comprehension

(Point to the story.) You're going to read this
story and then do the items. Remember to
write the answers in the blanks.

END OF LESSON 11

Note: Before presenting Reading lesson 16,
present Language lesson 11–15.

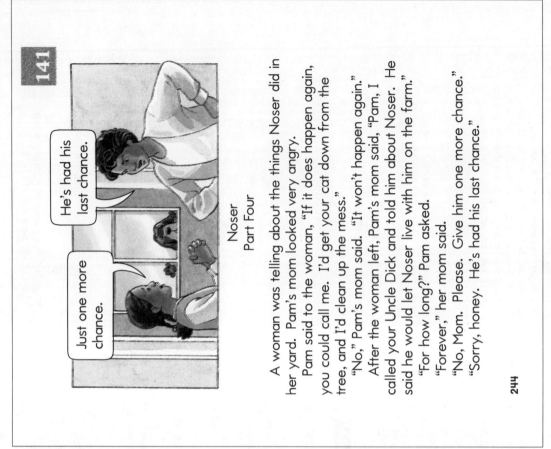

141

Just one more chance.

He's had his last chance.

Noser
Part Four

A woman was telling about the things Noser did in her yard. Pam's mom looked very angry.

Pam said to the woman, "If it does happen again, you could call me. I'd get your cat down from the tree, and I'd clean up the mess."

"No," Pam's mom said. "It won't happen again."

After the woman left, Pam's mom said, "Pam, I called your Uncle Dick and told him about Noser. He said he would let Noser live with him on the farm."

"For how long?" Pam asked.

"Forever," her mom said.

"No, Mom. Please. Give him one more chance."

"Sorry, honey. He's had his last chance."

244

141

1. <u>ma</u>ma
2. <u>angry</u>
3. <u>flashlight</u>
4. <u>driveway</u>

1. Dic<u>k</u>
2. <u>poli</u>ce
3. <u>offic</u>er
4. <u>c</u>oun<u>t</u>

1. <u>hero</u>
2. <u>baby</u>
3. <u>belongs</u>
4. <u>forever</u>

1. raccoon
2. gone
3. shoe
4. uncle
5. rushed
6. picture

1. touch
2. shovel
3. hugs
4. worry

243

141

Pam ran to her room and cried. At dinner, she tried to talk to her mom about keeping Noser, but her mom didn't change her mind.

Pam was sad that evening. She put a leash on Noser and took him for a walk. She was thinking that it might be her last walk with Noser.

Pam and Noser were three blocks from home when Pam saw a lot of police cars and people in front of a brown house. When she got closer, she asked a police officer, "Why are all these people around here?"

He said, "The baby girl who lives here is missing. Her mom was playing with her in the back yard. The mother went inside to answer the phone. When she went back to the yard, she found that the wind had blown the gate open. The baby was gone."

The police officer held up a little shoe. "This is the only thing she could find, one of the baby's shoes."

Pam thought for a moment and then said, "Maybe Noser can find her. Noser can find anything."

"Well . . . ," the police officer said and scratched his head. He looked around and then said, "I don't see how that would do any harm."

Pam said, "Hand me that shoe. I'll let Noser sniff it."

245

141

Smell the baby's shoe.

The police officer handed the shoe to Pam, and she held it in front of Noser. "Noser, this belongs to a baby . . . baby. Smell the baby's shoe."

Noser could tell from the way Pam was talking that she wanted him to find something. He wagged his tail. He sniffed the shoe she was holding. Then he sniffed the police officer's leg.

Pam tried to show Noser that he should think about the shoe, but he didn't seem to understand what she wanted.

More to come.

246

141

Clarabelle was in the hole she had dug. She told the other animals that she needed to eat. So the other animals got a lot of grass and dropped it into the hole. Clarabelle ate the grass and thanked the other animals. But she still wanted to get out of the hole. A sheep said, "Let's drop a long rope in the hole. Then we could pull Clarabelle out of the hole." So the animals got a rope from the barn and dropped one end in the hole. Clarabelle held onto that end. The other animals pulled and pulled as hard as they could pull. But they could not pull Clarabelle out of the hole.

1. Who needed to eat?
2. What did the other animals drop into the hole for her to eat?
3. What kind of animal had a new plan to get her out of the hole?
4. What did the animals drop into the hole?
5. Were the other animals able to pull Clarabelle out?

247

Worksheet 141

Fix up the picture so it matches this description:
- The dog sat on a log next to a green frog.
- There was another green frog near the bank of the stream.
- The dog was brown and black.
- Three jumping fish are in the stream.
- The tent was yellow.

- collar •   • land with water on all sides
- yesterday •   • the shade made by things
- gate •   • the day before today
- tomorrow •   • something that goes around a
                      dog's neck
- island •   • a door in a fence
- shadow •   • the day after today

Side 2

Worksheet 141

Name _____

1. Pam's mom told her that Noser would
   have to live with _____
   - Pam
   - Uncle Dick
   - Fluffy's owner

2. When Pam went for a walk, there were police cars and
   people near _____
   - a brown house
   - a white house
   - a red house

3. Who told Pam what happened there?
   - Bob
   - Uncle Dick
   - a police officer

4. Who was lost? _____
   - a dog
   - a baby
   - Fluffy

5. The police officer gave Pam the baby's _____
   - shoe
   - rattle
   - hat

6. Pam let Noser _____
   - smell it
   - carry it
   - hold it

7. Did Noser know what Pam wanted him to do? _____

Side 1

Lesson 141

Textbook

READING WORDS

Syllables

a. Open your textbook to lesson 141. Find the pig. ✓
• (Teacher reference:)

> 1. <u>ma</u>ma
> 2. <u>ang</u>ry
> 3. <u>flash</u>light
> 4. <u>drive</u>way

b. The first syllable of each word is underlined. You'll read the first syllable, then the whole word.
c. Word 1. The first syllable is **mah.** What's the first syllable? (Signal.) *mah.*
• What's the whole word? (Signal.) *Mama.* Yes, **mama** is another word for mother.
d. Word 2. What's the first syllable? (Signal.) *ang.*
• What's the whole word? (Signal.) *Angry.*
e. Word 3. What's the first syllable? (Signal.) *flash.*
• What's the whole word? (Signal.) *Flashlight.*
• What do you do with a flashlight? (Call on a child. Idea: *Use it to see in the dark.*)
f. Everybody, word 4. What's the first syllable? (Signal.) *drive.*
• What's the whole word? (Signal.) *Driveway.* Yes, you park a car in a **driveway.**
g. Let's read those words again the fast way.
• Word 1. What word? (Signal.) *Mama.*
• (Repeat for remaining words: **angry, flashlight, driveway.**)

READING WORDS

a. Find the haystack. ✓
• (Teacher reference:)

> 1. Di<u>ck</u>
> 2. poli<u>ce</u>
> 3. offi<u>cer</u>
> 4. c<u>ou</u>nt

b. You'll say the underlined combination, then the whole word.
c. Word 1 is a name. What does the combination say? (Signal.) *ck.*
• What's the name? (Signal.) *Dick.*
d. Word 2. What does the combination say? (Signal.) *sss.*
• What word? (Signal.) *Police.*
e. Word 3. What does the combination say? (Signal.) *sss.*
• What word? (Signal.) *Officer.*
f. Word 4. What does the combination say? (Signal.) *ou.*
• What word? (Signal.) *Count.* Yes, you **count** 1, 2, 3, 4.
g. Let's read those words again the fast way.
• Word 1. What word? (Signal.) *Dick.*
• (Repeat for remaining words: **police, officer, count.**)

READING WORDS

Syllables

a. Find the sheep. ✓
• (Teacher reference:)

> 1. <u>he</u>ro
> 2. <u>ba</u>by
> 3. <u>be</u>longs
> 4. <u>fore</u>ver

b. The first syllable in each word has a letter that says its name.
c. Word 1. That word is **hero.** What word? (Signal.) *Hero.* Yes, a **hero** is someone who does something very brave and wonderful.
• What's the first syllable? (Signal.) *he.*

- What's the whole word? (Signal.) *Hero.*
d. Word 2. What's the first syllable?
(Signal.) *bay.*
- What's the whole word? (Signal.) *Baby.*
e. Word 3. What's the first syllable?
(Signal.) *be.*
- What's the whole word? (Signal.)
Belongs.
f. Word 4. What's the first syllable?
(Signal.) *for.*
- What's the whole word? (Signal.)
Forever.
g. Let's read those words again the fast
way.
- Word 1. What word? (Signal.) *Hero.*
- (Repeat for remaining words: **baby,
belongs, forever.**)

EXERCISE 4
READING WORDS

a. Find the cow. ✓
- What do you think that cow's name is?
(Call on a child. *Clarabelle.*)
- (Teacher reference:)

> 1. raccoon
> 2. gone
> 3. shoe
> 4. uncle
> 5. rushed
> 6. picture

b. Everybody, word 1 is **raccoon.** What
word? (Signal.) *Raccoon.*
A **raccoon** is an animal that looks like it is
wearing a mask.
c. Word 2. What word? (Signal.) *Gone.*
d. Word 3. What word? (Signal.) *Shoe.*
e. Word 4. What word? (Signal.) *Uncle.*
f. Word 5. What word? (Signal.) *Rushed.*
g. Word 6. What word? (Signal.) *Picture.*
h. Let's read those words again the fast
way.
- Word 1. What word? (Signal.) *Raccoon.*
- (Repeat for remaining words: **gone,
shoe, uncle, rushed, picture.**)

EXERCISE 5
READING WORDS

a. Find the horse. ✓
- (Teacher reference:)

> 1. touch
> 2. shovel
> 3. hugs
> 4. worry

b. All these words have letters that make the
sound **uh.**
c. Spell word 1. Get ready. (Tap 5 times.)
T-O-U-C-H.
- What word? (Signal.) *Touch.*
d. Spell word 2. Get ready. (Tap 6 times.)
S-H-O-V-E-L.
- What word? (Signal.) *Shovel.*
Yes, a snow **shovel.**
e. Spell word 3. Get ready. (Tap 4 times.)
H-U-G-S.
- What word? (Signal.) *Hugs.*
Yes, **hugs** and kisses.
f. Spell word 4. Get ready. (Tap 5 times.)
W-O-R-R-Y.
- What word? (Signal.) *Worry.*
Don't **worry,** we'll get it.
g. Let's read those words again the fast way.
- Word 1. What word? (Signal.) *Touch.*
- (Repeat for remaining words: **shovel,
hugs, worry.**)

Individual Turns

- (Call on different children to read one or
two of the words on the page.)

EXERCISE 6

STORY READING

a. Find the story. ✓

b. You'll read the title of the story. Get ready. (Tap for each word.) *Noser . . . Part . . . Four.*

c. (Call on different children to read one or two sentences each.)

> A woman was telling about the things Noser did in her yard. Pam's mom looked very angry.
>
> Pam said to the woman, "If it does happen again, you could call me. I'd get your cat down from the tree, and I'd clean up the mess."
>
> "No," Pam's mom said. "It won't happen again."
>
> After the woman left, Pam's mom said, "Pam, I called your Uncle Dick and told him about Noser. He said he would let Noser live with him on the farm."
>
> "For how long?" Pam asked.
>
> "Forever," her mom said.
>
> "No, Mom. Please. Give him one more chance."
>
> "Sorry, honey. He's had his last chance."

d. Next page. ✓

> Pam ran to her room and cried. At dinner, she tried to talk to her mom about keeping Noser, but her mom didn't change her mind.
>
> Pam was sad that evening. She put a leash on Noser and took him for a walk. She was thinking that it might be her last walk with Noser.
>
> Pam and Noser were three blocks from home when Pam saw a lot of police cars and people in front of a brown house. When she got closer, she asked a police officer, "Why are all these people around here?"
>
> He said, "The baby girl who lives here is missing. Her mom was playing with her in the back yard. The mother went inside to answer the phone. When she went back to the yard, she found that the wind had blown the gate open. The baby was gone."

> The police officer held up a little shoe. "This is the only thing she could find, one of the baby's shoes."
>
> Pam thought for a moment and then said, "Maybe Noser can find her. Noser can find anything."
>
> "Well . . . . " the police officer said and scratched his head. He looked around and then said, "I don't see how that would do any harm."
>
> Pam said, "Hand me that shoe. I'll let Noser sniff it."

e. Next page. ✓

> The police officer handed the shoe to Pam, and she held it in front of Noser. "Noser, this belongs to a baby . . . baby. Smell the baby's shoe."
>
> Noser could tell from the way Pam was talking that she wanted him to find something. He wagged his tail. He sniffed the shoe she was holding. Then he sniffed the police officer's leg.
>
> Pam tried to show Noser that he should think about the shoe, but he didn't seem to understand what she wanted.
>
> **More to come.**

- (For no more than 6 errors, go to **Comprehension.**)
- (For 7 or 8 errors in the entire story, direct the rereading of the sentences in which mistakes occurred. Then go to **Comprehension.**)
- (For 9 or more errors, direct the rereading of the entire story. Then go to **Comprehension.**)

EXERCISE 7

COMPREHENSION

- Call on individuals to read one or two sentences each.
- Call on individuals to answer each question.

a. Now you'll read the story again, and I'll ask questions.

256   Lesson 141

b. Touch the title. ✓

NOSER
Part Four

A woman was telling about the things Noser did in her yard. Pam's mom looked very angry.

Pam said to the woman, "If it does happen again, you could call me. I'd get your cat down from the tree, and I'd clean up the mess."

"No," Pam's mom said. "It won't happen again."

- What did Pam say she would do? [Idea: *She would get the cat down from the tree and clean up the mess.*]
- Pam's mom seems sure that it won't happen again. What does that mean? [Idea: *She's going to get rid of Noser.*]

After the woman left, Pam's mom said, "Pam, I called your Uncle Dick and told him about Noser. He said he would let Noser live with him on the farm."

"For how long?" Pam asked.

"Forever," her mom said.

"No, Mom. Please. Give him one more chance."

"Sorry, honey. He's had his last chance."

- Who had Pam's mom called? [*Uncle Dick.*]
- Where did Uncle Dick live? [*On a farm.*]
- Where did Pam's mom say Noser was going to live? [Idea: *On Uncle Dick's farm.*]
- For how long? [*Forever.*]

- Look at the picture. What's Pam saying? [*Just one more chance.*]
- Who does she want to get one more chance? [*Noser.*]
- What's her mom saying? [*He's had his last chance.*]
- If he's had his last chance, how many more chances does he get? [*None.*]

c. Next page. ✓

Pam ran to her room and cried. At dinner, she tried to talk to her mom about keeping Noser, but her mom didn't change her mind.

Pam was sad that evening. She put a leash on Noser and took him for a walk. She was thinking that it might be her last walk with Noser.

Pam and Noser were three blocks from home when Pam saw a lot of police cars and people in front of a brown house. When she got closer, she asked a police officer, "Why are all these people around here?"

He said, "The baby girl who lives here is missing. Her mom was playing with her in the back yard. The mother went inside to answer the phone. When she went back to the yard, she found that the wind had blown the gate open. The baby was gone."

- Who told Pam what had happened at the brown house? [*A police officer.*]
- Why were there police cars around that house? [Idea: *Because the baby girl was missing.*]
- Where was the baby when the mother left her? [*In the back yard.*]
- Why did the mother leave the baby? [*To answer the phone.*]
- What was different about the gate when the woman returned? [*It was open.*]
- Where was the baby? [*Gone.*]

The police officer held up a little shoe. "This is the only thing she could find, one of the baby's shoes."

Pam thought for a moment and then said, "Maybe Noser can find her. Noser can find anything."

"Well . . . . " the police officer said and scratched his head. He looked around and then said, "I don't see how that would do any harm."

Pam said, "Hand me that shoe. I'll let Noser sniff it."

- What did the police officer show Pam? [*The baby's shoe.*]
- What did Pam think Noser might be able to do? [Idea: *Find the baby.*]

Lesson 141   257

d. Next page. ✓

> The police officer handed the shoe to Pam, and she held it in front of Noser. "Noser, this belongs to a baby . . . baby. Smell the baby's shoe."
> Noser could tell from the way Pam was talking that she wanted him to find something. He wagged his tail. He sniffed the shoe she was holding. Then he sniffed the police officer's leg.

- What did Noser do after he sniffed the shoe? [Sniffed the police officer's leg.]
- Do you think Noser knew what he was supposed to do? [No.]

> Pam tried to show Noser that he should think about the shoe, but he didn't seem to understand what she wanted.
> **More to come.**

- What could she do to get him to understand what she wanted him to find? (Accept reasonable suggestions.)

Smell the baby's shoe.

- Look at the picture. What's Pam doing in the picture? [Idea: *Holding the baby's shoe in front of Noser.*]
- What's she saying? [*Smell the baby's shoe.*]
- Does Noser seem to be interested? [*Yes.*]
- But what is he going to do right after he smells the shoe? [Idea: *Sniff the police officer's leg.*]
- We'll find out more next time.

Lined Paper

EXERCISE 8

SUMMARY OF INDEPENDENT WORK

Passage Reading
a. Find the passage. ✓
b. Later you'll read this passage and complete the items.

Worksheet 141

Story Items
a. Find the story items. ✓
b. Later you'll complete the items.

Illustrating Descriptions

a. Find the picture. ✓
b. Later you'll fix up the picture so it matches the description.

Description Matching Game

a. Find the description matching game. ✓
b. Later you'll draw lines to match the words with their descriptions.

Independent Work:

- Passage reading.
- Story items.
- Illustrating descriptions.
- Description matching game.

END OF LESSON 141

Note: Before presenting Reading lesson 146, present Language lesson 141–145.

LANGUAGE LESSON 141–145

Name

B.

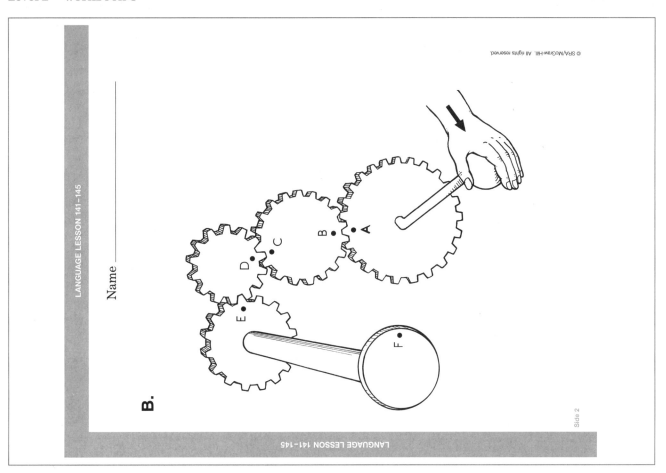

LANGUAGE LESSON 141–145

LANGUAGE LESSON 141–145

Name

A.

Goober	Paul
painted a pot	fed the pigs
sat on an apple	Fizz and Liz

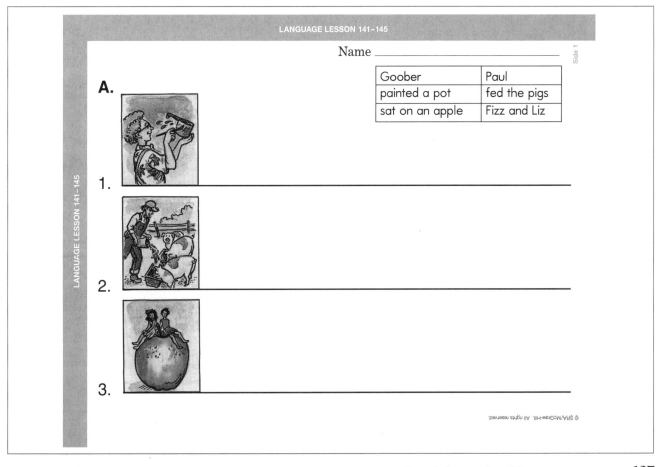

1. _____

2. _____

3. _____

Lesson 141–145

Present Language Lesson 141–145 before completing lesson 146.

Materials

- Each child will need a Language Lesson 141–145 worksheet, sides 1 and 2; and access to computer and reference books, exercise 5. Optional: Props for play, exercise 4.

Objectives

- Construct sentences for different illustrations. (Exercise 1)
- Draw arrows to show which direction gears and a wheel will move. (Exercise 2)
- Listen to part of a familiar story. (Exercise 3)
- Put on a play to show part of a familiar story. (Exercise 4)
- Use resources and references to build upon word meanings. (Exercise 5)

Worksheet 141–145

EXERCISE 1
SENTENCE CONSTRUCTION

A.

Goober	Paul
painted a pot	fed the pigs
sat on an apple	Fizz and Liz

1.
2.
3.

a. (Hold up Language Lesson 141–145 worksheet.)
- (Permit a brief discussion about Paul, Goober, Fizz, and Liz.)
- Everybody, find part A. ✓
- You're going to write sentences for the pictures. The words you'll use are in the boxes. I'll read those words.
- Touch the first word box. ✓
  It says: Goober.
- Next box: painted a pot. ✓
- Next box: sat on an apple. ✓
- Next box: Paul. ✓
- Next box: fed the pigs. ✓
- Last box: Fizz and Liz. ✓
- Those are the words you have to use for your sentences.

b. Touch picture 1. ✓
  Who is in that picture? (Signal.) *Paul.*
- So what will your sentence start with? (Signal.) *Paul.*
- Then your sentence will tell what Paul did in that picture.
c. Touch the two boxes that have the words for that sentence.
  (Observe children and give feedback.)
- Say the sentence for line 1. (Call on a child. *Paul painted a pot.)*
- Your turn: Write the sentence on the line for picture 1. Remember the capital and the period. Raise your hand when you're finished.
  (Observe children and give feedback.)
- (Write on the board:)

Paul painted a pot.

- Here's what you should have. Raise your hand if you got it right. ✓
d. Your turn: Write the sentence for picture 2. Then write the sentence for picture 3. Use the words in the boxes. Raise your hand when you're finished.
  (Observe children and give feedback.)
e. (Write on the board:)

2. Goober fed the pigs.
3. Fizz and Liz sat on an apple.

- Here's what you should have for picture 2 and picture 3. Raise your hand if you got them right. ✓
- That's great.

CONTINUOUS MOVEMENT

Gears

B.

a. Everybody, find part B. ✓
b. Make the arrows at A, B, C, D, E, and F in the picture. Raise your hand when you're finished.
   (Observe children and give feedback.)
• Everybody, is the handle moving up or down? (Signal.) *Down.*
• Touch A. ✓
   Which way is the gear turning at A? (Signal.) *Down.*
• Touch B. ✓
   Which way is the gear turning at B? (Signal.) *Up.*
• Touch C. ✓
   Which way is the gear turning at C? (Signal.) *Down.*
• Touch D. ✓
   Which way is the gear moving at D? (Signal.) *Up.*
• Touch E. ✓
   Which way is the gear moving at E? (Signal.) *Up.*
• Touch F. ✓
   Which way is the wheel moving at F? (Signal.) *Up.*
• Yes, it's moving the same direction as the arrow at E.
• Raise your hand if you got all the arrows right. ✓

STORY REVIEW

The Case of the Squashed Squash

• I'm going to re-read the last part of **The Case of the Squashed Squash.** Listen very carefully to the things that happen because we're going to put on a play.

THE CASE OF THE SQUASHED SQUASH

The rats had a wonderful feast. After the feast was over and everybody was so full of squash and walnuts and apples and berries and seeds and corn that they couldn't eat any more, the wise old rat stood up and said, "We can thank the gray rat—I mean Sherlock—for this fine feast. He figured out how the squash got squashed, and somehow he fixed things up so that there were two great squashes in our berry patch—not just one."

Sherlock stood up as straight as he could. He cleared his throat and said, "Well, this was a very difficult job. A detective without my skill would have been confused. That person would have used the wrong deductions. That detective would have figured out that Goober did it. After all, Goober's shoes made the footprints in the berry bushes, and Goober's overalls sat in the squash. Because I'm so good at deductions, I knew how to do them the right way. I knew that if Goober's **shoes** made the footprints, you couldn't say that **Goober** made the footprints. All you could say is that Goober's **shoes** made the footprints. I also knew that, if Goober's overalls sat on the squash, you couldn't say that Goober sat in the squash. All you could . . . "

"Enough talking," the wise old rat said. He was looking at Bertha. Her little body was rocking very fast, and it was easy to see that she was very, very unhappy.

The wise old rat said to her, "I can see that you don't agree with everything that Sherlock is saying."

She said, "Well . . . "

"Tell it the way it was," the wise old rat said.

"Yeah," the other rats shouted. "Tell it the way it was."

So she did just that. She told what had really happened.

As she talked, the other rats started staring at Sherlock with very unfriendly expressions. And Sherlock started to slouch. At first he slouched just a little bit. Then a little bit more. And finally he slouched right down into his chair.

When Bertha was finished, one of the rats said, "That Sherlock is a dirty liar."

"Yeah," another rat said. "A dirty liar. Let's clean him up."

So they rushed to Sherlock, picked him up, carried him to the pond, and splash.

And, while they were cleaning up Sherlock, the bluebirds moved into the feast area.

They said, "Wow, there's all kinds of squash and other good things to eat here."

And there was. There were lots of things that bluebirds love. So the bluebirds ate and ate. They ate walnuts and berries and corn and seeds and lots of yellow squash. Those bluebirds had their first annual fall feast.

Bertha said, "This is a fall feast for everybody." And she was almost right. But there was one person who wasn't very happy with the feast.

EXERCISE 4

PLAY

The Case of the Squashed Squash

a. Now we're going to put on a play. This play will take place during the fall feast. Sherlock will tell his version of what happened. Then Bertha will tell what really happened. Then the rats will carry Sherlock off to clean him up.

• We need somebody to play the wise old rat. (Identify the child.)

• We need somebody to play the part of Sherlock. This is a big part because Sherlock has to brag on and on about how he solved The Case of the Squashed Squash. (Identify the child.)

• We need somebody to play the part of Bertha. This is a very tough part because the story doesn't tell what Bertha said to the rat pack. (Identify the child.)

• The rest of us will play the part of the rat pack. At the end, some of us are going to rush over to Sherlock and take him away. We won't really pick Sherlock up. (Identify 4 or 5 children to take Sherlock away.)

b. (Arrange Sherlock, Bertha, and the wise old rat at the "head table." Arrange any of the optional props.)

• The wise old rat starts out by saying that we can thank Sherlock for this fine feast.

• Then Sherlock stands up very straight and tells how **he** wasn't fooled and how **he** made all the right deductions. While he's talking, Bertha gets madder and madder.

• Then the wise old rat interrupts Sherlock and asks Bertha why she doesn't agree with Sherlock.

• She tells what really happened. Then the rats call Sherlock a dirty liar and say that he should be cleaned up.

• Remember, the feast is over and everybody is full of squash.

c. Is everybody ready?

• Wise old rat, start. (Prompt children if necessary.)
(Cue: Sherlock to brag.)
(Cue: wise old rat to interrupt.)
(Cue: Bertha to tell what happened.)
(Cue: rats to call Sherlock a dirty liar.)

d. That was pretty good.

• (Optional:) Maybe we can do that part again some time with different actors.

COMPUTER AND REFERENCE BOOKS

a. (Write on the board:)

molars	bicuspids
cuspids	incisors

b. You've read about teeth. Here are the names of some teeth. (Read each name.)

• You're going to find out where these teeth are in your mouth or when you will get them.

c. (Assign children to two groups. The first group is to look up information about the teeth in the dictionary or encyclopedia. The second group is to use the computer lab to find information about the teeth. Both groups are to make up a report that answers the main questions and that presents other information about the teeth.)

71

A

1
1. Mr. Daniels
2. recognize
3. elevator
4. medicine
5. guess
6. dozen

2
1. silently
2. watering
3. heater
4. approached
5. fairly

3
1. clues
2. doctors
3. offices
4. drugs
5. typists
6. lawyers

4
1. cock your head
2. equipment
3. motorcycle
4. refinery
5. friendly
6. unfriendly

5
1. explain
2. insist
3. honest
4. crude
5. fifth

6
1. narrow
2. prison
3. polite
4. several
5. pipeline

B

Oil Wells

A well is a deep hole in the ground. The well has pipe in it so the hole stays open.

There are different types of wells.

• Some wells are fresh-water wells. These wells pump fresh water from under the ground.

Lesson 71 173

• Some wells are oil wells. These wells pump crude oil from under the ground.

Picture 1 shows a machine that is drilling a hole for a well.

If the machine keeps drilling, what type of liquid will it reach first?

If the machine keeps drilling past the fresh water, what kind of liquid will it reach next?

If the machine keeps drilling, what will it reach after the oil?

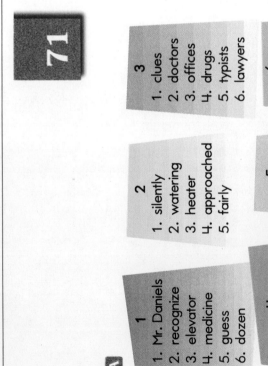

FRESH WATER
CRUDE OIL
SALT WATER

PICTURE 1

174 Lesson 71

If the well is an oil well, it pumps crude oil from the ground. Crude oil is a dark liquid that can be changed to make things like gasoline, motor oil, and plastic.

The crude oil is pumped from the well. Then it goes into a pipeline. The pipeline goes along the ground and carries the crude oil many miles to a refinery.

The refinery is a large place with strange-looking equipment and large tanks for holding oil.

The refinery changes crude oil into gasoline and other things.

Oil well

Pipeline

Refinery

PICTURE 2

Lesson 71   175

C Maria Tests Bertha's Talent

Bertha had a plan for helping Maria figure out where the water came from. You probably know what her plan was. Although Bertha didn't know too much about oil wells and refineries, she did know that she could smell the difference between water taken from the creek and water taken from water wells.

Bertha was sitting on Maria's porch. She said, "Maria, it's easy for me to tell if the water comes from the creek or from the well. I'll just smell it."

Maria looked slowly at Bertha and made a face. "What are you talking about?"

Bertha said, "Take me with you and I'll tell you where the water comes from."

Maria made another face. "How will you know where it comes from?"

"I told you. I'll smell it," Bertha said. Then she explained her talent. "I can tell about anything by smelling it. Honest I can."

Maria cocked her head and looked at Bertha. "What is this, a joke?" Maria asked.

Bertha said, "Give me a test. Get glasses of water from different places. I'll tell you where you got each glass of water." At first Maria didn't want to do it. "This is crazy," she kept saying. But Bertha kept insisting on the test. Finally Maria went into her house and came back with three

176   Lesson 71

D Number your paper from 1 through 19.

Skill Items

Lawyers with talent normally succeed.

1. What word means the opposite of **fail**?
2. What word names people who help us when we have questions about the law?
3. What word means **usually**?
4. What word refers to the special skills a person has?

Review Items

5. You can see drops of water on grass early in the morning. What are those called?

6. Which letter shows the coconut milk?
7. Which letter shows the inner shell?
8. Which letter shows the coconut meat?
9. Which letter shows the outer shell?

178   *Lesson 71*

---

glasses of water. She said, "You ⭐ can't feel them, or you may get some clues about where I got them."

Bertha said, "I don't have to feel them. The one on the left is from your water heater. The middle glass is from a watering can or something like that. That water has been sitting out for a couple of days. The water in the last glass came from a water jug or something in your refrigerator. It's been in the refrigerator for a long time, and it probably doesn't taste very good."

"I don't believe this," Maria said, and she tasted the water from the last glass. She made a face. "Oh, you're right. It's bad."

Suddenly Maria laughed, turned around, and looked at Bertha. She said, "I don't believe this." Then she said, "I don't believe this," three or four more times. "You're amazing. You are amazing. You are the most amazing person I have ever seen."

She kept talking very fast. She told about some of the amazing things that she had seen—a cow with two heads and a building over 3 hundred meters high. Finally, she said, "I once saw a man jump a motorcycle over twenty cars and that was amazing, but you are five times as amazing."

"Can I go with you?" Bertha asked.

"Yes, yes, yes, yes," Maria said. "This will be great."

MORE NEXT TIME

Lesson 71   177

---

15. Write the letter that shows a tugboat.
16. Write two letters that show ships.
17. Write two letters that show docks.

18. The place that is called Troy is now part of what country?
    • Greece   • Italy   • Turkey

19. Write the letters of the 4 kinds of weapons that soldiers used when they had battles with Troy.
    a. bows   c. arrows   e. spears   g. planes
    b. swords   d. rockets   f. guns   h. tanks

180   *Lesson 71*

---

10. All machines make it easier for someone to

11. You would have the most power if you pushed against one of the handles. Which handle is that?
12. Which handle would give you the least amount of power?

13. When people have very high fevers, how do they feel?
14. They may see and hear things that are not ▮.

Lesson 71   179

B Story Items

8. Gasoline comes from a liquid called _____

9. When Bertha first told Maria about her talent, did Maria believe her?

_____

10. How many glasses of water did Maria use to test Bertha's talent?

_____

11. **Underline** the items that tell where the water came from.

• fish bowl   • bath tub   • jug in refrigerator   • sink

• water heater   • frog pond   • watering can

12. Did Bertha pass Maria's test? _____

13. After the test, did Maria believe what Bertha said about her talent?

_____

14. Bertha will help Maria by telling where ▮▮▮▮ .

• the oil wells are   • the water came from   • the snow was

Review Items

15. The arrow by the handle shows which way it turns. Which arrow

shows the way the log moves? _____

16. Which arrow shows the way the vine moves? _____

▮ GO TO PART D IN YOUR TEXTBOOK

38   *Lesson 71*

71

Name _____

A

1. Name two kinds of wells. _____

Write these names on the picture to show where each liquid is: **crude oil, fresh water, salt water.**

2. _____

3. _____

4. _____

5. Fill in the boxes with the names for the **crude oil, pipeline, and refinery.**

6. Draw an arrow at A to show which way the crude oil is moving.

7. Draw an arrow at B to show which way the crude oil is moving.

Lesson 71   **37**

Lesson 71

EXERCISE 1
VOCABULARY REVIEW

a. You learned a sentence that tells how long she survived.
  • Everybody, say that sentence. Get ready. (Signal.) *She survived until she was rescued.*
  • (Repeat until firm.)
b. You learned a sentence that tells what the soldiers did.
  • Say that sentence. Get ready. (Signal.) *The soldiers protected their equipment.*
  • (Repeat until firm.)
c. Here's the last sentence you learned: Lawyers with talent normally succeed.
  • Everybody, say that sentence. Get ready. (Signal.) *Lawyers with talent normally succeed.*
  • (Repeat until firm.)
d. Everybody, what do we call people who help us when we have questions about the law? (Signal.) *Lawyers.*
  • What's another word for **usually?** (Signal.) *Normally.*
  • What word refers to the special skills a person has? (Signal.) *Talent.*
  • What word means the opposite of **fail?** (Signal.) *Succeed.*
e. Once more. Say the sentence that tells about lawyers with talent. Get ready. (Signal.) *Lawyers with talent normally succeed.*

EXERCISE 2
READING WORDS

Column 1

a. **Find lesson 71 in your textbook.** ✓
  • Touch column 1. ✓
  • (Teacher reference:)

1. Mr. Daniels	4. medicine
2. recognize	5. guess
3. elevator	6. dozen

b. Number 1 is the name **Mr. Daniels.** What name? (Signal.) *Mr. Daniels.*
c. Word 2 is **recognize.** What word? (Signal.) *Recognize.*

• When you **recognize** something that you see or feel, you know what it is. Here's another way of saying **She knew what the smell was: She recognized the smell.**
d. Your turn. What's another way of saying **She knew what the smell was?** (Signal.) *She recognized the smell.*
  • (Repeat step d until firm.)
e. What's another way of saying **She knew who the person was?** (Signal.) *She recognized the person.*
f. Word 3 is **elevator.** What word? (Signal.) *Elevator.*
  • Spell **elevator.** Get ready. (Tap for each letter.) *E-L-E-V-A-T-O-R.*
g. Word 4 is **medicine.** What word? (Signal.) *Medicine.*
  • Spell **medicine.** Get ready. (Tap for each letter.) *M-E-D-I-C-I-N-E.*
h. Word 5 is **guess.** What word? (Signal.) *Guess.*
  • Spell **guess.** Get ready. (Tap for each letter.) *G-U-E-S-S.*
i. Word 6 is **dozen.** What word? (Signal.) *Dozen.*
  • Spell **dozen.** Get ready. (Tap for each letter.) *D-O-Z-E-N.*
j. Let's read those words again, the fast way.
  • Number 1. What words? (Signal.) *Mr. Daniels.*
k. Word 2. What word? (Signal.) *Recognize.*
  • (Repeat for words 3–6.)
l. (Repeat steps j and k until firm.)

Column 2

m. Find column 2. ✓
  • (Teacher reference:)

1. silently	4. approached
2. watering	5. fairly
3. heater	

• All these words have endings.
n. Word 1. What word? (Signal.) *Silently.*
  • (Repeat for words 2–5.)
o. (Repeat step n until firm.)

Column 3

p. Find column 3. ✓
• (Teacher reference:)

1. clues	4. drugs
2. doctors	5. typists
3. offices	6. lawyers

• All these words end with the letter **S**.
q. Word 1. What word? (Signal.) *Clues.*
 • (Repeat for words 2–6.)
r. (Repeat step q until firm.)

Column 4

s. Find column 4. ✓
• (Teacher reference:)

1. cock your head	4. refinery
2. equipment	5. friendly
3. motorcycle	6. unfriendly

t. Number 1. What words? (Signal.) *Cock your head.*
• When you cock your head, you tilt it. Everybody, show me how you cock your head. ✓
u. Word 2. What word? (Signal.) *Equipment.*
 • (Repeat for words 3–6.)
v. Let's read those words again.
 • Number 1. What words? (Signal.) *Cock your head.*
w. Word 2. What word? (Signal.) *Equipment.*
 • (Repeat for words 3–6.)
x. (Repeat steps v and w until firm.)

Column 5

y. Find column 5. ✓
• (Teacher reference:)

1. explain	4. crude
2. insist	5. fifth
3. honest	

z. Word 1. What word? (Signal.) *Explain.*
• When you **explain** something, you **tell about it.** Here's another way of saying **She told about her talent: She explained her talent.**
a. Your turn. What's another way of saying **She told about her talent?** (Signal.) *She explained her talent.*
 • (Repeat step a until firm.)

b. What's another way of saying **He told about his plan?** (Signal.) *He explained his plan.*
c. Word 2. What word? (Signal.) *Insist.*
 • (Repeat for words 3–5.)
d. Let's read those words again.
 • Word 1. What word? (Signal.) *Explain.*
 • (Repeat for words 2–5.)
e. (Repeat step d until firm.)

Column 6

f. Find column 6. ✓
• (Teacher reference:)

1. narrow	4. several
2. prison	5. pipeline
3. polite	

g. Word 1. What word? (Signal.) *Narrow.*
 • (Repeat for words 2–5.)
h. (Repeat step g until firm.)

Individual Turns

(For columns 1–6: Call on individual students, each to read one to three words per turn.)

EXERCISE 3

COMPREHENSION PASSAGE

a. Find part B in your textbook. ✓
• You're going to read the next story about Bertha. First you'll read the information passage. It gives some facts about wells.
b. Everybody, touch the title. ✓
 • (Call on a student to read the title.) *[Oil Wells.]*
 • Everybody, what's the title? (Signal.) *Oil Wells.*
c. (Call on individual students to read the passage, each student reading two or three sentences at a time. Ask the specified questions as the students read.)

Oil Wells

A well is a deep hole in the ground. The well has pipe in it so the hole stays open.

• Why does the well have a pipe in it? (Call on a student. Idea: *So the hole stays open.*)

There are different types of wells.
• Some wells are fresh-water wells. These wells pump fresh water from under the ground.

• What do fresh-water wells do? (Call on a student. Idea: *Pump fresh water from under the ground.*)

• Some wells are oil wells. These wells pump crude oil from under the ground.

• What do oil wells do? (Call on a student. Idea: *Pump crude oil from under the ground.*)

Picture 1 shows a machine that is drilling a hole for a well.

PICTURE 1

• Everybody, touch the underground pipe in picture 1 and show how far down the well is already dug. ✓

If the machine keeps drilling, what type of liquid will it reach first?

• Everybody, touch the liquid it will reach first. ✓
• What kind of liquid is that? (Signal.) *Fresh water.*

If the machine keeps drilling past the fresh water, what kind of liquid will it reach next?

• Everybody, touch the liquid it will reach next. ✓
• What kind of liquid is that? (Signal.) *Crude oil.*

If the machine keeps drilling, what will it reach after the oil?

• Everybody, touch the liquid it will reach next. ✓
• What kind of liquid is that? (Signal.) *Salt water.*
• If you dig a well deep enough, you'll always hit salt water.

If the well is an oil well, it pumps crude oil from the ground. Crude oil is a dark liquid that can be changed to make things like gasoline, motor oil, and plastic.

• What can be made from crude oil? (Call on a student.) *Gasoline, motor oil, plastic.*

The crude oil is pumped from the well. Then it goes into a pipeline.

• Everybody, where does the crude oil go from the well? (Signal.) *Into a pipeline.*

The pipeline goes along the ground and carries the crude oil many miles to a refinery.

• Everybody, where does the pipeline take the crude oil? (Signal.) *To a refinery.*
• Is the refinery usually right next to the well? (Signal.) *No.*

The refinery is a large place with strange-looking equipment and large tanks for holding oil.
The refinery changes crude oil into gasoline and other things.

PICTURE 2

• What does the refinery do? (Call on a student. Idea: *Changes crude oil into gasoline and other things.*)
• Everybody, touch the crude oil underground in picture 2. ✓
• Now follow it up the pipe to the surface of the ground. ✓
• Now follow it in the pipeline to the other end of the pipeline. ✓

- What's the other end? (Signal.) *The refinery.*
- What does that refinery do to the crude oil? (Call on a student. Idea: *Changes it into gasoline and other things.*)
- The oil company that you're reading about is a refinery.

EXERCISE 4

STORY READING

a. Find part C in your textbook. ✓
- The error limit for this story is 9. Read carefully.
b. Everybody, touch the title. ✓
- (Call on a student to read the title.) *[Maria Tests Bertha's Talent.]*
- What's going to happen in this story? (Call on a student. Idea: *Maria will test Bertha's talent.*)
c. (Call on individual students to read the story, each student reading two or three sentences at a time. Ask questions marked **1.**)

- (**Correct errors:** Tell the word. Direct the student to reread the sentence.)
- (If the group makes more than 9 errors, direct the students to reread the story.)

d. (After the group has read the selection making no more than 9 errors, read the story to the students and ask questions marked **2.**)

Maria Tests Bertha's Talent

Bertha had a plan for helping Maria figure out where the water came from. You probably know what her plan was.

1. What do you think it was? (Call on a student. Idea: *Get water from the oil company and have Bertha smell it to see whether it came from the creek or water wells.*)

Although Bertha didn't know too much about oil wells and refineries, she did know that she could smell the difference between water taken from the creek and water taken from water wells.

2. Everybody, where was the company supposed to be taking water from? (Signal.) *Wells.*

2. Where did Maria think it was coming from? (Signal.) *The creek.*

Bertha was sitting on Maria's porch. She said, "Maria, it's easy for me to tell if the water comes from the creek or from the well. I'll just smell it."
Maria looked slowly at Bertha and made a face. "What are you talking about?"

1. Everybody, show me the kind of face Maria probably made. ✓
1. What was Maria thinking about Bertha? (Call on a student. Idea: *That she was strange or crazy.*)

Bertha said, "Take me with you and I'll tell you where the water comes from."
Maria made another face. "How will you know where it comes from?"
"I told you. I'll smell it," Bertha said. Then she explained her talent.

1. How would she do that? (Call on a student. Idea: *By telling Maria how she used her sense of smell.*)

"I can tell about anything by smelling it. Honest I can."
Maria cocked her head and looked at Bertha.

2. Everybody, show me how you cock your head. ✓

"What is this, a joke?" Maria asked.
Bertha said, "Give me a test. Get glasses of water from different places. I'll tell you where you got each glass of water." At first Maria didn't want to do it. "This is crazy," she kept saying. But Bertha kept insisting on the test.

2. What would she say to keep insisting on the test? (Call on a student. Idea: *Get glasses of water from different places and I'll tell you where each one came from.*)

Finally Maria went into her house and came back with three glasses of water. She said, "You can't feel them, or you may get some clues about where I got them."

Lesson 71 **119**

2. What kind of clues could you get by feeling the water glasses? (Call on a student. Idea: *Clues about temperature.*)

Bertha said, "I don't have to feel them. The one on the left is from your water heater.

2. What's a water heater? (Call on a student. Idea: *A machine that makes cold water get hot.*)

The middle glass is from a watering can or something like that.

2. What do you do with a watering can? (Call on a student. Idea: *Water plants and flowers.*)

That water has been sitting out for a couple of days. The water in the last glass came from a water jug or something in your refrigerator. It's been in the refrigerator for a long time, and it probably doesn't taste very good."
"I don't believe this," Maria said, and she tasted the water from the last glass. She made a face. "Oh, you're right. It's bad."

2. Everybody, show me the kind of face she made when she tasted the water. ✓

Suddenly Maria laughed, turned around, and looked at Bertha. She said, "I don't believe this." Then she said, "I don't believe this," three or four more times. "You're amazing. You are amazing. You are the most amazing person I have ever seen."
She kept talking very fast. She told about some of the amazing things that she had seen—a cow with two heads and a building over 3 hundred meters high. Finally, she said, "I once saw a man jump a motorcycle over twenty cars and that was amazing, but you are five times as amazing."

2. Maria is really excited. I'll read that part again. Listen to how she talks on and on.

Suddenly Maria laughed, turned around, and looked at Bertha. She said, "I don't believe this." Then she said, "I don't believe this," three or four more times. "You're amazing. You are amazing. You are the most amazing person I have ever seen."
She kept talking very fast. She told about some of the amazing things that she had seen—a cow with two heads and a building over 3 hundred meters high. Finally, she said, "I once saw a man jump a motorcycle over twenty cars and that was amazing, but you are five times as amazing."

"Can I go with you?" Bertha asked. "Yes, yes, yes, yes, yes," Maria said. "This will be great."
MORE NEXT TIME

1. Go back to the beginning of the story. Follow along while I read.
2. What do you think is going to happen? (Call on a student. Idea: *Maria will get Bertha to smell the water the oil company uses;* etc.)

EXERCISE 5

PAIRED PRACTICE

You're going to read aloud to your partner. Today the **B** members will read first. Then the **A** members will read from the star to the end of the story.
(Observe students and give feedback.)

End-of-Lesson Activities

INDEPENDENT WORK

Now finish your independent work for lesson 71. Raise your hand when you're finished. (Observe students and give feedback.)

WORKCHECK

a. (Direct students to take out their marking pencils.)
• We're going to check your independent work. Remember, if you got an item wrong, make an **X** next to the item. Don't change any answers.

b. (For each item: Read the item. Call on a student to answer it. If the answer is wrong, say the correct answer. Refer to the Answer Key for the correct answers.)

c. Now use your marking pencil to fix up any items you got wrong. Remember, all mistakes must be fixed up before you hand in your independent work.

WRITING-SPELLING

(Present Writing-Spelling lesson 71 after completing Reading lesson 71. See Writing-Spelling Guide.)

LANGUAGE ARTS GUIDE

(Present Language Arts lesson 71 after completing Reading lesson 71. See Language Arts Guide.)

Lesson 71 **121**

SPELLING

a. You've written words that have the sound **oy.** You can add endings to those words. You just write the word and then write the ending. To write the word **boiling,** you write **boil** and then write **I-N-G: B-O-I-L-I-N-G.**
• To write the word **joyful,** you write **joy** and then **F-U-L: J-O-Y-F-U-L.**

b. You're going to write words on lined paper. Number your paper from 1 through 5. ✔

c. Word 1 is **pointing.** Stop **pointing** at people. What word? **(Signal.)** *Pointing.*
• Write the word **pointing.** ✔

d. Word 2 is **coiled.** The rope was **coiled** up in the corner. What word? **(Signal.)** *Coiled.*
• Write the word **coiled.** ✔

e. Word 3 is **joyful.** It was a **joyful** time of the year. What word? **(Signal.)** *Joyful.*
• Write the word **joyful.** ✔

f. Word 4 is **boiler.** The engine room had a large **boiler.** What word? **(Signal.)** *Boiler.*
• Write the word **boiler.** ✔

g. Word 5 is **boys.** We saw the **boys.** What word? **(Signal.)** *Boys.*
• Write the word **boys.** ✔

h. Check your work. Make an **X** next to any word you got wrong.

i. Word 1. Spell **pointing.** Get ready. **(Tap for each letter.)** *P-O-I-N-T-I-N-G.*
• (Repeat for: **2. coiled, 3. joyful, 4. boiler, 5. boys.**)

SENTENCE COPYING

a. (Write on the board:)

Maria asked, "How did you know that?"

b. You're going to write this sentence.
• (Call on a student to read the sentence.)

c. Everybody, turn your paper over. ✔
• Copy the sentence on the top line. Do it quickly.
(Observe students and give feedback.)

d. Pencils down. You're going to copy the sentence as many times as you can in three minutes. Get ready. Go. **(Time the students. At the end of three minutes, say:)** Stop. Pencils down.
• (Call on individual students.) How many times did you copy the sentence?

Name _____

B. All the words in the box below begin with the letter E. Underline the second letter in each word. Then write the words in alphabetical order.

eraser	evening
enormous	escape
edge	eggs
easy	eyes

1. _____
2. _____
3. _____
4. _____
5. _____
6. _____
7. _____
8. _____

Name _____

Lesson 71

CALIFORNIA

Redding

Shasta National Forest

Shasta Lake

A. Read each item to yourself. Write fact or opinion.

1. Redding is a city in California. _____
2. Redding is the nicest place to live. _____
3. Redding is not one of the largest cities in California. _____
4. Redding is close to Shasta Lake. _____
5. Many tourists stop in Redding. _____
6. All other cities should try to be more like Redding. _____
7. There are mountains to the north of Redding. _____
8. Redding has great weather during all times of the year. _____
9. If you like places where there's a lot to do, you'll love Redding. _____
10. The trees around Redding are the best in the world. _____
11. There is a lot of farmland to the south of Redding. _____
12. Everybody you'll meet in Redding is very friendly. _____

Lesson 71

Materials: Each student will need a copy of the worksheets for lesson 71
(blackline masters 17 and 18).

EXERCISE 1
FACT VS. OPINION

Lesson 71

A. Read each item to yourself. Write fact or opinion.

1. Redding is a city in California. _____
2. Redding is the nicest place to live. _____
3. Redding is not one of the largest cities in California. _____
4. Redding is close to Shasta Lake. _____
5. Many tourists stop in Redding. _____
6. All other cities should try to be more like Redding. _____
7. There are mountains to the north of Redding. _____
8. Redding has great weather during all times of the year. _____
9. If you like places where there's a lot to do, you'll love Redding. _____
10. The trees around Redding are the best in the world. _____
11. There is a lot of farmland to the south of Redding. _____
12. Everybody you'll meet in Redding is very friendly. _____

**B. All the words in the box below begin with the letter E. Underline the
second letter in each word. Then write the words in alphabetical
order.**

eraser	evening
enormous	escape
edge	eggs
easy	eyes

1. _____
2. _____
3. _____
4. _____
5. _____
6. _____
7. _____
8. _____

a. Find part A on your worksheet. ✔
• The map shows Redding, California, and the area around Redding. The population of Redding is about 80 thousand people. That's not one of the larger cities in California. But a lot of tourists stop in Redding because there is a big lake nearby and to the north there are great mountains.

b. All of the statements below the map are about Redding. Some of the statements are true. Those are **facts.** Some of the statements are **opinions.** They are not facts. If you ask different people, you'll get different opinions. Remember, if you can show that something is true, it is a fact. If you can't show it's true, it's an opinion.

c. Statement 1: Redding is a city in California. Everybody, is that a **fact** or is that an **opinion?** (Signal.) *Fact.*

d. Statement 2: Redding is the nicest place to live. Is that a **fact** or is that an **opinion?** (Signal.) *Opinion.*

e. Everybody, work the rest of the items. Read each item to yourself. Write **fact** or **opinion.**

f. (After the students complete the items, do a workcheck. For each item: Read the item. Call on a student to say the answer. If the answer is wrong, say the correct answer.)

Answer Key: 1. fact **2.** opinion **3.** fact
4. fact **5.** fact **6.** opinion **7.** fact **8.** opinion
9. opinion **10.** opinion **11.** fact **12.** opinion

71

EXERCISE 2
ALPHABETICAL ORDER

a. (Tell the students when they should complete the items in part B.)

b. (After the students complete the items, write the alphabetized list on the board:)

1. easy	5. eraser
2. edge	6. escape
3. eggs	7. evening
4. enormous	8. eyes

• Check your work. Here's the list you should have. Fix up any mistakes. ✔

21

A

1
1. mukluks
2. wrist
3. hailstone
4. playfully

2
1. gulped
2. gently
3. owed
4. wavy
5. kneeled
6. dents

3
1. rose
2. sight
3. marble
4. dove

B

Facts About Clouds

You have read about a big storm cloud. Here are facts about clouds:

• Clouds are made up of tiny drops of water

• In clouds that are very high, the water drops are frozen. Here is how those clouds look.

Picture 1

Picture 2

• Some clouds are storm clouds. They are flat on the bottom, but they go up very high. Sometimes they are five miles high.

Picture 3

• Some kinds of clouds may bring days of bad weather These are low, flat clouds that look like bumpy blankets.

104   *Lesson 21*

VOCABULARY SENTENCES

Lessons 1–70

1. The horses became restless on the dangerous route.
2. Scientists do not ignore ordinary things.
3. She actually repeated that careless mistake.
4. The smell attracted flies immediately.
5. The rim of the volcano exploded.
6. The new exhibit displayed mysterious fish.
7. She automatically arranged the flowers.
8. They were impressed by her large vocabulary.
9. He responded to her clever solution.
10. The patent attorney wrote an agreement.
11. The applause interrupted his speech.
12. She selected a comfortable seat.
13. Without gravity, they were weightless.
14. She demonstrated how animals use oxygen.
15. Lava erupted from the volcano's crater.
16. The incredible whales made them anxious.
17. The boring speaker disturbed the audience.

352   *Vocabulary Sentences*

The arrows in picture 3 show how the winds move inside a storm cloud. The winds move water drops to the top of the cloud. The drops freeze. When a drop freezes, it becomes a tiny hailstone. The tiny hailstone falls to the bottom of the cloud. At the bottom of the cloud, the tiny hailstone gets covered with more water. Then it goes up again and freezes again. Now the hailstone is a little bigger. It keeps going around and around in the cloud until it gets so heavy that it falls from the cloud. Sometimes it is as big as a baseball. Sometimes it is smaller than a marble.

If you want to see how many times a hailstone has gone to the top of the cloud, break the hailstone in half. You'll see rings. Each ring shows one trip to the top of the cloud. Count the rings and you'll know how many times the hailstone went through the cloud. Hailstone A went through the cloud three times.

How many times did Hailstone B go through the cloud?

Hailstone A   Hailstone B

C The Killer Whales Wait

Oomoo took off one of her boots. She kneeled down and slammed the boot against the surface of the ice. The boot made a loud spanking sound. Oolak watched for a moment, then took off one of his boots and slapped it against the surface of the ice. "Maybe they'll hear this," Oomoo said. "I hope they do," she added. But she knew that it was still raining a little bit and that the rain made noise. She also knew that she and Oolak were far from shore—too far. They were more than a mile from the tent. She guessed that the sounds they made with their boots were lost in the rain and the slight breeze that was still blowing from the south.

From time to time, Oomoo glanced out to the ocean. She hoped that she would see the killer whales

Lesson 21   105

moving far away. She hoped that the sound of the boots would scare them away. But each time she looked in their direction, she saw them moving back and forth, just past the top of the C-shaped ice floe.

Suddenly, Oolak tugged on Oomoo's shoulder and pointed toward the whales. His eyes were wide. He looked as if he was ready to cry. "I know," Oomoo said. Her voice was almost a whisper. "Just keep trying to signal," she said. "Maybe the people on the shore will hear us."

As she pounded her boot against the surface of the ice, she stared toward the shore. She wanted to see a kayak moving silently through the rain. She wanted to hear the signal of a bell ringing. She wanted to . . . .

Suddenly, she saw something white moving through the water. At first, she thought that it was a chunk of ice. But no, it couldn't be. It was not moving the way ice moves. It was very hard to tell what it was through the light rain. It wasn't a kayak. It wasn't a long boat. It was . . . Usk.

Usk ★ was swimming directly toward the ice chunk. And he was moving very fast.

"Usk!" Oomoo yelled as loudly as she could. "Usk!" She stood up and waved her arms.

106   *Lesson 21*

The huge polar bear caught up to the ice chunk when it was not more than a hundred meters away from the killer whales. "Will they go after Usk?" Oolak asked.

"They'll go after Usk if they're hungry," Oomoo replied. "We've got to get out of here fast."

The huge bear swam up to the ice chunk, put his huge paws on the surface, and started to climb onto it. When he tried that, he almost tipped it over.

"No," Oomoo said. "Stay down." She tried to push him back. He rolled into the water and made a playful circle. "Give me your laces," Oomoo said to Oolak. Oomoo and Oolak untied the laces from their boots. These laces were long, thick straps of animal skin. Oomoo tied all the laces together. Quickly, she glanced back. The ice chunk was less than a hundred meters from the killer whales.

She called Usk. He playfully swam around the ice chunk, rolling over on his back and slapping the water with his front paws. Oomoo waited until Usk got close to the shore side of the ice chunk. Then she slipped the laces around his neck. "Hang on tight," she told Oolak, and handed him one end of the laces. She and Oolak sat down on the ice chunk and tried to dig

Review Items

Kotzebue

Big Trout Lake

Key
0   500 miles

6. The map shows a route. What state is at the north end of the route?
7. What country is at the south end of the route?
8. About how many miles is the route?

9. Female animals fight in the spring to protect ▮.
10. Name 2 kinds of Alaskan animals that are dangerous in the spring.
11. Is it easier to fly alone or with a large flock?
12. Flying near the back of a large flock is like riding your bike ▮.
    • with the wind   • against the wind

108   *Lesson 21*

---

their heels into dents in the surface of the ice.

"Play sled," she told Usk. "Play sled. Go home."

At first, Usk just rolled over and almost got the laces tangled in his front paws. "Home," Oomoo repeated. "Play sled and go home."

Usk stayed next to the ice chunk, making a playful sound. "Home," Oomoo shouted again.

Then Usk seemed to figure out what he was supposed to do. Perhaps he saw the fins of the killer whales. He got low in the water and started to swim toward shore.

Lesson 21   107

D Number your paper from 1 through 12.

Story Items

1. What were Oomoo's boot laces made of?
2. What did Oomoo do with the laces after she tied them together?
3. What did she want Usk to do?
4. Did Usk immediately understand what he was supposed to do?
5. What did Usk start doing at the end of the story?

A

Name _____

1. What are clouds made of?
2. What kind of cloud does picture A show?
3. Write the letter of the clouds that may stay in the sky for days at a time.
4. Write the letter of the storm clouds.
5. Write the letter of the clouds that have frozen drops of water.
6. Write the letter of the clouds that may be five miles high.
7. Look at cloud A. At which number does a drop of water start?
8. What happens to the drop at the number 2?
9. Draw 2 arrows on cloud A to show how a hailstone forms and returns to 1.

10. If you break a hailstone in half, what will you see inside the hailstone?

11. The picture shows half of a hailstone. How many times did the stone go through a cloud?

Lesson 21   37

B   Story Items

12. Oomoo slapped her boot on the ice to make noise. Why did she want the people on shore to hear the noise?
13. Why did she want the killer whales to hear the noise?
14. Was Oomoo sure that someone would hear her?
15. About how far was the ice chunk from the tent?
16. About how far was the ice chunk from the killer whales?

Review Items

17. Write **north**, **south**, **east** and **west** in the correct boxes.
18. In which direction is ocean current J moving?
19. In which direction is ocean current K moving?
20. Which direction is the wind coming from?
21. Make an arrow above ice chunk L to show the direction the current will move the ice chunk.
22. Make an arrow above ice chunk M to show the direction the current will move the ice chunk.

GO TO PART D IN YOUR TEXTBOOK.

Lesson 21

38

Lesson 21

EXERCISE 1
VOCABULARY

a. **Find page 352 in your textbook.** ✓
- Touch sentence 4. ✓
- This is a new vocabulary sentence. It says: The smell attracted flies immediately. Everybody, say that sentence. Get ready. (Signal.) *The smell attracted flies immediately.*
- Close your eyes and say the sentence. Get ready. (Signal.) *The smell attracted flies immediately.*
- (Repeat until firm.)

b. The smell **attracted** flies. If the smell attracted flies, the smell really interested the flies and pulled them toward the smell. Everybody, what word means **really interested** the flies? (Signal.) *Attracted.*

c. The sentence says the smell attracted flies **immediately. Immediately** means **right now.** Everybody, what word means **right now?** (Signal.) *Immediately.*

d. Listen to the sentence again: The smell attracted flies immediately. Everybody, say that sentence. Get ready. (Signal.) *The smell attracted flies immediately.*

e. What word means **really interested** the flies? (Signal.) *Attracted.*
- What word means **right now?** (Signal.) *Immediately.*

EXERCISE 2
READING WORDS
Column 1

a. Find lesson 21 in your textbook. ✓
- Touch column 1. ✓
- (Teacher reference:)

1. **mukluks**	3. **hailstone**
2. **wrist**	4. **playfully**

b. Word 1 is **mukluks.** What word? (Signal.) *Mukluks.*
- Spell **mukluks.** Get ready. (Tap for each letter.) *M-U-K-L-U-K-S.*
- Mukluks are very warm boots that Eskimos wear.

c. Word 2 is **wrist.** What word? (Signal.) *Wrist.*
- Spell **wrist.** Get ready. (Tap for each letter.) *W-R-I-S-T.*
- Your wrist is the joint between your hand and your arm. Everybody, touch your wrist. ✓

d. Word 3. What word? (Signal.) *Hailstone.*

e. Word 4. What word? (Signal.) *Playfully.*

f. Let's read those words again, the fast way.
- Word 1. What word? (Signal.) *Mukluks.*
- (Repeat for words 2–4.)

g. (Repeat step f until firm.)

Column 2

h. Find column 2. ✓
- (Teacher reference:)

1. **gulped**	4. **wavy**
2. **gently**	5. **kneeled**
3. **owed**	6. **dents**

i. All these words have an ending.

j. Word 1. What word? (Signal.) *Gulped.*
- When you gulp something, you swallow it quickly. Here's another way of saying **She swallowed the water quickly: She gulped the water.**
- What's another way of saying **They swallowed their food quickly?** (Signal.) *They gulped their food.*
- Word 2. What word? (Signal.) *Gently.*
- Things that are gentle are the opposite of things that are rough. Everybody, what's the opposite of **a rough touch?** (Signal.) *A gentle touch.*
- What's the opposite of someone who behaves roughly? (Signal.) *Someone who behaves gently.*
- (Repeat until firm.)
- Word 3. What word? (Signal.) *Owed.*
- Something that you owe is something that you must pay. If you owe five dollars, you must pay five dollars. If you owe somebody a favor, you must pay that person a favor.

- Word 4. What word? (Signal.) *Wavy.*
- (Repeat for: **5. kneeled, 6. dents.**)

k. Let's read those words again, the fast way.
- Word 1. What word? (Signal.) *Gulped.*
- (Repeat for: **2. gently, 3. owed, 4. wavy, 5. kneeled, 6. dents.**)
l. (Repeat step k until firm.)

Column 3

m. Find column 3. ✓
- (Teacher reference:)

1. rose	3. marble
2. sight	4. dove

n. Word 1. What word? (Signal.) *Rose.*
- Something that moves up today rises. Something that moved up yesterday **rose.** Everybody, what do we say for something that moves up today? (Signal.) *Rises.*
- What do we say for something that moved up yesterday? (Signal.) *Rose.*
- Word 2. What word? *Sight.*
- A sight is something you see. A terrible sight is something terrible that you see. Everybody, what do we call something **wonderful** that you see? (Signal.) *A wonderful sight.*
- Word 3. What word? (Signal.) *Marble.*
- Word 4 rhymes with **stove.** What word? (Signal.) *Dove.*
o. Let's read those words again.
- Word 1. What word? (Signal.) *Rose.*
- (Repeat for words 2–4.)
p. (Repeat step o until firm.)

Individual Turns

(For columns 1–3: Call on individual students, each to read one to three words per turn.)

EXERCISE 3

COMPREHENSION PASSAGE

a. Find part B in your textbook. ✓
- You're going to read the next story about Oomoo and Oolak. First, you'll read the information passage. It gives some facts about clouds.
b. Everybody, touch the title. ✓
- (Call on a student to read the title.) *[Facts About Clouds.]*

- Everybody, what's the title? (Signal.) *Facts About Clouds.*
c. (Call on individual students to read the passage, each student reading two or three sentences at a time. Ask the specified questions as the students read.)

Facts About Clouds
You have read about a big storm cloud. Here are facts about clouds:
Clouds are made up of tiny drops of water.

- Everybody, say that fact. Get ready. (Signal.) *Clouds are made up of tiny drops of water.*

In clouds that are very high, the water drops are frozen. Here is how those clouds look.

Picture 1   Picture 2

- Everybody, in what kind of clouds are the water drops frozen? (Signal.) *In clouds that are very high.*
- Touch a high cloud. ✓
- Those clouds are very pretty in the sunlight because the light bounces off the tiny frozen drops.

Some kinds of clouds may bring days of bad weather. These are low, flat clouds that look like bumpy blankets.

- Everybody, what kind of clouds may bring days of bad weather? (Signal.) *Low, flat clouds.*
- Does that kind of cloud pass over quickly? (Signal.) *No.*
- Touch a low, flat cloud. ✓
- How long may that kind of cloud be around? (Call on a student. Idea: *Days.*)

Some clouds are storm clouds. They are flat on the bottom, but they go up very high. Sometimes they are five miles high.

118 *Lesson 21*

- Tell me how a storm cloud looks. (Call on a student. Idea: *It's flat on the bottom and it goes up very high.*)
- Everybody, how high is the top of a big storm cloud sometimes? (Signal.) *Five miles.*

The arrows in picture 3 show how the winds move inside a storm cloud. The winds move water drops to the top of the cloud.

- Everybody, touch the number **1** that is inside the cloud. ✓
- That's where a drop of water starts. The wind blows it up to the top of the cloud. Everybody, follow the arrow to the top of the cloud and then stop. ✓
- Tell me about the temperature of the air at the top of the cloud. Get ready. (Signal.) *It's freezing cold.*
- So what's going to happen to the drop? (Call on a student. Idea: *It will freeze.*)

The drops freeze. When a drop freezes, it becomes a tiny hailstone.

- Everybody, what do we call a drop when it moves up and freezes? (Signal.) *A tiny hailstone.*

The tiny hailstone falls to the bottom of the cloud.

- Everybody, touch the number **2** in the cloud. ✓
- That's where the drop freezes. Now it falls down. Everybody, follow the arrow down. ✓
- What's the temperature like at the bottom of the cloud? (Signal.) *It's warm.*

At the bottom of the cloud, the tiny hailstone gets covered with more water. Then it goes up again and freezes again.

- Everybody, when it gets to the top of the cloud, what's going to happen to the water that is covering it? (Signal.) *It will freeze.*

Now the hailstone is a little bigger. It keeps going around and around in the cloud until it gets so heavy that it falls from the cloud. Sometimes it is as big as a baseball. Sometimes it is smaller than a marble.

- Everybody, touch the number **1** in the cloud. ✓
- Pretend that your finger is a drop. Show me a drop that goes around inside the cloud four times. Each time it goes through the top of the cloud, say: "It freezes." Go. ✓

If you want to see how many times a hailstone has gone to the top of the cloud, break the hailstone in half. You'll see rings.

- Everybody, what will you see inside the hailstone? (Signal.) *Rings.*

Each ring shows one trip to the top of the cloud. Count the rings and you'll know how many times the hailstone went through the cloud. Hailstone A went through the cloud three times.

- The rings are numbered. Everybody, count the rings in hailstone A out loud, starting with the center circle. Get ready. (Signal.) *One, two, three.*

How many times did Hailstone B go through the cloud?

- Everybody, figure out the answer. Remember to count the outside ring. (Wait.)
- How many times? (Signal.) *Seven.*

EXERCISE 4

STORY READING

a. Find part C in your textbook. ✓
- The error limit for group reading is 12 errors.
b. Everybody, touch the title. ✓
- (Call on a student to read the title.) *[The Killer Whales Wait.]*
- Everybody, what's the title? (Signal.) *The Killer Whales Wait.*

- Where were Oolak and Oomoo when we left them? (Call on a student. Idea: *Floating on an ice chunk.*)

c. (Call on individual students to read the story, each student reading two or three sentences at a time. Ask the specified questions as the students read.)

- (Correct errors: Tell the word. Direct the student to reread the sentence.)
- (If the group makes more than 12 errors, direct the students to reread the story.)

The Killer Whales Wait
Oomoo took off one of her boots. She kneeled down and slammed the boot against the surface of the ice.

- Why do you think she was doing that? (Call on a student. Idea: *She was trying to make noise so someone would hear her.*)
- Why didn't she yell? (Call on a student. Ideas: *She was losing her voice; nobody could hear her.*)

The boot made a loud spanking sound. Oolak watched for a moment, then took off one of his boots and slapped it against the surface of the ice. "Maybe they'll hear this," Oomoo said. "I hope they do," she added. But she knew that it was still raining a little bit and that the rain made noise. She also knew that she and Oolak were far from shore—too far. They were more than a mile from the tent. She guessed that the sounds they made with their boots were lost in the rain and the slight breeze that was still blowing from the south.

- Everybody, did she think that the people on the shore would hear the sounds? (Signal.) *No.*
- About how far away were these people? (Signal.) *Over a mile.*
- Why didn't she think they would hear the signal? (Call on a student. Idea: *Because the wind and rain were louder than the signal.*)

From time to time, Oomoo glanced to the ocean. She hoped that she would see the killer whales moving far away. She hoped that the sound

of the boots would scare them away. But each time she looked in their direction, she saw them moving back and forth, just past the top of the C-shaped ice floe.

- How do you think that made her feel? (Call on a student. Idea: *Afraid.*)

Suddenly, Oolak tugged on Oomoo's shoulder and pointed toward the whales. His eyes were wide. He looked as if he was ready to cry. "I know," Oomoo said.

- What does she mean when she says, "I know?" (Call on a student. Idea: *She knew the whales were there.*)

Her voice was almost a whisper. "Just keep trying to signal," she said. "Maybe the people on the shore will hear us."

- Everybody, had Oolak noticed the whales before? (Signal.) *No.*
- Why did he look as if he was ready to cry? (Call on a student. Idea: *Because he was afraid of the killer whales.*)

As she pounded her boot against the surface of the ice, she stared toward the shore. She wanted to see a kayak moving silently through the rain. She wanted to hear the signal of a bell ringing. She wanted to . . . .

- She stopped thinking about those things. I wonder why.

Suddenly, she saw something white moving through the water.

- What do you think it is? (Call on individual students. Ideas: *Another ice chunk; a boat; an animal;* etc.)

At first, she thought that it was a chunk of ice. But no, it couldn't be. It was not moving the way ice moves. It was very hard to tell what it was through the light rain. It wasn't a kayak. It wasn't a long boat. It was . . . Usk.

Usk ★ was swimming directly toward the ice chunk. And he was moving very fast.

"Usk!" Oomoo yelled as loudly as she could. "Usk!" She stood up and waved her arms.

The huge polar bear caught up to the ice chunk when it was not more than a hundred meters away from the killer whales. "Will they go after Usk?" Oolak asked.

- Everybody, who does he think might go after Usk? (Signal.) *The killer whales.*
- How close are they to the whales now? (Call on a student. Idea: *About 100 meters.*)

"They'll go after Usk if they're hungry," Oomoo replied. "We've got to get out of here fast."

The huge bear swam up to the ice chunk, put his huge paws on the surface, and started to climb onto it. When he tried that, he almost tipped it over.

- Why? (Call on a student. Idea: *Because he was so heavy.*)

"No," Oomoo said. "Stay down." She tried to push him back. He rolled into the water and made a playful circle. "Give me your laces," Oomoo said to Oolak. Oomoo and Oolak untied the laces from their boots. These laces were long, thick straps of animal skin. Oomoo tied all the laces together. Quickly, she glanced back. The ice chunk was less than a hundred meters from the killer whales.

She called Usk. He playfully swam around the ice chunk, rolling over on his back and slapping the water with his front paws.

- What does Usk want to do? (Call on a student. Idea: *Play.*)

Oomoo waited until Usk got close to the shore side of the ice chunk.

- Everybody, which side did he move to? (Signal.) *The shore side.*

- What do you think Oomoo's going to do? (Call on a student. Idea: *Get Usk to help them get back to shore.*)

Then she slipped the laces around his neck. "Hang on tight," she told Oolak, and handed him one end of the laces. She and Oolak sat down on the ice chunk and tried to dig their heels into dents in the surface of the ice.

"Play sled," she told Usk. "Play sled. Go home."

- Read the rest of the story to yourself. Find out two things. Find out what Usk did at first. Find out something he may have seen that made him stop being playful. Raise your hand when you're done.

At first, Usk just rolled over and almost got the laces tangled in his front paws. "Home," Oomoo repeated. "Play sled and go home."

Usk stayed next to the ice chunk, making a playful sound. "Home," Oomoo shouted again.

Then Usk seemed to figure out what he was supposed to do. Perhaps he saw the fins of the killer whales. He got low in the water and started to swim toward shore.

- (After all students have raised their hands:)
- What did Oomoo keep telling Usk to do? (Call on a student. Ideas: *Go home; play sled.*)
- Everybody, did Usk do that at first? (Signal.) *No.*
- What did he do? (Call on a student. Idea: *Rolled over.*)
- What may Usk have seen that made him stop being playful? (Call on a student. Idea: *The fins of the killer whales.*)
- What did Usk do then? (Call on a student. Idea: *Swam toward shore.*)
- Everybody, look at the picture. What are Oomoo and Oolak hanging on to? (Signal.) *The laces.*
- Point on the picture to show the direction Usk is moving. ✓

Lesson 21 **121**

EXERCISE 5

PAIRED PRACTICE

You're going to read aloud to your partner. Today the **B** members will read first. Then the **A** members will read from the star to the end of the story.
(Observe students and give feedback.)

End-of-Lesson Activities

INDEPENDENT WORK

Now finish your independent work for lesson 21. Raise your hand when you're finished. (Observe students and give feedback.)

WORKCHECK

a. (Direct students to take out their marking pencils.)
  • We're going to check your independent work. Remember, if you got an item wrong, make an **X** next to the item. Don't change any answers.

b. (For each item: Read the item. Call on a student to answer it. If the answer is wrong, say the correct answer. Refer to the Answer Key for the correct answers.)
c. Now use your marking pencil to fix up any items you got wrong. Remember, all mistakes must be fixed up before you hand in your independent work.

LANGUAGE ARTS

(Present Language Arts lesson 21 after completing Reading lesson 21. See Language Arts Guide.)

ACTIVITIES

(Present Activity 2 after completing Reading lessons 21. See Activities Across the Curriculum.)

> **Note:** A special project occurs after lesson 22. See page 128 for the materials you'll need.

122 Lesson 21

Name _____

Lesson 21

Use an encyclopedia to answer these questions.

1. Why is New Orleans sometimes called "Crescent City"? _____

   _____

2. What do reindeer eat? _____

3. What things did Alexander Graham Bell invent? _____

4. In what years was the Civil War fought? _____

5. Which letter has the fewest topics listed in the index, **Q, T** or **Z**? _____

Lesson 22

An atlas shows maps of different places in the world and gives information about these places. If you wanted to know how far Virginia is from Indiana, you could find that information in an atlas. If you wanted to know which states touch Illinois, you could find that information in an atlas. If you wanted to know the names of the four highest mountains in Alaska, you could find that.

An atlas has a table of contents and an index to help you find the map you're looking for.

Use an atlas to answer these questions.

1. Which of the Great Lakes touches Ohio? _____

2. What is the capital of France? _____

3. What's the highest mountain in Alaska? _____

4. What river is the border between Illinois and Iowa? _____

5. What **3** seas touch Greece? _____

BLM 17 139

Lesson 21

Materials: Each student will need a copy of worksheet 21 (blackline master 17) and access to an encyclopedia.

RESOURCE BOOKS
ENCYCLOPEDIA

> **Lesson 21**
>
> Use an encyclopedia to answer these questions.
>
> 1. Why is New Orleans sometimes called "Crescent City"? _____
> _____
> 2. What do reindeer eat? _____
> 3. What things did Alexander Graham Bell invent? _____
> 4. In what years was the Civil War fought? _____
> 5. Which letter has the fewest topics listed in the index, **Q, T** or **Z?** _____

a. You learned that an encyclopedia is a set of books that tells about any topic you could name. How are the topics in an encyclopedia arranged? **(Call on a student. Idea:** *In alphabetical order.***)**

b. You're going to find the answers to the questions in an encyclopedia.

• Item 1: Why is New Orleans sometimes called "Crescent City"? Everybody, what topic will you look up in the index of the encyclopedia? **(Signal.)** *New Orleans.*

• Item 2: What do reindeer eat? Everybody, what topic will you look up? **(Signal.)** *Reindeer.*

• Item 3: What things did Alexander Graham Bell invent? Everybody, what topic will you look up? **(Signal.)** *Alexander Graham Bell.*

• Item 4: In what years was the Civil War fought? Everybody, what topic will you look up? **(Signal.)** *Civil War.*

• Item 5: Which letter has the fewest topics listed in the index **Q, T** or **Z?** Everybody, what part of the encyclopedia will you use to find the answer? **(Signal.)** *Index.*

c. (Tell the students when they should complete the items.)

d. (After the students complete the items, do a workcheck. For each item: Read the item. Call on a student to answer it. If the answer is wrong, say the correct answer.)

Answer Key: 1. Idea: Because the original part of the town was crescent shaped.
2. Idea: Plants **3.** Telephone, photo-phone, graphophone **4.** 1861 to 1865 **5.** Z

ACTIVITY 2

Lesson 21

Science: Tracking the Weather

Materials: Blackline Master 2, writing materials

Objective: Students will observe, record, and summarize weather conditions in their area for one week.

Directions: Ask students to read the directions and the information on Blackline Master 2. Then have students work in pairs to complete the daily weather chart for one week. If students do not have a thermometer to measure the temperature outside, provide that information for them.

Have students write on a separate sheet of paper a paragraph that summarizes the weather this week—number of clear days, range of temperatures, and so on.

Evaluation/Answers: Chart information should be based on accurate, verifiable data.

ACTIVITY 2:   Tracking the Weather

Directions: Observe and note the weather changes in your area for one week. Use the chart below to track the weather.

At the end of the week, write a paragraph summarizing the weather changes that took place during the week.

Day	Date	High Temperature	Low Temperature	Cloud Cover	Wind Direction	Rain or Snow
1						
2						
3						
4						
5						
6						
7						

76

A WORD LISTS

1
Hard Words
1. soothe
2. persuade
3. pirates
4. poverty
5. conceal
6. dread
7. hasty

2
Compound Words
1. shipwreck
2. horseback
3. anybody
4. halfway
5. courtyard
6. folktale

3
Word Practice
1. ridicule
2. Beauty
3. cautious
4. fatigue
5. excuses
6. ridiculed
7. countries
8. furniture

4
Vocabulary Review
1. vanish
2. original
3. insane
4. glossy
5. dimple
6. greedy
7. victim

5
Vocabulary Preview
1. desolate
2. persuade
3. terrify
4. selfish
5. soothe
6. poverty

B VOCABULARY FROM CONTEXT

1. There was nothing within a hundred miles of this lonely, **desolate** place.
2. She was good at talking people into doing things, but she could not **persuade** anybody to go to the beach with her.
3. The old house was frightening, and the sounds within it **terrified** me.
4. She seemed to be kind, but she was really very **selfish** and thought of nobody but herself.
5. He was so upset that nothing we could do would comfort or **soothe** him.
6. At first he was wealthy, but then he lost all his wealth and found himself in **poverty**.

Lesson 76   75

C STORY BACKGROUND

Folktales

The next story you will read is a folktale called "Beauty and the Beast." Like myths, folktales are old stories that people told aloud before someone wrote them down. But folktales are usually much newer than myths. The myths you have just read, for example, take place about three thousand years ago. In comparison, "Beauty and the Beast" takes place just a few hundred years ago.

Another difference is that myths usually include gods and goddesses, but folktales do not. Instead, folktales often have witches, wizards, or other kinds of magic.

"Beauty and the Beast" is one of the most famous folktales of all time. Many movies have been made of the story, and many writers have retold it in their own words. The story comes from France, a large country in Europe.

D READING

Beauty and the Beast
Chapter 1

Once upon a time there lived a merchant who was enormously rich. The merchant had six sons and six daughters, and he would let them have anything they wanted.

But one day their house caught fire and burned to the ground, with all the splendid furniture, books, pictures, gold, silver, and precious goods it contained. Yet this was only the beginning of their misfortune. Shortly after the fire, the merchant lost every ship he had upon the sea, either because of pirates, shipwrecks, or fire. Then he heard that the people who worked for him in distant countries had stolen his money. At last, he fell into great poverty.

All the merchant had after those misfortunes was a little cottage in a desolate place a hundred miles from the town in which he used to live. He moved into the cottage with his children. They were in de-

76   *Lesson 76*

spair at the idea of leading such a different life. The cottage stood in the middle of a dark forest, and it seemed to be the most dismal place on earth.

The children had to cultivate the fields to earn their living. They were poorly clothed, and they missed the comforts and amusements of their earlier life. Only the youngest daughter tried to be brave and cheerful. She had also been sad at first, but she soon recovered her good nature. She set to work to make the best of things. But when she tried to persuade her sisters to join her in dancing and singing, they ridiculed her and said that this miserable life was all she was fit for. But she was far prettier and more clever than they were. She was so lovely that she was called Beauty.

After two years, their father received news that one of his ships, which he had believed to be lost, had come safely into port with a rich cargo. All the sons and daughters at once thought their poverty would be over, and they wanted to set out directly for the town. But their father was more cautious, so he decided to go by himself. Only Beauty had any doubt that they would soon be rich again. The other daughters gave their father requests for so many jewels and dresses that it would have taken a fortune to buy them. But Beauty did not ask for anything. Her father noticed her silence and said, "And what shall I bring for you, Beauty?"

"The only thing I wish for is to see you come home safely," she answered.

This reply angered her sisters, who thought she was accusing them of asking for costly things. But her father was pleased. Still, he told her to choose something.

"Well, dear Father," she said, "since you insist upon it, I want you to bring me a rose. I have not seen one since we came here, and I love them very much." ◆

So the merchant set out on horseback and reached the town as quickly as possible. But when he got there, he found out that his partners had taken the goods the ship had brought. So he found himself poorer than when he had left the cottage. He had only enough money to buy food on his journey home. To make matters worse, he left town during terrible weather. The storm was so bad that he was exhausted with cold and fatigue before he was halfway home. Night came on, and the deep snow and bitter frost made it impossible for the merchant's horse to carry him any further.

The merchant could see no houses or lights. The only shelter he could find was the hollow trunk of a great tree. He crouched there all night long. It was the longest night he had ever known. In spite of his weariness, the howling of the wolves kept him awake. And when the day broke, he was not much better off, for falling snow had covered up every path, and he did not know which way to turn.

At last, he made out some sort of path, and he started to follow it. It was rough and slippery, so he kept falling down. But the path soon became easier, and it led him to a row of trees that ended at a splendid castle. It seemed very strange to the merchant that no snow had fallen in the row of trees. Stranger still, the trees were fruit trees, and they were covered with apples and oranges. ★

The merchant walked down the row of trees and soon reached the castle. He called, but nobody answered. So he opened the door and called again. Then he climbed

up a flight of steps and walked through several splendid rooms. The pleasant warmth of the air refreshed him, and he suddenly felt very hungry; but there seemed to be nobody in this huge palace who could give him anything to eat.

The merchant kept wandering through the deep silence of the splendid rooms. At last, he stopped in a room smaller than the rest, where a bright fire was burning next to a couch. The merchant thought this room must be prepared for someone, so he sat down to wait. But very soon he fell into a heavy sleep.

His extreme hunger wakened him after several hours. He was still alone, but

a good dinner had been set on a little table. The merchant had eaten nothing for an entire day, so he lost no time in beginning his meal, which was delicious. He wondered who had brought the food, but no one appeared.

After dinner, the merchant went to sleep again. He woke completely refreshed the next morning. There was still no sign of anybody, although a fresh meal of cakes and fruit was sitting on the little table at his elbow. The silence began to terrify the merchant, and he decided to search once more through the rooms. But it was no use. There was no sign of life in the palace. Not even a mouse could be seen.

E MAIN IDEA

For each paragraph, write a sentence that tells the complete main idea.

1. Saturday finally arrived. Janet took her camera out of her closet. Then she went outside to look for her friends. When she had found everybody, she told them to stand together on her porch. She looked through her camera and told everybody to stand closer together. Finally, she said, "Smile," and pressed the button on the camera. The camera went "click," and some of Janet's friends made faces.

2. William liked rowing boats. Last spring, William visited Swan Lake. He rented a rowboat for the whole day. He hopped into the boat and started to pull the oars. The boat started across the lake. William could see the boat rental place getting farther and farther away. William kept rowing. He looked at people fishing and at birds flying near the water. He had fun seeing how fast he could row. After a long time, he came to the opposite side of the lake.

F COMPREHENSION

Write the answers.

1. Why were most of the merchant's children greedy and spoiled?
2. Name at least three ways that Beauty was different from her sisters.
3. Why do you think Beauty asked her father for a rose?
4. Why did the merchant get lost on the way home?
5. Name at least three strange things about the palace.

G WRITING

What objects do you think are beautiful?

• Pick an object that you think is beautiful, such as a flower, a painting, or a river. Then write a poem about the object. Describe what the object looks like and tell why you think it's beautiful.

Lesson 76

79

76

Name ___

A STORY DETAILS

Write the answers.

1. At the beginning of the story, how rich was the merchant?

2. How many children did the merchant have?

3. What happened to his house?

4. What kind of house did the family move into?

5. Before her father left for town, what did Beauty ask him to bring back?

6. What kinds of things did the other children ask for?

7. Where did the merchant sleep during the storm?

8. What was strange about the row of trees the merchant found?

9. Why was the palace so silent?

B VOCABULARY

Write the correct words in the blanks.

shrewd	calculate
witty	century
appetite	secure
inhabitant	sympathy
discontented	defeat

1. Lillian was so ___ with her job that she quit.

2. The wise man made many ___ decisions.

3. A ___ is a long time.

4. The experts could not ___ the number of stars in the sky.

5. She was glad to see the food because she had an enormous ___.

6. The cat was ___ from dogs as long as it stayed inside the house.

7. After the child fell, her mother held her and showed great ___.

Lesson 76   151

C SEQUENCING

Put the following events in the correct order by numbering them from **1** to **5**.

___ The merchant found a palace.

___ The merchant spent the night in a tree.

___ The merchant moved to a cottage.

___ The merchant's house burned down.

___ The merchant went back to the town.

D RELATED FACTS

Write which Greek god each statement describes. Choose **Hermes**, **Poseidon**, or **Zeus.**

1. The god of the sky

2. The god of the ocean

3. The god of travelers

E STORY REVIEW

Write whether each statement describes **The Miraculous Pitcher** or **The Golden Touch.**

1. Zeus appeared in this story.

2. The main character was a king.

3. One of the characters had a magic staff.

4. One of the characters was changed into a statue.

5. The story showed how evil greed can be.

6. The story showed why you should be kind to strangers.

GO TO PART E IN YOUR TEXTBOOK.

152   Lesson 76

Lesson 76

BEFORE READING

Have students find lesson 76, part A, in their textbooks.

HARD WORDS

1. Everybody, find column 1. ✓
 • The words in this column are hard words from your textbook stories.

1. soothe	5. conceal
2. persuade	6. dread
3. pirates	7. hasty
4. poverty	

2. Word 1 is **soothe.** Everybody, what word? (Signal.) *Soothe.*
 • (Repeat for every word in the column.)
3. Let's read these words again.
4. Word 1. Everybody, what word? (Signal.) *Soothe.*
 • (Repeat for every word in the column.)
5. (Repeat the column until firm.)

COMPOUND WORDS

1. Everybody, find column 2. ✓
 • All these compound words consist of two short words.

1. shipwreck	4. halfway
2. horseback	5. courtyard
3. anybody	6. folktale

2. Word 1. Everybody, what's the first short word? (Signal.) *Ship.*
 • Everybody, what's the compound word? (Signal.) *Shipwreck.*
 • (Repeat for every word in the column.)
3. (Repeat the column until firm.)

WORD PRACTICE

1. Everybody, find column 3. ✓
 • We're going to practice these words.

1. ridicule	5. excuses
2. Beauty	6. ridiculed
3. cautious	7. countries
4. fatigue	8. furniture

2. Word 1. Everybody, what word? (Signal.) *Ridicule.*
 • (Repeat for every word in the column.)
3. (Repeat the column until firm.)

VOCABULARY REVIEW

1. Everybody, find column 4. ✓
 • You've learned the meaning for all these words.

1. vanish	5. dimple
2. original	6. greedy
3. insane	7. victim
4. glossy	

2. Word 1. Everybody, what word? (Signal.) *Vanish.*
 • (Repeat for every word in the column.)
3. (Repeat the column until firm.)
4. Now let's talk about what the words mean.

Word 1

1. Word 1 is **vanish.**
 • What does **vanish** mean? (Idea: *Disappear.*)
2. Everybody, what's another way of saying **The mysterious stranger disappeared**? (Signal.) *The mysterious stranger vanished.*

Word 2

1. Word 2 is **original.**
 • What is an **original**? (Idea: *Something that is not a copy of anything else.*)

Lesson 76   **77**

Word 3

1. Word 3 is **insane.**
- What does **insane** mean? (Idea: *Crazy.*)
2. Everybody, what's another way of saying **He had a crazy desire for wealth**? (Signal.) *He had an insane desire for wealth.*

Word 4

1. Word 4 is **glossy.**
- What does **glossy** mean? (Idea: *Smooth and shiny.*)

Word 5

1. Word 5 is **dimple.**
- What is a **dimple**? (Idea: *A little dent in your cheek or chin.*)

Word 6

1. Word 6 is **greedy.**
- What does **greedy** mean? (Idea: *You are never satisfied with what you have.*)

Word 7

1. Word 7 is **victim.**
- What is a **victim**? (Idea: *A person who is harmed.*)

EXERCISE 5

VOCABULARY PREVIEW

1. Everybody, find column 5. ✓
- First we'll read the words in this column. Then we'll read the words in sentences.

1. desolate	4. selfish
2. persuade	5. soothe
3. terrify	6. poverty

2. Word 1. Everybody, what word? (Signal.) *Desolate.*
- (Repeat for every word in the column.)
3. (Repeat the column until firm.)

EXERCISE 6

VOCABULARY FROM CONTEXT

1. Everybody, find part B. ✓
- These sentences use the words you just read.
2. We're going to use the rest of the sentence to figure out the meaning of the word in bold type.

Sentence 1

1. There was nothing within a hundred miles of this lonely, **desolate** place.

1. (Call on a student to read the sentence.)
- What could **desolate** mean? (Ideas: *Gloomy; barren; uninhabited.*)

Sentence 2

2. She was good at talking people into doing things, but she could not **persuade** anybody to go to the beach with her.

1. (Call on a student to read the sentence.)
- What could **persuade** mean? (Idea: *Convince.*)

Sentence 3

3. The old house was frightening, and the sounds within it **terrified** me.

1. (Call on a student to read the sentence.)
- What could **terrified** mean? (Idea: *Greatly frightened.*)

Sentence 4

4. She seemed to be kind, but she was really very **selfish** and thought of nobody but herself.

1. (Call on a student to read the sentence.)
- What could **selfish** mean? (Idea: *Concerned only with herself.*)

Sentence 5

5. He was so upset that nothing we could do would comfort or **soothe** him.

1. (Call on a student to read the sentence.)
- What could **soothe** mean? (Ideas: *Relax; make him feel better.*)

Sentence 6

6. At first he was wealthy, but then he lost all his wealth and found himself in **poverty**.

1. (Call on a student to read the sentence.)
- What could **poverty** mean? (Ideas: *Without money; the state of being poor.*)

READING

EXERCISE 7
STORY BACKGROUND

1. Everybody, find part C. ✓
2. (Call on individual students to read two or three sentences each.)
3. (After students complete each section, ask the questions for that section.)

Folktales

The next story you will read is a folktale called "Beauty and the Beast." Like myths, folktales are old stories that people told aloud before someone wrote them down. But folktales are usually much newer than myths. The myths you have just read, for example, take place about three thousand years ago. In comparison, "Beauty and the Beast" takes place just a few hundred years ago.

Another difference is that myths usually include gods and goddesses, but folktales do not. Instead, folktales often have witches, wizards, or other kinds of magic.

- Who were the gods in the myths you have read? (Ideas: *Zeus, Hermes; the stranger in "The Golden Touch."*)
- Who can name some folktales that have witches or wizards? (Ideas: *Cinderella; Sleeping Beauty; Snow White; Hansel and Gretel.*)

"Beauty and the Beast" is one of the most famous folktales of all time. Many movies have been made of the story, and many writers have retold it in their own words. The story comes from France, a large country in Europe.

- How many of you have seen a movie of "Beauty and the Beast"? (Have students raise their hands.)
- The version you will read is different from the movie versions.

EXERCISE 8
READING ALOUD

1. Everybody, find part D. ✓
- The error limit for this lesson is 10.
2. (Call on individual students to read two or three sentences each.)

3. (After students complete each section, ask the questions for that section.)

Beauty and the Beast
Chapter 1

Once upon a time there lived a merchant who was enormously rich. The merchant had six sons and six daughters, and he would let them have anything they wanted.

- What do merchants do? (Idea: *Buy and sell things.*)
- How many children did the merchant have in all? (Response: *Twelve.*)
- How do you think those children might behave if they got everything they wanted? (Ideas: *They might be spoiled; they might be ungrateful.*)

But one day their house caught fire and burned to the ground, with all the splendid furniture, books, pictures, gold, silver, and precious goods it contained. Yet this was only the beginning of their misfortune. Shortly after the fire, the merchant lost every ship he had upon the sea, either because of pirates, shipwrecks, or fire. Then he heard that the people who worked for him in distant countries had stolen his money. At last, he fell into great poverty.

- Name some things that went wrong for the merchant. (Ideas: *His house burned down; he lost all his ships; the people who worked for him stole his money.*)
- How rich was the merchant after all this misfortune? (Ideas: *He wasn't rich; he was poor.*)

All the merchant had after those misfortunes was a little cottage in a desolate place a hundred miles from the town in which he used to live. He moved into the cottage with his children. They were in despair at the idea of leading such a different life. The cottage stood in the middle of a dark forest, and it seemed to be the most dismal place on earth. The children had to cultivate the fields to earn their living. They were poorly clothed, and they missed the comforts and amusements of their earlier life. Only the youngest daughter tried to be brave and cheerful. She had also been sad at first, but she soon recovered her good nature. She set to work to make the best of things. But when she tried to persuade her sisters to join her in dancing and singing, they ridiculed her and said that this miserable life was all she was fit for. But she was far prettier and more clever than they were. She was so lovely that she was called Beauty.

- Why do you think working was especially hard for these children? (Idea: *Because they were used to having servants do all the work.*)
- What's the title of this story? (Response: *Beauty and the Beast.*)
- Who do you think one of the main characters will be? (Response: *Beauty.*)
- Who will the other main character be? (Response: *The Beast.*)

After two years, their father received news that one of his ships, which he had believed to be lost, had come safely into port with a rich cargo. All the sons and daughters at once thought their poverty would be over, and they wanted to set out directly for the town. But their father was more cautious, so he decided to go by himself. Only Beauty had any doubt that they would soon be rich again. The other daughters gave their father requests for so many jewels and dresses that it would have taken a fortune to buy them. But Beauty did not ask for anything. Her father noticed her silence and said, "And what shall I bring for you, Beauty?"

"The only thing I wish for is to see you come home safely," she answered.

This reply angered her sisters, who thought she was accusing them of asking for costly things. But her father was pleased. Still, he told her to choose something.

"Well, dear Father," she said, "since you insist upon it, I want you to bring me a rose. I have not seen one since we came here, and I love them very much." ◆

- What did Beauty's sisters ask for? (Idea: *Jewels and dresses.*)
- Why do you think Beauty asked for a rose? (Ideas: *Because she loved roses; because roses are beautiful; because roses don't cost much money.*)

SILENT READING

1. Read the rest of the chapter to yourselves and be ready to answer some questions.

So the merchant set out on horseback and reached the town as quickly as possible. But when he got there, he found out that his partners had taken the goods the ship had brought. So he found himself poorer than when he had left the cottage. He had only enough money to buy food on his journey home. To make matters worse, he left town during terrible weather. The storm was so bad that he was exhausted with cold and fatigue before he was halfway home. Night came on, and the deep snow and bitter frost made it impossible for the merchant's horse to carry him any further.

The merchant could see no houses or lights. The only shelter he could find was the hollow trunk of a great tree. He crouched there all night long. It was the longest night he had ever known. In spite of his weariness, the howling of the wolves kept him awake. And when the day broke, he was not much better off, for falling snow had covered up every path, and he did not know which way to turn.

At last, he made out some sort of path, and he started to follow it. It was rough and slippery, so he kept falling down. But the path soon became easier, and it led him to a row of trees that ended at a splendid castle. It seemed very strange to the merchant that no snow had fallen in the row of trees. Stranger still, the trees were fruit trees, and they were covered with apples and oranges. ★

The merchant walked down the row of trees and soon reached the castle. He called, but nobody answered. So he opened the door and called again. Then he climbed up a flight of steps and walked through several splendid rooms. The pleasant warmth of the air refreshed him, and he suddenly felt very hungry; but there seemed to be nobody in this huge palace who could give him anything to eat.

The merchant kept wandering through the deep silence of the splendid rooms. At last, he stopped in a room smaller than the rest, where a bright fire was burning next to a couch. The merchant thought this room must be prepared for someone, so he sat down to wait. But very soon he fell into a heavy sleep.

His extreme hunger wakened him after several hours. He was still alone, but a good dinner had been set on a little table. The merchant had eaten nothing for an entire day, so he lost no time in beginning his meal, which was delicious. He wondered who had brought the food, but no one appeared.

After dinner, the merchant went to sleep again. He woke completely refreshed the next morning. There was still no sign of anybody, although a fresh meal of cakes and fruit was sitting on the little table at his elbow. The silence began to terrify the merchant, and he decided to search once more through the rooms. But it was no use. There was no sign of life in the palace. Not even a mouse could be seen.

- What bad news did the merchant discover when he reached the town? (Idea: *His partners had taken everything off the ship.*)
- What was the weather like when he started back home? (Idea: *Cold and snowy.*)
- Why did he have trouble finding his way in the morning? (Idea: *Snow had covered up the path.*)
- What was unusual about the row of trees? (Ideas: *They had no snow on them; they had fruit on them.*)
- What was unusual about the castle? (Ideas: *Nobody was there; a fire was burning by itself; food appeared while the merchant was sleeping.*)
- Why did the merchant search through the palace the next day? (Ideas: *To see if anybody was there; to find the owner.*)
- Who do you think the castle belongs to? (Ideas: *The Beast; a witch; a wizard.*)

EXERCISE 10
PAIRED PRACTICE

1. Now you'll read in pairs.
- Whoever read second the last time will read first today.
- Remember to start at the diamond and switch at the star.
2. (Observe students and answer questions as needed.)

AFTER READING

EXERCISE 11
INDEPENDENT WORK

1. Do all the items in your workbook and textbook for this lesson.
2. (The independent work in this lesson includes the following activities.)
- Story details
- Vocabulary
- Sequencing
- Related facts
- Story review
- Main idea
- Comprehension
- Writing

EXERCISE 12
WORKCHECK

1. (Using the Answer Key, read the questions and answers for the workbook.)
2. (Have students read their answers for the textbook activities.)
3. (Have two or three students read their writing assignments aloud. Comment on each assignment.)
4. (Have students correct and turn in their work.)

LANGUAGE ARTS GUIDE

(Students should complete the appropriate exercises in the *Language Arts Guide* after completing lesson 76. See *Language Arts Guide* for details.)

Lesson 76 **81**

76

Lesson 76

Name _____

The children saw a shovel.

Picture A   **Picture B**

Rewrite the sentence so that it tells about each picture. Add the words in the yard.

1. Picture A _____

_____

_____

2. Picture B _____

_____

_____

Lesson 76

VARYING SENTENCE STRUCTURE:
Inserting Phrases

1. Look at your worksheet for lesson 76. ✔

- You're going to rewrite a sentence so it tells about different pictures. The sentence you'll rewrite is **The children saw a shovel.** You'll add the words **in**

the yard so the sentence tells about either picture A or picture B.

2. Look at picture A. What's in the yard? (Signal.) *A shovel.*
- Rewrite the sentence so it tells about picture A. Put the words **in the yard** in the sentence. Make sure they are in the right place. Raise your hand when you're finished.
  (Observe students and give feedback.)
- (Write on the board:)

> **The children saw a shovel in the yard.**

- Check your work. Here's what you should have for picture A: **The children saw a shovel in the yard.**
- Raise your hand if you got it right.
3. Rewrite the sentence so it tells about picture B. Raise your hand when you're finished.
  (Observe students and give feedback.)
- (Write on the board:)

> **The children in the yard saw a shovel.**

- Check your work. Here's what you should have for picture B: **The children in the yard saw a shovel.**
- Those children outside the yard didn't see a shovel.
- Raise your hand if you got it right. ✔
4. Remember, if the **shovel** is in the yard, you put the words **in the yard** right after **shovel.** If the **children** are in the yard, you put the words **in the yard** right after **children.**

57

A WORD LISTS

1
Hard Words
1. heron
2. trio
3. Sylvia
4. wilderness
5. gallant
6. pigeon

2
Word Practice
1. Circe
2. Calypso
3. Scylla

3
New Vocabulary
1. heron
2. foster parent
3. huckleberry
4. bough
5. gallant
6. trio
7. game

B VOCABULARY DEFINITIONS

1. **heron**—Herons are birds that wade through water and eat frogs and fish. Herons usually have tall, thin legs and a long, S-shaped neck. The picture shows a *white heron*.
   • Describe a heron.

2. **foster parent**—A *foster parent* is somebody who brings up a child but is not the child's real parent.
   • What do we call somebody who brings up a child but is not the child's real parent?

3. **huckleberry**—A *huckleberry* is a small purple or black berry that grows on bushes.
   • What is a huckleberry?

4. **bough**—A *bough* of a tree is a branch of the tree.
   • What is a branch of a tree?

5. **gallant**—Somebody who is *gallant* is brave and noble.
   • What's another way of saying *He was a noble warrior?*

6. **trio**—A *trio* is a group of three.
   • What's another way of saying *A group of three went to the river?*

7. **game**—Wild animals that are hunted are called *game*.
   • What do we call wild animals that are hunted?

C READING

A White Heron
by Sarah Orne Jewett*
Part 1

Focus Question: How did Sylvia feel about living on her foster mother's farm?

The woods were filled with shadows one June evening, but a bright sunset still glimmered faintly among the trunks of the trees. A girl named Sylvia was driving a cow from the pasture to her home. Sylvia had spent more than an hour looking for the cow and had finally found her hiding behind a huckleberry bush.

Sylvia and the cow were going away from the sunset and into the dark woods. But they were familiar with the path, and the darkness did not bother them.

Sylvia wondered what her foster mother, Mrs. Tilley, would say because they were so late. But Mrs. Tilley knew how difficult it was to find the cow. She had chased the beast many times herself. As she waited, she was only thankful that Sylvia could help her. Sylvia seemed to love the out-of-doors, and Mrs. Tilley thought that being outdoors was a good change for an orphan girl who had grown up in a town.

The companions followed the shady road. The cow took slow steps, and the girl took very fast ones. The cow stopped at the brook to drink, and Sylvia stood still and waited. She let her bare feet cool themselves in the water while the great twilight moths struck softly against her. She waded on through the brook as the cow moved away, and she listened to the waterbirds with pleasure.

There was a stirring in the great boughs overhead. They were full of little birds that seemed to be wide awake and going about their business. Sylvia began to feel sleepy as she walked along. However, it was not much farther to the house, and the air was soft and sweet.

She was not often in the woods so late as this. The darkness made her feel as if she were a part of the gray shadows and the moving leaves. She was thinking how long it seemed since she had first come to her foster mother's farm a year ago. Sylvia wondered if everything was still going on in the noisy town just the same as when she had lived there. ◆

It seemed to Sylvia that she had never been alive at all before she came to live at her foster mother's farm. It was a beautiful place to live, and she never wished to go back to the town. The thought of the children who used to chase and frighten her made her hurry along the path to escape from the shadows of the trees.

* Adapted for young readers

Suddenly, she was horror-struck to hear a clear whistle not very far away. It was not a bird's whistle. It sounded more like a boy's. Sylvia stepped aside into the bushes, but she was too late. The whistler had discovered her, and he called out in a cheerful voice, "Hello, little girl, how far is it to the road?"

Trembling, Sylvia answered quietly, "A long distance."

She did not dare to look at the tall young man, who carried a gun over his shoulder. But Sylvia came out of the bushes and again followed the cow, while the young man walked alongside her.

"I have been hunting for some birds," the stranger said kindly, "and I have lost my way. Don't be afraid," he added gallantly. "Speak up and tell me what your name is and whether you think I can spend the night at your house and go out hunting early in the morning."

Sylvia was more alarmed than before. Would her foster mother blame her for this? She hung her head, but she managed to answer "Sylvia" when her companion again asked her name.

Mrs. Tilley was standing in the doorway when the trio came into view. The cow gave a loud moo as if to explain the situation.

Mrs. Tilley said, "Yes, you'd better speak up for yourself, you naughty old cow! Where'd she hide herself this time, Sylvia?" But Sylvia kept silent.

The young man stood his gun beside the door and dropped a heavy gamebag next to it. Then he said good evening to Mrs. Tilley. He repeated his story and asked if he could have a night's lodging.

"Put me anywhere you like," he said. "I must be off early in the morning, before day, but I am very hungry indeed. Could you give me some milk?"

"Dear sakes, yes," said Mrs. Tilley. "You might do better if you went out to the main road, but you're welcome to what we've got. I'll milk the cow right now, and you make yourself at home. Now step round and set a plate for the gentleman, Sylvia!"

Sylvia promptly stepped. She was glad to have something to do, and she was hungry herself.

D INFERENCE

Write the answers for items 1–8.

You have to answer different types of questions about the passages you read. Some questions are answered by words in the passage. Other questions are not answered by words in the passage. You have to figure out the answer by making a deduction.

The following passage includes both types of questions.

More about Ecology

Two hundred years ago, many people were not concerned with ecology. They believed there was no end to the different types of wildlife, so they killed wild animals by the hundreds of thousands. When we look back on these killings, we may feel shocked. But for the people who lived two hundred years ago, wild animals seemed to be as plentiful as weeds.

Because of these killings, more than a hundred types of animals have become extinct since 1800. An animal is extinct when there are no more animals of that type.

One type of extinct animal is the passenger pigeon. At one time, these birds were so plentiful that flocks of them used to blacken the sky. Now the passenger pigeon is gone forever. Think of that. You will never get to see a living passenger pigeon or any of the other animals that have become extinct. The only place you can see those animals is in a museum, where they are stuffed and mounted.

1. Are house cats extinct?
2. Is that question answered by **words** or a **deduction?**
3. Name one type of extinct animal.
4. **Words** or **deduction?**
5. How many types of animals have become extinct since 1800?
6. **Words** or **deduction?**
7. The dodo bird is extinct. How many animals of that type are alive today?
8. **Words** or **deduction?**

E DEDUCTIONS

Write the answers about the deductions.
Oliver believed that if he studied, he would pass the test. Oliver studied for the test.
1. So, what did Oliver believe would happen?

Nadia believed that if you ate an apple a day you would stay healthy. Nadia ate an apple every day.
2. So, what did Nadia believe would happen?

F VOCABULARY REVIEW

unprecedented
maneuver
devoted
spurn
endured
regard

For each item, write the correct word.
1. When you move skillfully, you ▇▇ .
2. When you consider something, you ▇▇ it.
3. Something that has never occurred before is ▇▇ .

G COMPREHENSION

Write the answers.
1. How did Sylvia feel about living on her foster mother's farm?
2. Why didn't Sylvia like the town?
3. Why do you think Sylvia didn't dare to look at the young man?
4. How do you think Sylvia feels about hunting? Explain your answer.
5. What do you think will happen in the next part of the story?

H WRITING

Where would you rather live, on a farm or in a town? Write an essay that explains your answer. Try to answer the following questions:
• What are the advantages of living on a farm?
• What are the disadvantages of living on a farm?
• What are the advantages of living in a town?
• What are the disadvantages of living in a town?
• Where would you rather live? Why?
Make your essay at least sixty words long.

57

A STORY DETAILS

Write or circle the answers.

1. Sylvia was — who lived on a farm.
   • a vacationer • a farmhand • an orphan

2. Where had Sylvia lived before coming to the farm?

3. Sylvia thought she had never been — at all before coming to the farm.
   • scared • alive • punished

4. Which place did Sylvia enjoy more, the town or the farm?

5. How had the children in town treated Sylvia?

6. What was the young man doing in the woods?

7. Was Sylvia bold or shy?

8. What was the name of the person who owned the farm?

9. That person was Sylvia's —.
   • employer • mother • foster parent

B VOCABULARY

Write the correct words in the blanks.

> regarded   suitable
> appealed   humiliating
> unprecedented maneuvered

1. The starving boy _____ to the sympathy of the crowd.

2. They _____ the criminal as a dangerous person.

3. He _____ the shopping cart past the fallen cans.

4. The pitcher made an _____ number of strikeouts.

C FIGURATIVE LANGUAGE

For each statement, write **simile, metaphor,** or **exaggeration.**

1. Her face was like a pale star.

2. The apartment was a prison.

3. The day was like a dream.

Lesson 57   113

D DEDUCTIONS

Complete each deduction.
Every element has an atomic weight. Argon is an element.

1. What's the conclusion about argon?

Horses eat grass. A palomino is a horse.

2. What's the conclusion about a palomino?

E CHARACTER TRAITS

Write whether each phrase describes **Sylvia, Mrs. Tilley,** or **the stranger.**

1. Very shy

2. Whistled loudly

3. An orphan

4. Owned a farm

5. Felt like a part of the woods

6. Hunted for animals

F COMPARISONS

Write **Odyssey** if the event occurred in *The Odyssey*. Write **Yarn** if the event occurred in "Mystery Yarn."

1. Telemachus was one of the suitors.

2. Telemachus helped defeat the suitors.

3. The suitors took a test that involved unwinding string.

4. The suitors took a test that involved a bow and arrow.

▶ GO TO PART D IN YOUR TEXTBOOK.

Lesson 57   114

Lesson 57

BEFORE READING

Have students find lesson 57, part A, in their textbooks.

EXERCISE 1
HARD WORDS

1. Look at column 1.
   - These are hard words from your textbook stories.

1.	heron	4.	wilderness
2.	trio	5.	gallant
3.	Sylvia	6.	pigeon

2. Word 1 is **heron**. Everybody, what word? (Signal.) *Heron.*
   - (Repeat this procedure for every word in the column.)
3. Let's read the words again.
4. Word 1. Everybody, what word? (Signal.) *Heron.*
   - (Repeat this procedure for every word in the column.)
5. (Repeat the column until firm.)

EXERCISE 2
WORD PRACTICE

1. Look at column 2.
   - We're going to practice these words.

1.	Circe	3.	Scylla
2.	Calypso		

2. Word 1. Everybody, what word? (Signal.) *Circe.*
   - (Repeat this procedure for every word in the column.)
3. (Repeat the column until firm.)

EXERCISE 3
NEW VOCABULARY

1. Look at column 3.
   - First we'll read the words in this column. Then we'll read their definitions.

1.	heron	5.	gallant
2.	foster parent	6.	trio
3.	huckleberry	7.	game
4.	bough		

2. Word 1. Everybody, what word? (Signal.) *Heron.*
   - (Repeat this procedure for every word in the column.)
3. (Repeat the column until firm.)

EXERCISE 4
VOCABULARY DEFINITIONS

1. Everybody, find part B. ✓
   - These are definitions for the words you just read.
2. (For each word, call on a student to read the definition and the item. Then ask the student to complete the item.)

1. **heron**—*Herons* are birds that wade through water and eat frogs and fish. Herons usually have tall, thin legs and a long, S-shaped neck. The picture shows a *white heron*.
   - Describe a heron.

   - What's the answer? (Ideas: *It has tall, thin legs and a long, S-shaped neck; it wades through water and eats frogs and fish.*)

2. **foster parent**—A *foster parent* is somebody who brings up a child but is not the child's real parent.
   - What do we call somebody who brings up a child but is not the child's real parent?

   - What's the answer? (Response: *A foster parent.*)

3. **huckleberry**—A *huckleberry* is a small purple or black berry that grows on bushes.
   - What is a huckleberry?

   - What's the answer? (Idea: *A small purple or black berry that grows on bushes.*)

4. **bough**—A *bough* of a tree is a branch of the tree.
   • What is a branch of a tree?

• What's the answer? (Response: *A bough.*)

5. **gallant**—Somebody who is *gallant* is brave and noble.
   • What's another way of saying *He was a noble warrior*?

• What's the answer? (Response: *He was a gallant warrior.*)

6. **trio**—A *trio* is a group of three.
   • What's another way of saying *A group of three went to the river*?

• What's the answer? (Response: *A trio went to the river.*)

7. **game**—Wild animals that are hunted are called *game*.
   • What do we call wild animals that are hunted?

• What's the answer? (Response: *Game.*)

EXERCISE 5

INFERENCE

1. Everybody, turn to part D at the end of today's story. ✓
• (Call on individual students to read several sentences each.)
• (At the end of each section, present the questions for that section.)

Write the answers for items 1–8.
  You have to answer different types of questions about the passages you read. Some questions are answered by words in the passage. Other questions are *not* answered by words in the passage. You have to figure out the answer by making a deduction.

• What do you use to answer the first kind of question? (Idea: *Words in the passage.*)
• What do you use to answer the second kind of question? (Idea: *A deduction.*)

The following passage includes both types of questions.
More about Ecology
  Two hundred years ago, many people were not concerned with ecology. They believed there was no end to the different types of wildlife, so they killed wild animals by the hundreds of thousands. When we look back on these killings, we may feel shocked. But for the people who lived two hundred years ago, wild animals seemed to be as plentiful as weeds.
  Because of these killings, more than a hundred types of animals have become extinct since 1800. An animal is extinct when there are no more animals of that type.
  One type of extinct animal is the passenger pigeon. At one time, these birds were so plentiful that flocks of them used to blacken the sky. Now the passenger pigeon is gone forever. Think of that. You will never get to see a living passenger pigeon or any of the other animals that have become extinct. The only place you can see those animals is in a museum, where they are stuffed and mounted.
1. Are house cats extinct?

• What's the answer? (Response: *No.*)

2. Is that question answered by **words** or a **deduction**?

• What's the answer? (Response: *Deduction.*)
• That's right, the passage does not contain this sentence: "House cats are not extinct." You figure out the answer by making a deduction.
• Here's the deduction: **Animals are extinct when there are no more animals of that type. There are still many house cats. Therefore, house cats are not extinct.**

3. Name one type of extinct animal.

• What's the answer? (Response: *The passenger pigeon.*)

4. **Words** or **deduction**?

• Is the question answered by **words** or by a **deduction**? (Response: *Words.*)

Lesson 57   **273**

- Read the sentence that contains words that answer the question. (Response: *One type of extinct animal is the passenger pigeon.*)

5. How many types of animals have become extinct since 1800?

- What's the answer? (Response: *More than a hundred.*)

6. **Words** or **deduction**?

- Is the question answered by **words** or by a **deduction**? (Response: *Words.*)
- Read the sentence that contains the words that answer the question. (Response: *Because of these killings, more than a hundred types of animals have become extinct since 1800.*)

7. The dodo bird is extinct. How many animals of that type are alive today?

- What's the answer? (Idea: *None.*)

8. **Words** or **deduction**?

- Is the question answered by **words** or by a **deduction**? (Response: *Deduction.*)
- Here's the deduction: **Animals are extinct when there are no more animals of that type. The dodo bird is extinct. Therefore, there are no more animals of that type.**
- You'll write the answers later.

READING

EXERCISE 6

FOCUS QUESTION

1. Everybody, find part C. ✓
2. What's the focus question for today's lesson? (Response: *How did Sylvia feel about living on her foster mother's farm?*)

EXERCISE 7

READING ALOUD (OPTIONAL)

1. We're going to read aloud to the diamond.
- (Call on individual students to read several sentences each.)

A White Heron
by Sarah Orne Jewett
Part 1
Focus Question: How did Sylvia feel about living on her foster mother's farm?

The woods were filled with shadows one June evening, but a bright sunset still glimmered faintly among the trunks of the trees. A girl named Sylvia was driving a cow from the pasture to her home. Sylvia had spent more than an hour looking for the cow and had finally found her hiding behind a huckleberry bush.

Sylvia and the cow were going away from the sunset and into the dark woods. But they were familiar with the path, and the darkness did not bother them.

Sylvia wondered what her foster mother, Mrs. Tilley, would say because they were so late. But Mrs. Tilley knew how difficult it was to find the cow. She had chased the beast many times herself. As she waited, she was only thankful that Sylvia could help her. Sylvia seemed to love the out-of-doors, and Mrs. Tilley thought that being outdoors was a good change for an orphan girl who had grown up in a town.

The companions followed the shady road. The cow took slow steps, and the girl took very fast ones. The cow stopped at the brook to drink, and Sylvia stood still and waited. She let her bare feet cool themselves in the water while the great twilight moths struck softly against her. She waded on through the brook as the cow moved away, and she listened to the waterbirds with pleasure.

There was a stirring in the great boughs overhead. They were full of little birds that seemed to be wide awake and going about their business. Sylvia began to feel sleepy as she walked along. However, it was not much farther to the house, and the air was soft and sweet.

She was not often in the woods so late as this. The darkness made her feel as if she were a part of the gray shadows and the moving leaves. She was thinking how long it seemed since she had first come to her foster mother's farm a year ago. Sylvia wondered if everything was still going on in the noisy town just the same as when she had lived there. ◆

EXERCISE 8

SILENT READING

1. Read the rest of the lesson to yourselves and be ready to answer some questions.

It seemed to Sylvia that she had never been alive at all before she came to live at her foster mother's farm. It was a beautiful place to live, and she never wished to go back to the town. The thought of the children who used to chase and frighten her made her hurry along the path to escape from the shadows of the trees.

Suddenly, she was horror-struck to hear a clear whistle not very far away. It was not a bird's whistle. It sounded more like a boy's. Sylvia stepped aside into the bushes, but she was too late. The whistler had discovered her, and he called out in a cheerful voice, "Hello, little girl, how far is it to the road?"

Trembling, Sylvia answered quietly, "A long distance."

She did not dare to look at the tall young man, who carried a gun over his shoulder. But Sylvia came out of the bushes and again followed the cow, while the young man walked alongside her.

"I have been hunting for some birds," the stranger said kindly, "and I have lost my way. Don't be afraid," he added gallantly. "Speak up and tell me what your name is and whether you think I can spend the night at your house and go out hunting early in the morning." ★

Sylvia was more alarmed than before. Would her foster mother blame her for this? She hung her head, but she managed to answer "Sylvia" when her companion again asked her name.

Mrs. Tilley was standing in the doorway when the trio came into view. The cow gave a loud moo as if to explain the situation.

Mrs. Tilley said, "Yes, you'd better speak up for yourself, you naughty old cow! Where'd she hide herself this time, Sylvia?" But Sylvia kept silent.

The young man stood his gun beside the door and dropped a heavy gamebag next to it. Then he said good evening to Mrs. Tilley. He repeated his story and asked if he could have a night's lodging.

"Put me anywhere you like," he said. "I must be off early in the morning, before day, but I am very hungry indeed. Could you give me some milk?"

"Dear sakes, yes," said Mrs. Tilley. "You might do better if you went out to the main road, but you're welcome to what we've got. I'll milk the cow right now, and you make yourself at home. Now step round and set a plate for the gentleman, Sylvia!"

Sylvia promptly stepped. She was glad to have something to do, and she was hungry herself.

- How did Sylvia feel about living on her foster mother's farm? (Ideas: *She loved being outdoors; the farm made her feel alive.*)
- Why didn't Sylvia like the town? (Ideas: *The other children made fun of her; it was noisy and crowded.*)
- Why do you think Sylvia didn't dare to look at the young man? (Ideas: *She was afraid of him; he was a stranger; she was shy.*)
- How do you think Sylvia feels about hunting? Explain your answer. (Ideas: *She probably doesn't like hunting because she loves living things; she probably doesn't like hunting because guns are noisy.*)
- What do you think will happen in the next part of the story? (Ideas: *The stranger will ask Sylvia to go hunting with him; the stranger will rob Sylvia and her foster mother.*)

EXERCISE 9

PAIRED PRACTICE (OPTIONAL)

1. Now you'll read in pairs.
- Whoever read second the last time will read first today.
- Remember to start at the diamond and switch at the star.
2. (Observe students and answer questions as needed.)

Lesson 57

Materials: Each student will need a copy of the worksheet for lesson 57 (Blackline Master 57).

EXERCISE 1
PAST-TENSE VERBS

57

Lesson 57

Name _____

- Past-tense verbs express actions that have already happened.
- Past-tense verbs are usually formed by adding **d** or **ed** to the base verb.
- The form of past-tense verbs is the same for both singular and plural subjects.

A. Write the past-tense form of the verb to finish the sentence.

1. mow   Jamael _____ yards all last summer.

2. wait   Betsy _____ twenty minutes for Howard.

3. explore   The tourists _____ the mission ruins.

4. watch   I _____ in horror as the wall tumbled.

5. help   Kyle _____ his grandmother clean her attic.

B. For each item, circle the verb. Write **present** or **past** to show its tense.

Tense

1. Gordon erased the first paragraph of his essay.   _____

2. Do you object to the plan?   _____

3. Jeanne boasted about her new computer.   _____

4. Leslie talks too much!   _____

5. Suzi smiles easily.   _____

202   BLM 57

---

1. Look at your worksheet for lesson 57. ✔
- The box has some more information about verb tense. I'll read what it says. Follow along:

  - **Past-tense** verbs express actions that have already happened.
  - Past-tense verbs are usually formed by adding **d** or **ed** to the base verb.
  - The form of past-tense verbs is the same for both singular and plural subjects.

  What's the name for verbs that express actions that have already happened? (Signal.) *Past tense.*

- How do you form past-tense verbs? (Idea: *By adding **d** or **ed** to the base verb.*)

2. Find part A on your worksheet. ✔
- For each item, you'll write the past-tense form of the verb to finish the sentence.
- For Item 1, the verb is **mow**: **Jamael _____ yards all last summer.** What's the past tense of **mow**? (Signal.) *Mowed.*
- Yes. You should finish the sentence by writing **mowed** on the blank.
3. Complete the items. Raise your hand when you've finished.
   (Observe students and give feedback.)
4. (After the students complete the items, do a workcheck. For each item, call on a student to say and spell the past-tense verb form and read the complete sentence. If an answer is wrong, give the correct answer.)

Answer Key: (Part A:) 1. mowed
2. waited **3.** explored **4.** watched **5.** helped

EXERCISE 2
PRESENT- AND PAST-TENSE VERBS

1. Find part B on your worksheet. ✔
- For each item, circle the verb. Write **present** or **past** to show its tense. Raise your hand when you've finished.
   (Observe students and give feedback.)
2. (After the students complete the items, do a workcheck. For each item, call on a student to say the verb, read the complete sentence, and identify the verb tense. If an answer is wrong, give the correct answer.)

Answer Key: (Part B:) 1. erased, past
2. object, present **3.** boasted, past **4.** talks, present **5.** smiles, present